California Politics

Fourth Edition

CQ Press, an imprint of SAGE, is the leading publisher of books, periodicals, and electronic products on American government and international affairs. CQ Press consistently ranks among the top commercial publishers in terms of quality, as evidenced by the numerous awards its products have won over the years. CQ Press owes its existence to Nelson Poynter, former publisher of the *St. Petersburg Times,* and his wife Henrietta, with whom he founded Congressional Quarterly in 1945. Poynter established CQ with the mission of promoting democracy through education and in 1975 founded the Modern Media Institute, renamed The Poynter Institute for Media Studies after his death. The Poynter Institute (*www.poynter.org*) is a nonprofit organization dedicated to training journalists and media leaders.

In 2008, CQ Press was acquired by SAGE, a leading international publisher of journals, books, and electronic media for academic, educational, and professional markets. Since 1965, SAGE has helped inform and educate a global community of scholars, practitioners, researchers, and students spanning a wide range of subject areas, including business, humanities, social sciences, and science, technology, and medicine. A privately owned corporation, SAGE has offices in Los Angeles, London, New Delhi, and Singapore, in addition to the Washington DC office of CQ Press.

California Politics

A Primer

Fourth Edition

Renée B. Van Vechten
University of Redlands

Los Angeles | London | New Delhi
Singapore | Washington DC

Los Angeles | London | New Delhi
Singapore | Washington DC

FOR INFORMATION:

CQ Press

An Imprint of SAGE Publications, Inc.

2455 Teller Road

Thousand Oaks, California 91320

E-mail: order@sagepub.com

SAGE Publications Ltd.

1 Oliver's Yard

55 City Road

London, EC1Y 1SP

United Kingdom

SAGE Publications India Pvt. Ltd.

B 1/I 1 Mohan Cooperative Industrial Area

Mathura Road, New Delhi 110 044

India

SAGE Publications Asia-Pacific Pte. Ltd.

3 Church Street

#10-04 Samsung Hub

Singapore 049483

Acquisitions Editor: Michael Kerns

Development Editor: Nancy Matuszak

Editorial Assistant: Zachary Hoskins

eLearning Editor: Allison Hughes

Production Editor: Laura Barrett

Copy Editor: Michelle Ponce

Typesetter: Hurix System (P) Ltd.

Proofreader: Tricia Currie-Knight

Indexer: Teddy Diggs

Cover Designer: Gail Buschman

Marketing Manager: Jennifer Jones

Printed in the United States of America

Library of Congress Cataloging-in-Publication Data

Names: Van Vechten, Renée, author.

Title: California politics : a primer / Renée B. Van Vechten.

Description: Fourth edition | Los Angeles : CQ Press, [2017] | Includes index.

Identifiers: LCCN 2015037796 | ISBN 9781483375595 (pbk. : alk. paper)

Subjects: LCSH: California—Politics and government.

Classification: LCC JK8716 .V36 2017 | DDC 320.4794–dc23 LC record available at http://lccn.loc.gov/2015037796

This book is printed on acid-free paper.

16 17 18 19 20 10 9 8 7 6 5 4 3 2 1

Contents

SAGE was founded in 1965 by Sara Miller McCune to support the dissemination of usable knowledge by publishing innovative and high-quality research and teaching content. Today, we publish over 900 journals, including those of more than 400 learned societies, more than 800 new books per year, and a growing range of library products including archives, data, case studies, reports, and video. SAGE remains majority-owned by our founder, and after Sara's lifetime will become owned by a charitable trust that secures our continued independence.

Los Angeles | London | New Delhi | Singapore | Washington DC

Preface

Drought. The word whispers across parched lands, from south to north, east to west. Drought has transformed major portions of the agricultural and food industries, fisheries, and energy production; influenced how residents design and maintain their homes; and should force everyone to think differently about the resources that too often are taken for granted. Drought—not just a meteorological or hydrological event, but a political issue that will reverberate through every region for years to come—for even if heavy winter rains refill some reservoirs, the water is unlikely to fall naturally where it's needed critically, and storms will beget new problems such as flooding and mudslides.

Other developments on social, economic, and political fronts have *occasionally* managed to displace water-related issues from the headlines (Who won the World Series and the NBA Finals?), and Democratic lawmakers have joined the assiduous Governor Jerry Brown in approaching intractable problems creatively. What have they done lately? Together they've widened health care access for low-income children and adults, extended drivers' licenses to undocumented immigrants, raised the minimum wage to $10 an hour, used surpluses to reduce the state's long-term indebtedness, installed an Earned Income Tax Credit for the poorest working adults, created an amnesty program for individuals who have racked up court-related late fees, and begun to overhaul elections by making voter registration automatic (effective January 2016), instituting election-day registration, and making voting-by-mail the norm (the latter are under development). Not everyone is pleased with their work of course: the Democrats in charge have managed to further alienate opponents of illegal immigration, who fear that extending benefits such as health care to undocumented children will encourage waves of new immigrants; they've also hit a nerve with "anti-vaxxers"—those opposed to mandatory vaccination for schoolchildren—by eliminating exemptions for personal beliefs as of July 2015. They've hardly begun to deal with the state's infrastructure backlog that's about a half-a-trillion dollars and have done little to avoid a potential pension calamity: at current rates, the public retirement system that is underfunded by tens of billions of dollars may not be able to sustain the thousands of people who are depending on it. Brown himself called the 2015–16 budget "precariously balanced." Yet it's clear that government is working better than it was even five years ago; a stronger economy combined with Jerry Brown's cautious restraint have helped bring spending back in line with revenues, and the state is better positioned for the next recession, whenever it hits.

Brown revels in the challenges of running what is effectively one of the world's largest countries, and has helped shift attention to the work of government and away from its blatant failings. Now that Brown has demonstrated that the mammoth state *is* governable, it behooves us to ask, what does "better government" entail? What would a high-functioning, effective governing system for this state require? No government can satisfy all of its constituents, but is there a consensus about the criteria for a satisfactory grade? This short text, *California Politics: A Primer,* attempts to outline the puzzle that is California politics, providing readers with analytical tools to piece together an answer to these overarching questions. By emphasizing how history, political culture, rules, and institutions influence choices that lie at the heart of governing, the text moves beyond mere recitation of facts, pressing the reader to think about how these forces conspire to shape politics today and how they will determine the state of affairs tomorrow. It asks the reader to consider what effective government is—and isn't.

Because this book is intended to provide the essentials of California politics, brevity and wide scope eclipse detail and depth. Yet what is included presents a tidy snapshot for understanding how the state is governed and how its politics work. Timely examples succinctly clarify trends and concepts, but because of limitations on space, some developments are given short attention or a passing mention. Instructors may read these as cues for further elaboration in class. Heavy emphasis on visuals in the form of figures, charts, graphs, maps, and photos also allows readers to discern the basics quickly, but readers should also take time to uncover the clues to understanding politics and tease out the rich patterns contained in these illustrations and in the accompanying captions. Some of these graphics, such as the cartograms, suggest to the reader novel ways of perceiving current trends.

What's New to the Fourth Edition

Fully updated chapters that contain recent examples and research enrich this fourth edition of *California Politics: A Primer*. Particular attention has been paid to the apolitical habits of younger generations, policy responses to the drought, electoral innovations for connecting voters to politics (including consequences of the Top Two Primary), considerations on the emerging impacts of restructured term limits, and developments in the still-underfunded courts and the criminal justice system (prison realignment). A small change has also been made to the discussion about administrative organization: Government Operations has been reclassified as a superagency, and Corrections and Rehabilitation has been shifted to the superdepartment category. The book's tone also reflects a more upbeat feeling about the state's outlook, a sentiment that more and more Californians share (as measured by the Public Policy Institute of California in their series of public opinion surveys).

Several informative maps have been added, and graphics have been updated for this edition wherever possible, incorporating data releases by the U.S. Census Bureau, state agencies, and public affairs research organizations. It should be noted that some agencies have undergone data transitions and have not produced some annual reports as of this writing (CalTrans, Department of Corrections Statistical Unit). Many of the current graphics are incorporated into PowerPoint lecture slides that are designed to provide instructors with helpful guidance and guideposts for classroom instruction. Instructors should go to http://study.sagepub.com/california4e to register and download materials, including

- A **test bank**, available in Respondus, offers a diverse set of test questions for every chapter to help effectively assess students' progress and understanding.
- Editable, chapter-specific Microsoft® **PowerPoint® slides** offer you complete flexibility in easily creating a multimedia presentation for your course.
- All **graphics from the book,** in PowerPoint, PDF, and JPG, are available for use while lecturing, in discussion groups, or for importing into test material.

Acknowledgments

The clean and vigorous style in which this book is written is meant to engage the reader in an unending discussion of California politics that makes plenty of room for other participants. Those who have been essential to enlarging the debate by making this book possible are the expert crew at CQ Press, namely Charisse Kiino, director extraordinaire; Nancy Matuszak, perpetually insightful, optimistic, and skillful development editor, who should be thanked repeatedly for the expert way she applies gentle pressure under stressful conditions; and an adroit and exceptionally talented production and marketing team that includes Laura Barrett, Jennifer Jones, and Amy Whitaker. The book's continued success is testament to their professional prowess, and my gratitude and admiration for their word-smithing talents are limitless. I also extend sincere thanks to those colleagues who have taken the time to provide essential feedback on previous editions, especially Shaun Bowler, whose first review was invaluable; Rick Battson for his thorough review of the second edition; and Mark Petracca, an adviser for the ages, as well as numerous reviewers whose insights and advice provided the thrust for improvements: Monica Galligan, California State University, Monterey Bay; Wesley Hussey, California State University, Sacramento; Kristen J. Huyck, Mt. San Jacinto Community College District; Sarah John, California State University, Fullerton; Vincent Latino, California State University, Sacramento; Uyen, MA, Evergreen Valley College; and Eileen M. Morris, California State University, Chico. I also extend my thanks to the many extraordinary public employees of California who helped provide critical source material for the book, from the staff of the Legislative Analyst's Office to the Secretary of the Senate and many in between. Brian Ebbert, of the Assembly Clerk's Office, deserves special mention for his considerate responses to my requests for information, as do Patrick Johnston, Alison Dinmore, and Mark Stivers; their insights have helped clarify my thoughts and writing about state politics immeasurably. Many thanks as well to Dean Bonner and his colleagues at the Public Policy Institute of California for their first-rate research and assistance. I'm also indebted to the inimitable Bill Stokes, who remains the consummate Sacramento host and jazz impresario. I am blessed with a caring family, to whom this effort is dedicated: my parents, Ann and Joe, loving and faithful exemplars who taught me to find meaning in otherwise ordinary things; my mother-in-law, Ruth, who epitomizes generosity; my visionary, stabilizing, talented husband and partner, Charlie, who deserves a standing ovation for his exceptional patience with my unremitting work schedule; and Ava and Zachary, whose smiles, growth, and progress are a source of joy. May they someday reap the benefits of their Snapchat, Crossy Road, and Minecraft training and help create the "budget surpluses" of tomorrow, contributing resourcefully to a political community in which they take pride.

Introduction

California could be considered one of the ten largest countries in the world. Only six or seven other nations had a larger gross domestic product than California in 2014, and its $2.3 trillion economy rivals those of Italy and Brazil.[1] With a population nearing 39 million, the state boasts 4 million more people than Canada.[2] As many billionaires live in California as in Russia; only China and the United States have more.[3] Its territorial spread includes breathtaking coastlines, fertile farmland both natural and human-made, deserts, the highest and lowest points in the continental United States, dense urban zones, twenty-one mountain ranges, and ancient redwood forests—a resource-rich expanse with boundaries that could accommodate a dozen east coast states.

California sparks global trends, and national and world events permeate—and sometimes temporarily overwhelm—the state's politics. Immigration, climate change, drought, terrorism, pandemics, world-wide economic tides, and wave after wave of other factors push and pull on those who make policy decisions for one of the world's most diverse political communities. Unlike most democratic governments, however, elected officials share the responsibility for policymaking with ordinary Californians who make laws through the initiative process at the state and local levels. This **hybrid political system** (a combination of direct and representative democracy) provides an outlet for voters' general distrust of politicians and dissatisfaction with representative government but tends to promote decision making without compromises.

If **politics** is a process through which people with differing goals and ideals try to manage their conflicts by working together to allocate values for society—which requires bargaining and compromise—then California's system is vulnerable not only to failures of governance but also to repeated attempts to fix what's perceived as broken. Over the last hundred-plus years, the initiative process has permitted voters, wealthy corporations, and interest groups to perform a series of historical experiments on the state's political system, from restyling elections to retuning taxation rates to rebooting the legislature's membership through term limits. Some of these reforms, which are discussed throughout this book, are celebrated as triumphs. Proposition 13 in 1978, for example, deflated ballooning property tax rates for homeowners (now limited to 1 percent of the property's sale price) and arrested rate increases, an arrangement that voters guard watchfully to this day.

Reforms also tend to produce unanticipated consequences that demand further repairs. Property owners may covet the low property tax rates that Prop 13 guarantees, but it has led to chronic underfunding of education and heavy reliance on user fees for public services, as well as unequal tax bills across every neighborhood. Local governments still face a backlog of critical infrastructure projects that continues to swell along with the population. Meanwhile, citizens' loathing of taxes and their exasperation with politicians persist.

California's bulging population ensures that public issues exist on a massive scale. More than one of every eight U.S. residents lives in California, and one of every four Californians is foreign-born. When economic recession hit in the mid-2000s, multibillion-dollar budget gaps were commonplace and reached a high-water mark of $27 billion under Governor Schwarzenegger. Deficits were patched through gargantuan loans, the placement of state workers on unpaid leaves (furloughs), and the slashing of state services. Unemployment rates exceeding 12 percent outstripped the

FIGURE 1.1 Gross Domestic Product, 2014 (in millions)

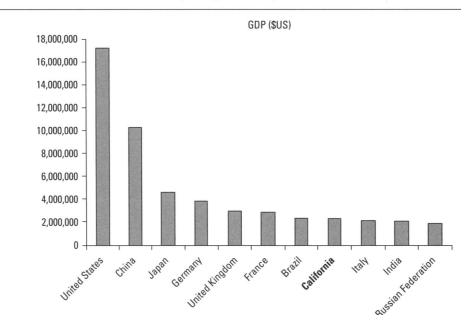

Sources: World Bank, "Gross Domestic Product 2014," World Development Indicators Database, http://databank.worldbank.org/data/download/GDP.pdf; U.S. Department of Commerce, Bureau of Economic Analysis, "BEARFACTS: GDP for California," http://www.bea.gov/regional/bearfacts/action.cfm?geoType=3&fips=06000&areatype=06000.

national averages.[4] Now, even though the economy is on the upswing, 85 percent of Californians continue to describe unemployment as a serious problem in 2015, and half (50 percent) of Californians describe the state's economy as being in bad times rather than good (only 33 percent are optimistic).[5] Prisons remain overcrowded by tens of thousands of inmates, although incarceration rates have shrunk from all-time highs by federal court order as many nonviolent criminals have been shifted to county jails and paroled.

Drought, long-term and pervasive, has gripped the entire state, and heavy rains are unlikely to erase all its impacts. In 2014, California became the last state in the nation to require local management plans for groundwater, and not long after, Governor Jerry Brown mandated 25 percent water usage cutbacks for counties and cities. The state was also contending with an 11 trillion-gallon deficit caused by rain- and snowfall shortages,[6] painfully visible in cracked-earth river basins, bathtub-type rings created by falling lake levels, and an almost nonexistent Sierra Nevada snowpack that is arguably the state's most critical reservoir, the main source of the southland's water. Overpumping of groundwater is causing land to sink faster than ever, a phenomenon called *subsidence* that buckles roads, irrigation canals, bridges, and pipes, costing state and local governments millions to fix.

Mandatory restrictions have spurred close examinations of water rights belonging not only to all drought-stricken western states but also to three separate rights-holders within the state: the *environment* (restoring or sustaining habitat, ensuring water quality, and so forth, which guzzles half of the state's water), *people*, including individual consumers and companies, and *agriculture*. Media stories have sensationalized ongoing battles over water allocations from the complex Sacramento–San Joaquin River Delta estuary located east of San Francisco, which feeds farms in the Central Valley and is also diverted to protect a unique environment in which endangered species such as a small fish called the Delta smelt subsist. Reports have spotlighted growers who replenish the nation's breadbasket but purportedly use 80 percent of water used by humans and businesses and pay far less for the lower-quality water they use, further annoying residents who feel that local water agency restrictions on urban consumption are unfair. Farmers point out that food safety should come first: "We have to feed families, but we don't have to golf."[7] Meanwhile, local water agencies are busily devising ways to incentivize conservation and penalize higher water consumption by urban users.

The availability, cost, distribution, storage, and cleanliness of freshwater represent a fraction of the complex, interrelated issues that state and local elected officials deal with year-round. Drought is merely one dimension of climate change, a large-scale phenomenon that also intensifies the risk of wildfire; affects whether California can produce the wines and food that the world enjoys; alters delicate ecosystems; and invites invasive pests that carry infectious diseases—all of which have impacts on human health, affordable housing, and employment, to name just a few areas of concern for policymakers. Californians also face a daunting list of challenges brought about by natural population growth and immigration, as deteriorating infrastructure in the form of sewers, roads, bridges, storm drains, water storage and treatment facilities, aging schools, and jails compete for the public's limited attention and money. Current infrastructure needs are estimated to exceed $500 billion.[8] These policy issues, along with other pressing challenges, are catalogued in the concluding chapter.

Water scarcity also highlights how different interests compete through the political process to get what they want. Governing officials must balance private and public interests, and they work hard to fix problems experienced by their constituents—a job that also requires them to balance the needs of their own districts against those of their city, county, or the entire state. This grand balancing act is but one reason California politics often appears irrational, but, like the U.S. government, the system

THE FOUR SEASONS iN CALiFORNiA

EARTHQUAKE

BRUSHFIRE

MUDSLIDE

BUT HEY, THE HARMONIC KARMA IN THIS PLACE AND THE SUNSETS? WOW, AWESOME!

DENIAL

© raesidecartoon.com

was designed that way, mostly through deliberate choice but also through the unintended consequences of prior decisions. California's crazy quilt of governing institutions reflects repeated attempts to manage conflicts that result from millions of people putting demands on a system that creates both winners and losers—not all of whom give up quietly when they lose. As happens at the federal level, state officials tend to respond to the most persistent, organized, and well-funded members of society; on the other hand, losers in California can reverse their fortunes by skillfully employing the tools of direct democracy to sidestep elected officials altogether.

Principles for Understanding California Politics

It may seem counterintuitive given the depth of its problems, but California politics can be explained and understood logically—although the results of the process are just as often frustrating and irresponsible as they are praiseworthy and necessary. In short, the fundamental concepts of **choice, political culture, institutions, collective action, rules,** and **history** can be used to understand state politics just as they are used to understand national or even local democratic politics. These concepts are used throughout this book to explain how governing decisions are made by Californians or on their behalf and to provide a starting point for evaluating California's political system: does it work as intended? Do citizens have realistic expectations about what problems government can solve, the services or values it provides, and how efficiently or cheaply it can do so? How do we measure "successful" politics?

We begin with the premise that **choices** are at the heart of politics. Citizens make political choices explicit when they decide not to participate in an election or when they cast a vote, but they also make implicit political choices when they throw aluminum cans in a recycling bin or send their children to private schools. Legislators' jobs consist of a series of choices that involve choosing what to say, which issues to ignore, whose recommendations to take, which phone calls to return, and how to word a law or cast a vote.

BOX 1.1   Comparative FAST FACTS on California

	California	New York	United States
Capital:	Sacramento	Albany	Washington, DC
Statehood:	September 9, 1850 (31st state)	July 26, 1788 (11th state)	Declared independence from Great Britain July 4, 1776
Number of U.S. House members:	53	27 (–2 from 2000)	435
Number of counties:	58 (since 1879)	62	50 states
Largest city by population:	Los Angeles, 3,957,022*	New York City, 8,175,133**	New York
Total population:	38,715,000*	19,746,227**	318,857,056**
Percentage of foreign-born persons:**	27.0	22.1	12.9
Median annual household income:**	$61,094	$58,003	$50,502
Percentage of persons living below poverty level:**	15.9	15.3	15.9

*California Department of Finance, "California Grew by 358,000 Residents in 2014," press release (May 1, 2015), http://www.dof.ca.gov/research/demographic/reports/estimates/e-1/documents/E-1_2015PressRelease.pdf. The U.S. Census Bureau estimated the figure to be 38,802,500 as of July 1, 2014.

**Current U.S. and New York population figures based on U.S. 2010 census, monthly population estimates as of July 1, 2014. U.S. Census Bureau, American FactFinder, "Monthly Population Estimates for the United States as of July 1, 2014," http://factfinder.census.gov/faces/nav/jsf/pages/community_facts.xhtml. Income, national origin, and poverty rates based on U.S. Census Bureau, American Community Survey, 3-year estimates, accessed June 2015.

Ethnic Makeup of California:

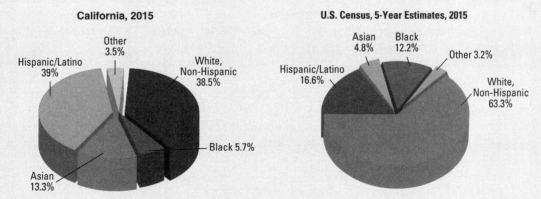

California, 2015

Other 3.5%
Hispanic/Latino 39%
White, Non-Hispanic 38.5%
Black 5.7%
Asian 13.3%

U.S. Census, 5-Year Estimates, 2015

Asian 4.8%
Black 12.2%
Other 3.2%
Hispanic/Latino 16.6%
White, Non-Hispanic 63.3%

Sources: California Department of Finance, "Report P-2: Population Projections by Race/Ethnicity, and 5-year Age Groups, 2010–2060" (December 2014), http://www.dof.ca.gov/research/demographic/reports/projections/P-2. "Other" includes Hawaiian/Pacific Islander, American Indian, and "more than two races." U.S. figures from U.S. Census Bureau, American FactFinder, based on American Community Survey, 2009–2013 five-year estimates.

In large and diverse societies that are crammed with people who are motivated by different goals, interests, and values, a successful political system provides a process for narrowing choices to a manageable number and allows many participants to reconcile their differences as they make choices together. The decisions that emerge from this process express the customs, values, and beliefs about government that a society holds and give that political system a distinct culture—a **political culture** that varies from state to state. Three of the features that define California's political culture are a historical fondness for reforming the political system, a preference for Democratic officials but general detachment from political parties, and an aversion to politicians—themes that will resurface throughout this book.

Political systems also facilitate compromises, trade-offs, and bargains that lead to acceptable solutions or alternatives. **Institutions** help organize this kind of action. Political institutions are organizations built to manage conflict by defining particular roles and rules for those who participate in them. In short, they bring people together to solve problems on behalf of society. Democratic elections are a good example: there are rules about who can vote and who can run for office, how the process will be controlled, and how disputes resulting from them will be resolved. Through institutions like elections, **collective action** (working together for mutual benefit) can take place. The same can be said of other institutions—such as traffic courts and political parties—for in each, people work together to solve their problems and allocate goods for a society.

Rules also matter. **Rules** define who has power and how they may legitimately use it, and rules create incentives for action or inaction. For instance, in the legislature, a majority political party must cater to the minority party's demands in order to secure a few decisive votes when a two-thirds supermajority vote is required, whereas they can choose to ignore the minority when simple majority rules are in place.

Rules are also the results of choices made throughout **history,** and over time a body of rules will change and grow in response to cultural shifts, natural disasters, scandals, economic trends, and other forces, creating further opportunities and incentives for political action. Enormous economic tides that define eras (think "The Great Recession" or "The Great Depression") exert especially powerful forces in politics because behemoth governments are not designed to respond nimbly to rapid and unanticipated changes; budgets and programs are planned months and years in advance, with history providing clues to decision makers about probable developments. Sudden readjustments, particularly those made in hard times, will reverberate far into the future.

Thus, recognizing that both choices and the rules that condition them are made within a given historical context goes a long way toward explaining each state's distinctive political system. A state's political culture also contributes to that distinctiveness. These are the elements that make New York's state government so different from the governments of Nevada, Georgia, and every other state, and we should keep them in mind as we consider how California's governing institutions developed. In essence, a unique set of rules, its culture, and its history are key to understanding California politics. They help explain the relationship between Californians and their government, how competing expectations about "successful" politics propel change, and why elected officials tend to have such a hard time running the state.

For years, online bloggers to *New York Times* editors opined that California was on that brink of collapse, that it was "ungovernable," but Governor Jerry Brown has snuffed out those critiques as balanced, on-time budgets have materialized on his watch, and budget surpluses have mounted—facts that certainly affirm the importance of a strong economy but also solid leadership, both of which have contributed to his generally high approval ratings (58 percent in mid-2015, ratings he has maintained since late 2013).[9]

The steps of the state capitol in Sacramento serve as the location where California governors are sworn into office at least every four years and provide a daily stage for public rallies and demonstrations.

It remains to be seen whether Brown is merely holding a tidal wave of problems at bay, as debts pile up (see chapter 8) and deferred maintenance projects accumulate. The people's general discontent with politicians and politics also handicap government's capacity to solve the state's pressing problems, address piecemeal decisions of the past, and hinder representatives' ability to plan sufficiently for the future. Still, Californians' hope that things can be better motivates them to keep testing the limits of their political machinery. Moreover, Brown has demonstrated that political leadership is possible and he has originated his own brand of "successful" politics. This book explores the reasons for the contemporary state of affairs and pushes the reader to ask what successful politics requires, whether those conditions are present in California, and what it will take to enable California's government to serve the public's interests effectively, comprehensively, and sensibly over the long term.

Notes

1. See Jason Sisney and Justin Garosi, "2014 GDP: California Ranks 7th or 8th in the World," Legislative Analyst's Office, July 1, 2015, http://www.lao.ca.gov/LAOEconTax/Article/Detail/90. See also World Bank, "Gross Domestic Product 2014," World Development Indicators Database, http://databank.worldbank.org/data/download/GDP.pdf; U.S. Department of Commerce, Bureau of Economic Analysis, "Interactive Data" (state GDP, TOTAL industries number), http://www.bea.gov.

2. The Department of Finance estimated the total population to be 38,715,000 on January 1, 2015. Source: State of California, Department of Finance, *E-1 Population Estimates for Cities, Counties and the State with Annual Percent Change—January 1, 2014 and 2015,* Sacramento, California, May 2015.

3. Dan Alexander, "California Leads All States (and All but Two Countries) with 111 Billionaires," *Forbes,* March 7, 2014, http://www.forbes.com/sites/danalexander/2014/03/07/california-leads-all-states-and-all-but-2-countries-with-111-billionaires.

4. The seasonally adjusted rate was 12.2 percent for February through April, 2010. Rates were 12.7 percent in California for January 2010, versus 10.6 percent in the same month nationally. Sources: California Employment Development Department, "Unemployment Rates (Labor Force), 2000-2015," California Employment Development Department, http://www.labormarketinfo.edd.ca.gov/cgi/dataanalysis/labForceReport.asp?menuchoice=LABFORCE, and Bureau of Labor Statistics, "Labor Force Statistics from the Current Population Survey," U.S. Department of Labor, August 24, 2015, http://data.bls.gov/timeseries/LNS14000000.

5. Mark DiCamillo and Mervin Field, "Release #2508," *The Field Poll,* May 28, 2015, http://www.field.com/fieldpollonline/subscribers/Rls2508.pdf. Respondents in this report were a randomly selected subsample of 1,664 California adults, with a total response subset of 478 registered voters; the poll's margin of error was ±4.6 percent. Interviews took place April 23–May 16, 2015.

6. "NASA Data Underscore Severity of California Drought," NASA Jet Propulsion Laboratory, California Institute of Technology, December 14, 2014, http://www.jpl.nasa.gov/news/news.php?feature=4412.

7. Quoted in Jesse Marx and Ian James, "Farm Water Use Comes Under Scrutiny," *The Desert Sun,* April 20, 2015, http://www.desertsun.com/story/news/environment/2015/04/20/farm-water-use-comes-scrutiny/26076211.

8. Jose Cisneros, "California's Crumbling Infrastructure: An Urgent Priority," League of California Cities, *Western City Magazine,* February 2014, http://www.westerncity.com/Western-City/February-2014/PresMsg-CA-Crumbling-Infrastructure.

9. Mark DiCamillo and Mervin Field, "Release #2507," *The Field Poll,* May 27, 2015, http://www.field.com/fieldpollonline/subscribers/Rls2507.pdf. The respondents were 1,664 California adults, including 1,044 registered voters; interviews took place April 23–May 16, 2015. The poll's margin of error was ±3.2 percent.

CHAPTER 2

Critical Junctures

California's Political History in Brief

Early California

The contours of California's contemporary political landscape began to take shape in 1542, when Spanish explorer Juan Cabrillo claimed the Native American lands now known as San Diego for a distant monarchy, thereby paving the way for European settlements along the West Coast. Aided by Spanish troops, colonization accompanied the founding of Catholic missions throughout Baja (lower) and then Alta (northern) California. These missions, as well as military presidios (army posts), were constructed along what became known as El Camino Real, or the King's Highway, a path that roughly followed a line of major tribal establishments. Over the next two hundred years, native peoples were either subordinated or decimated by foreign diseases, soldiers, and ways of life, and the huge mission complexes and ranches, or rancheros, that replaced these groups and their settlements became the focal points for social activity and economic industry in the region.

The western lands containing California became part of Mexico when that country gained independence from Spain in 1821, and for more than two decades, Mexicans governed the region, constructing presidios and installing military leaders to protect the cities taking shape up and down the coast. Following the Mexican-American War of 1848 that ended with the Treaty of Guadalupe Hidalgo, California became the new U.S. frontier astride a new international border. The simultaneous discovery of gold near Sacramento provoked an onslaught of settlers in what would be the first of several significant population waves to flood the West Coast during the next 125 years. The rush to the Golden State was on.

MAP 2.1 California's Missions

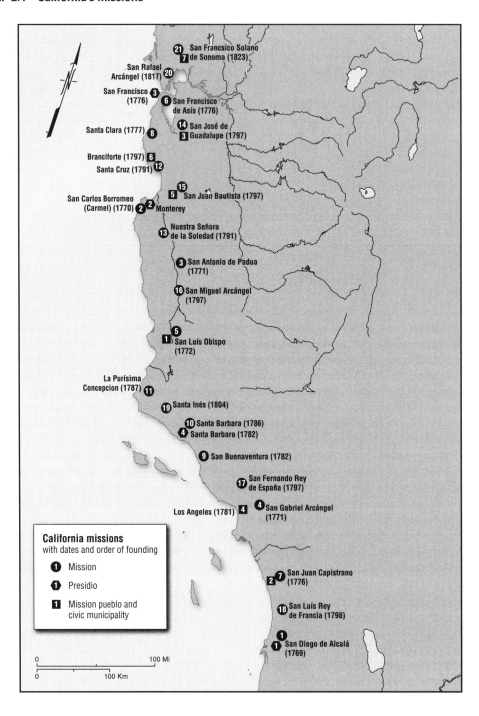

San Francsico Solano de Sonoma (1823) — 21 / 7

San Rafael Arcángel (1817) — 20

San Francisco (1776) — 3

San Francisco de Asís (1776) — 6

Santa Clara (1777) — 8

San José de Guadalupe (1797) — 14 / 3

Branciforte (1797) — 6

Santa Cruz (1791) — 12

San Carlos Borromeo (Carmel) (1770) — 2 / 2 Monterey

San Juan Bautista (1797) — 5 / 15

Nuestra Señora de la Soledad (1791) — 13

San Antonio de Padua (1771) — 3

San Miguel Arcángel (1797) — 16

San Luís Obispo (1772) — 1 / 5

La Purísima Concepcion (1787) — 11

Santa Inés (1804) — 19

Santa Barbara (1786) — 10

Santa Barbara (1782) — 4

San Buenaventura (1782) — 9

San Fernando Rey de España (1797) — 17

Los Angeles (1781) — 4

San Gabriel Arcángel (1771) — 4

San Juan Capistrano (1776) — 2 / 7

San Luís Rey de Francia (1798) — 18

San Diego de Alcalá (1769) — 1 / 1

California missions
with dates and order of founding

1 Mission

1 Presidio

1 Mission pueblo and civic municipality

0 ————— 100 Mi

0 ————— 100 Km

The Rise of the Southern Pacific Railroad

Spurning slavery and embracing self-governance, a group of pregold-rush settlers and mayors convened to write a state constitution in 1849; a year later, the U.S. Congress granted the territory statehood, and shortly thereafter Sacramento became the state's permanent capital. Although gold had already lured nearly one hundred thousand adventurers to the state in less than two years, the region remained a mostly untamed and distant outpost, separated from the East Coast by treacherous terrain and thousands of miles of ocean travel. Growing demand for more reliable linkages to the rest of the United States led to the building of the transcontinental railroad in 1869, an undertaking that resulted in the importation of thousands of Chinese laborers and millions of acres of federal land grants to a few railroad companies. Eleven million acres in California were granted to the Southern Pacific Railroad alone.[1]

The wildly successful enterprise not only opened the West to rapid development but also consolidated economic and political power in the Central Pacific Railroad, later renamed the Southern Pacific Railroad. Owned by barons Collis Huntington, Mark Hopkins, Leland Stanford, and Charles Crocker—the "Big Four"—through the early 1900s the Southern Pacific extended its reach to virtually all forms of shipping and transportation. This had direct impacts on all major commercial activity within the state, from wheat prices to land values and from bank lending to the availability

© Everett Collection Historical / Alamy

Enduring persistent racial discrimination, punishing conditions, and a lack of labor and safety protections, Chinese immigrants laid thousands of miles of railroad tracks during the 1880s and early 1900s.

of lumber. The railroad barons' landholdings enabled them to control the prosperity or demise of entire towns near rail lines throughout the West. Power didn't come cheap, however, and they fostered "friendships" in the White House, Congress, the state court system, and of course throughout local and state governments by finding every influential person's "price." As famously depicted in Edward Keller's illustration "The Curse of California," which appeared in San Francisco's *The Wasp* on August 19, 1882, the "S.P." (Southern Pacific Railroad) dominated every major sector of the state's economy—and politics—like a determined octopus.

Progressivism

The Southern Pacific's hold over California government during the late 1800s cannot be overestimated. One historian describes the situation in this way:

> For at least a generation after the new constitution went into effect [in 1879] the great majority of Californians believed that the influence of the railroad extended from the governor's mansion in Sacramento to the lowest ward heeler in San Francisco, and that the machine determined who should sit in city councils and on boards of supervisors; who should be sent to the House of Representatives and to the Senate in Washington; what laws should be enacted by the legislature, and what decisions should be rendered from the bench.[2]

The Southern Pacific's grip over California industry and politics was finally smashed, bit by bit, by muckraking journalists whose stories were pivotal in the passing of new federal regulations aimed at breaking monopolies; by the prosecution of San Francisco's corrupt political boss, Abe Ruef; and by the rise of a national political movement known as "Progressivism" that quickly took root in California. Governor Hiram Johnson (1911–1917) personified the idealistic Progressive spirit through his focus on eliminating every private interest from government and restoring power to the people.

To that end, Governor Johnson spearheaded an ambitious reform agenda that addressed a wide range of social, political, and economic issues that were attracting the attention of Progressives in other U.S. states. His agenda was not only grounded in a fundamental distrust of political parties, which had been hijacked by the Southern Pacific in California, but also built on an emerging philosophy that government could be run like a business, with efficiency as a clear objective. Workers' rights, municipal ownership of utility companies, universal education, environmental conservation, morals laws, and the assurance of fair political representation topped the list of items Johnson tackled with the help of the California legislature after he entered office in 1911.

Changes in electoral laws directly targeted the ties political parties had to both the railroads and potential voters. Although **secret voting** had become state law in 1896, the practice was strengthened and enforced as a means to control elections and ensure fairness. The ability of party bosses to "select and elect" the candidates for political offices was undercut with the establishment of **direct primary elections,** in which any party member could become a candidate for office and gain the nomination of his fellow party members through a regular party election. The legislature also reclassified local elected offices as **"nonpartisan,"** meaning that the party affiliations of candidates did not appear on

THE CURSE OF CALIFORNIA.

the ballot if they were running for municipal offices, such as city councils or local school boards, or for judgeships. Efficiency, the Progressives believed, demanded that voters and officials be blind to partisanship, because petty divisions wasted valuable time and resources, and the important concern was who was the best person for a position, not his political affiliation.

A more ingenious method of controlling parties was accomplished through a new law that allowed **cross-filing,** which meant that any candidate's name could appear on any party's primary election ballot without the candidate's party affiliation being indicated. In effect, Republicans could seek the Democrats' nomination and vice versa, thereby allowing candidates to be nominated by more than one party. This rule, which remained on the books until 1959, initially helped Progressives but later allowed Republicans to dominate state politics despite state party registration that favored the Democrats after 1934.

Civil service exams were also instituted, which changed the hiring of local and state government employees from a system based on patronage (*who* one knew) to one based on merit (*what* one knew about a position and *how well* one knew it). But perhaps the most important political reform the Progressives instituted was a transformation of the relationship citizens had to California government. They accomplished this first by guaranteeing **women the right to vote** and then by adopting the tools of **direct democracy**: the **recall**, the **referendum**, and the **initiative** process (discussed in chapter 3). By vesting the people with the power to make laws directly—even new laws that could override those already in place—Progressives redistributed political power and essentially redesigned the basic structure of government. No longer was California a purely representative democracy; it now had a **hybrid government** that combined direct and representative forms of democracy. Elected officials would now compete with the people and special interests for power through the initiative process. The Progressives had triggered the state's first giant political earthquake.

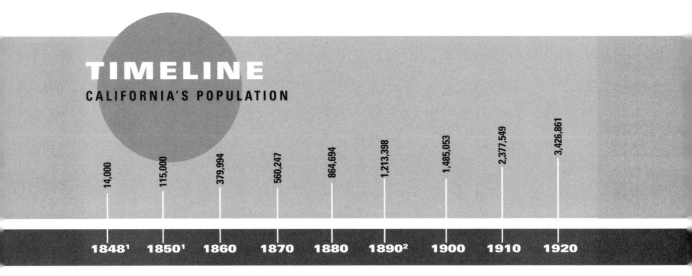

TIMELINE
CALIFORNIA'S POPULATION

1848[1]	1850[1]	1860	1870	1880	1890[2]	1900	1910	1920
14,000	115,000	379,994	560,247	864,694	1,213,398	1,485,053	2,377,549	3,426,861

[1] Source for population estimates 1848–1850: Andrew Rolle, *California: A History* (Wheeling, IL: Harlan Davidson, 2003).
[2] Population estimates from 1848–1880 are for nonnative populations. Native populations were not included in the U.S. census prior to 1890.

It should be noted that the Progressives' efforts to widen access to political power did not extend to every group in California, and some of the laws they passed were specifically designed to exclude certain people from decision making and restrict their political power. The most egregious examples reflected the White majority's racial hostility toward Chinese-born and other Asian-born residents, which took the form of "Alien Land Laws" that denied landownership, full property rights, and other civil rights to anyone of Asian descent—laws that would not be removed from the state's books for another half century.

The Power of Organized Interests

Ironically, the Progressives' attacks on political parties and the Southern Pacific created new opportunities for other kinds of special interests to influence state government. Cross-filing produced legislators with minimal party allegiances, and by the 1940s, these individuals had come to depend heavily on lobbyists for information and other "diversions" to supplement their meager $3,000 annual salary. The legendary Artie Samish, head of the liquor and racetrack lobbies from the 1920s to the 1950s, personified the power of the "third

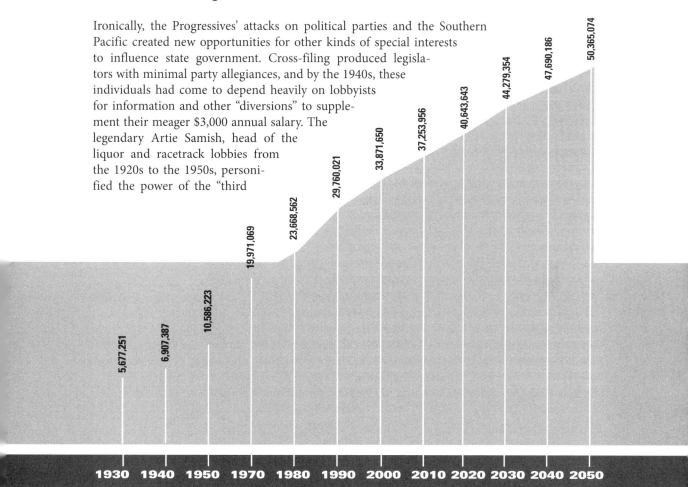

| 1930 | 1940 | 1950 | 1970 | 1980 | 1990 | 2000 | 2010 | 2020 | 2030 | 2040 | 2050 |

5,677,251
6,907,387
10,586,223
19,971,069
23,668,562
29,760,021
33,871,650
37,253,956
40,643,643
44,279,354
47,690,186
50,365,074

Source for population estimates 1860–2015: U.S. Census Bureau.

Source for population estimates 2020–2050: California Department of Finance, Demographic Research Unit.

house" (organized interests represented in the lobbying corps) in his ability to control election outcomes and tax rates for industries he represented. "I am the governor of the legislature," he brazenly boasted in the 1940s. "To hell with the governor of California."[3] He was convicted and jailed for corruption not long after making this statement, but his personal downfall hardly disturbed the cozy relationships between lobbyists and legislators that continued to flourish in—and taint—California state politics.

Growth and Industrialization in the Golden State

To outsiders, the image of California as a land of mythical possibility and wealth persisted even as the Great Depression took hold in the 1930s. As depicted in John Steinbeck's *The Grapes of Wrath,* hundreds of thousands of unskilled American migrants from the mid- and southwestern Dust Bowl ("Okies" as they were pejoratively called by Californians) flooded the state, provoking a stinging social backlash that lasted at least until war production created new labor demands. The Depression also helped breathe life into what was neither the first nor the last unconventional political movement: in 1934, outspoken writer and socialist Upton Sinclair easily won the Democratic nomination for governor by waging an "End Poverty in California" (EPIC) campaign, which promised relief for lower- and middle-class Californians through a radical tax plan. His near-win mobilized conservatives, inspired left-wing Democrats to fortify social programs, and propelled the first modern attack ads—the media-driven smear campaign—into being.

Rapid urban and industrial development during the first decades of the twentieth century accompanied the invention of the automobile and the step-up in oil production preceding World War II. Ribbons of roads and highways wrapped new towns and tied them to swelling cities, and people kept arriving in California at spectacular rates. Industrialization during World War II restored the state's golden image, bringing defense-related jobs, federal funds, manufacturing, construction, and a prosperity that only accelerated postwar. The building sector boomed while orange trees blossomed. To address labor shortages, the federal "Bracero" program created a new agricultural labor force by facilitating the entry of Mexican laborers into the United States, beckoning millions of men and their families to the country. Their efforts laid the foundations for California's thriving modern agribusiness sector.

Tract-housing developments materialized at an unprecedented rate and so did demands for roads, water, schools, and other critical infrastructure. In 1947, the state fanned the spread of "car culture" with an ambitious ten-year highway plan that cost $1 million per working day. Flood control and colossal irrigation projects begun in the 1860s had transformed the San Francisco Bay and the Sacramento–San Joaquin River Delta region from wetlands filled with wildlife into a labyrinth of levees, tunnels, canals, and dams that allowed midcentury farmers to feed expanding populations. Los Angeles continued to invent itself by sprawling across floodplains with manufacturing plants and neighborhoods that depended on water imported from the north, triggering "water wars" that continue to this day. Infrastructure spending centered on moving water to the thirsty south via the State Water Project (SWP), the building of schools, establishing a first-class university system, and keeping freeways flowing—priorities that governors Earl Warren and Edmund "Pat" Brown (Jerry Brown's father) advanced through the early 1960s.

The Initiative Process Takes Hold

The political landscape was also changing dramatically midcentury. Cross-filing, which had severely disadvantaged the Democrats for forty years, was effectively eliminated through a 1952 initiative that required candidates' party affiliations to be printed on primary election ballots. With this important change, Democrats finally realized majority status in 1958 with Pat Brown in the governor's office and control of both legislative houses.

Several U.S. Supreme Court cases also necessitated fundamental changes in the way that Californians were represented in both the state and national legislatures. Between 1928 and 1965, the state employed the "federal plan," modeling its legislature on the U.S. Congress, with an upper house based on geographic areas (counties rather than states) and a lower house based on population. Although many attempts had been made to dismantle the plan because it produced gross overrepresentation of northern and inland rural interests and severe underrepresentation of southern metropolitan residents in the state Senate (three-fourths of sitting senators represented low-density rural areas), it remained in place until a federal court struck it down; per the U.S. Supreme Court ruling in *Reynolds v. Sims* (1964), the California system was found to violate the "one person–one vote" principle.[4] After 1965, political influence passed from legislators representing the north to those representing the south and also from rural to urban interests. Moreover, putting legislators in charge of redrawing their own districts reopened the possibility for gerrymandering, the practice of manipulating district boundaries to virtually ensure the reelection of incumbents and the continuation of the majority party in power.

The revival of parties in the legislature during the 1960s was greatly assisted by the Democratic Speaker of the California State Assembly, "Big Daddy" Jesse Unruh, who understood how to influence the reelection of loyal partisans by controlling the flow of campaign donations and called money the "mother's milk of politics."[5] Unruh also helped orchestrate an overhaul of the legislature through Proposition 1A, a measure designed to "Update the State!" via constitutional cleanup in 1966. Prop 1A professionalized the lawmaking body by endowing it with the "three S's": higher *salary*, many more *staff*, and year-round *session*. The intent was to create a legislative body that could separate itself from the enticements of lobbyists by giving it the necessary resources to compete on more equal footing with the executive branch, and 73.5 percent of California voters welcomed the political shake-up. Lawmakers' annual pay doubled to $16,000 to reflect their new full-time status, and assistants were hired to write and analyze bills.

Professionalization transformed the legislature into a highly paid, well-staffed institution that quickly gained a reputation as a policy and political reform leader among the states. In 1971, the legislature was described as possessing "all the characteristics that a legislature should have," having "proved itself capable of leading the nation in the development of legislation to deal with some of our most critical problems."[6] It didn't take long for the shine to fade, however, as the legislature appeared to let certain taxation policies fly out of control in the mid-1970s.

Propelled by anger over the legislature's inability to reconcile skyrocketing property taxes and a multibillion-dollar state budget surplus, voters revolted against "spendthrift politicians" who "will not act to reduce . . . property taxes."[7] Fully realizing the energizing power of a grassroots political movement through the initiative process, citizens overwhelmingly approved Prop 13, which limited annual property tax to 1 percent of a property's assessed value.[8] Prop 13 forever changed the rules regarding taxation and state budgeting by imposing a two-thirds vote requirement to raise either state or local taxes, a rule that both empowers a minority determined to forestall any tax increases and can significantly jeopardize the legislature's ability to pass balanced budgets on time. Prop 13 sparked the dramatic use of the initiative process that continues today.

The faith in self-governance and mistrust of politicians that spurred Progressives into action and citizens to approve Prop 13 continued to cause political tremors in California politics. The view that citizens were more trustworthy than their representatives only intensified during the 1980s after three legislators were convicted of bribery in an FBI sting labeled "Shrimpscam" (a fictitious shrimp company "paid" legislators to introduce bills favoring the company), reinforcing the perception that Sacramento was full of corrupt, self-indulgent politicians. State lawmakers' reputation for being "arrogant and unresponsive" only grew as the power of incumbency (simply being an elected official) and membership turnover in the legislature stagnated. In 1990, they found themselves targeted by Proposition 140 (discussed in chapter 4), which imposed term limits on all elected state constitutional officers, eliminating the chance to develop long careers in a single, elected state office.

Parties and elections have also been targeted through ballot initiatives. In the tradition of cross-filing, allowing all persons to vote in any political party's primary election regardless of party membership was attempted in 1996, but Proposition 198's blanket primary was overturned by the U.S.

AP Photo/Lennox McLendon

The passage of Proposition 13 in June 1978 opened a new chapter in California history, demonstrating the power of the initiative and the strength of antitax forces. The initiative's authors, Howard Jarvis and Paul Gann (not pictured here), led the antitaxation effort. Prop 13's strict limits on property taxes sparked similar "taxpayer revolts" across the United States.

Supreme Court. This idea finally succeeded as a "voter preference primary" law in 2010, or what is better known as the "Top Two Primary" (Prop 14; more will be said about this later). Importantly, in that same year voters transferred the authority to draw electoral district lines (boundaries defining the geographic areas that legislators represent) from lawmakers to a citizen commission (Prop 11).

Voters have also altered policymaking processes through changes in the rules. Proposition 98, enacted in 1988, significantly constrains the legislature by mandating that public schools (grades K–12) and community colleges receive an amount equal to roughly 40 percent of the state's general fund budget each year. Proposition 39, approved in 2000, affects the voters' ability to approve school bonds by lowering the supermajority requirement to 55 percent (from two-thirds). The recently passed Proposition 26 recategorizes most "fees" as taxes, subject to a two-thirds supermajority approval, and Proposition 25 allows legislators to pass the state budget with a simple majority vote (down from a two-thirds supermajority) but denies legislators a paycheck if they fail to pass the budget on time. This sampling of reforms reveals a firmly established reform tradition that will continue to reshape California's government.

Hyperdiversity in a Modern State

Hybrid government reinforces California's distinctiveness, but probably no condition defines politics in California more than the state's great human diversity, which is as much a source of rich heritage and culture as it is the root of competing and sometimes divisive political pressures. Differences stemming from ethnicity, race, religion, age, sexuality, ideology, socioeconomic class, and geography (to name but a few sources) do not inevitably breed conflict; however, these differences often are the source of intense political clashes in the state. The political realm is where these differences are expressed as divergent goals and ideals in the search for group recognition, power, or public goods, and the vital challenge for California's political representatives and institutions is to aggregate interests rather than aggravate them.

A post–World War II baby boom inflated the state's population even as waves of immigration and migration throughout the mid- to late twentieth century produced minor political tremors. A marked national population shift from the Rust Belt to the Sun Belt boosted California's economy, as well as its population, over the latter half of the twentieth century. Another wave of people from Southeast Asia arrived during the late 1960s to the mid-1970s, following the Vietnam War, and the most recent influx of immigrants occurred during the 1980s and 1990s, when the state's economic prosperity encouraged large-scale migration from Mexico and other Latin and Central American countries.

Immigration, legal and illegal, as well as natural population growth, have therefore produced a hyperdiverse state in which many groups vie for political legitimacy and attention, for public services and goods, and for power and influence. California is home to the largest Asian population in the United States, including Southeast Asians, who are among the fastest-growing groups in the state.[9] Having displaced Whites in 2015 as the state's largest ethnic group, Latinos now constitute 40 percent of the state's population.[10] Still underrepresented at the polls, Latinos have yet to realize their political power in California. How will they shake off political disinterest? What kinds of political earthquakes, if any, will eventual shifts toward new voting groups produce?

Continually changing demographic patterns help drive public policy debates, as they often raise questions about what it means to be a citizen. Impassioned campaigns have been waged over whether to make English the state's official language (approved by 73.2 percent of voters in 1986), whether to teach children only in English (passed by 60.9 percent of voters in 1998 as Proposition 227), whether to deny citizenship to children born in the state to undocumented workers (a federal constitutional issue), and whether to allow undocumented immigrants the ability to obtain in-state tuition rates or Cal Grants (the California Development, Relief, and Education for Alien Minors Act, known as the DREAM Act, was signed into law in 2011). AB 60, a law passed in 2013, allows undocumented immigrants to obtain driver's licenses, something many Californians have opposed for symbolic and practical reasons, though this right has already been enabled in the District of Columbia and nine other states, including Colorado and Illinois.[11] The Department of Motor Vehicles (DMV) estimates that at least 1.5 million applicants will receive this specially designated license before 2018.[12]

Residential patterns also raise questions about cultural assimilation versus cultural preservation. Some subpopulations tend to concentrate geographically, forming "Little Saigons," "Chinatowns," or barrios. "Communities of interest" such as these have performed the historical role of absorbing foreign laborers and refugees, including the approximately fifty thousand Vietnamese who arrived after the Vietnam War and the approximately three million Latinos who joined family members in the United States as part of a 1986 federal amnesty program. Chinatown in San Francisco remains the

AP Photo/Gosia Wozniacka

Children at Jefferson Elementary School in Sanger, a city near Fresno, are among the state's plurality (40 percent) Latino population. In 2013–14 they represented more than half (53 percent) of all students enrolled in California K–12 schools, whereas non-Hispanic Whites were 25 percent, Asian and Pacific Islanders were 11.5 percent, and African Americans were 6 percent.

largest enclave of its kind, with the largest concentration of ethnic Chinese outside China. The dual trends of "balkanization" (communities separated by race or ethnicity) and "White flight" (the movement of Caucasians out of urban zones and to the inland counties) have become more pronounced during recent decades and have political implications, particularly for voting (see chapter 9).

The sheer volume of basic and special needs created by this hyperdiversity has tended to outstrip government capacity in the areas of public education, legal and correctional services, infrastructure development, environmental protection, public welfare, and health services. Population growth will continue to animate budget and policy debates, providing plenty of fissures that will test the foundations of state government.

Recalling a Governor

The constant energy of gradual population change contrasts sharply with the sudden jolts that unexpected events can send through a political system. The most significant political earthquake of the new millennium in California hit in 2003 with the recall of Governor Gray Davis, a dizzying, circus-like event that solidified the state's image as a national outlier. The mild-mannered, uncharismatic Governor Davis had gained a reputation as a "pay-to-play" politician who rewarded friendly public employee unions with generous contracts and was blamed for skyrocketing electricity bills, tripling the car tax, and overdue budgets that contained accounting gimmicks.[13] After Republican U.S. representative Darrell Issa infused the recall effort with more than $1 million, enough signatures were gathered to trigger a special recall election.

For the first time ever, Californians would be asked if they wanted to keep their governor or replace him, and if enough voters wanted to replace him, they would have the opportunity to choose a successor. Hundreds of potential candidates jostled for attention, including actor Arnold Schwarzenegger, who surprised Jay Leno and the audience of *The Tonight Show* by announcing his candidacy during an appearance on the show.

The spectacular election season lasted only seventy-six days (a normal cycle is about twice as long), during which time the candidates spent $80 million, captivated the mainstream media, and participated in televised debates. On October 7, 2003, 55.4 percent of voters selected "yes" on the recall question, and 48.7 percent chose Schwarzenegger from among 135 candidates on the ballot to replace Davis. With 61.2 percent of registered voters having participated in the election, a high turnout historically speaking, Californians demonstrated that they'd had enough "politics as usual" by exploiting the tools of direct democracy to shake up their government once again.

Pushing Ahead with More Reforms

Arnold Schwarzenegger's approach to governing involved centrist appeals to Californians on common themes such as the environment and reforming government, and he will probably be best remembered for signing AB 32, the nation's first law to regulate greenhouse gas emissions. Today AB 32 is being enacted through a public cap-and-trade system of carbon emissions credits and other carbon gas-related mandates, and it survived a public referendum to dismantle it.[14] He may also be remembered for a jaw-dropping $27 billion budget deficit that mushroomed on his watch and colossal loans the state borrowed to plug budget gaps—loans that will take billions of dollars and several decades to pay off.

Elections remained at the epicenter of political change throughout Schwarzenegger's two terms. The 2008 presidential election drew the highest voter turnout in almost thirty years, ensuring future shake-ups with voters' approval of the Voters FIRST Act (Proposition 11), an initiative that stripped lawmakers of their responsibility for redrawing state legislative districts and mandated that a new nonpartisan citizens' commission assume the job; a later initiative added congressional redistricting to the commission's duties. Schwarzenegger also appealed to the people through two special elections, but these proved ineffective as voters rejected all of his proposals but one: a measure preventing legislators from receiving pay raises when a budget deficit is anticipated.

More big tremors were promised with voters' approval of the "Top Two Primary" (Prop 14 in 2010). Through this adaptation of the open primary, or "jungle primary" as some call it, *all* registered voters, including independents, may choose among all candidates running for different offices, not just their own parties' candidates. The new rules force the top two vote-getters for every seat into a runoff in the November general election. Thus, in November 2012, a total of 28 U.S. House, state Senate, and Assembly contests—some extremely aggressive—pitted Democrats against fellow Democrats, or set Republicans against fellow Republicans.[15] The same scenario played out in November 2014, with twenty-five same-party match-ups. Advocates of Prop 14 hoped that more moderates would replace strident ideologues who tend to resist compromise, but so far there is little evidence that the electoral changes have greatly reduced polarization (which is the inclination for members of both parties to occupy the far right or left ends of the ideological spectrum) or have significantly moderated legislative politics.[16] However, observers point to specific cases in which the more moderate candidates were selected over their competitors in the general election, and more members of the state legislature now associate with the "moderate caucus."[17] Additionally, the new system allows independents, or "no party preference" voters, to participate fully in primary elections. Over time, researchers will be able to verify or invalidate these preliminary conclusions and measure how deep lawmakers' ideological fault lines run under the new system.

Democratic Government and the Return of Jerry Brown

Adding to the seismic proportions of the 2010 election was the reelection of Jerry Brown as governor after almost thirty years, the only person to hold that office for a third, and eventually fourth, term.

One of the most striking facts about Edmund G. "Jerry" Brown is that he was one of the youngest governors in California history when he assumed office in 1975 at age thirty-six, and he became the oldest governor when he retook the oath of office in 2011 at age seventy-two—overtaking his own record with his final reelection at age seventy-six. An experienced statesman whose résumé includes having been a candidate for the U.S. presidency three times, secretary of state in the 1970s, Oakland mayor, and state attorney general immediately before retaking the governorship, Brown spent the first years of his new tenure wrangling the state's deficit-plagued budget into balance by slicing spending and seeking a voter-approved tax measure to fund public education (Prop 30). By sharply reducing public services that fellow Democrats considered sacred, including health care and education, and by using the initiative process to help enact his agenda, he showed that he would govern with calculated moderation. Brown has resisted big expansions in government programs that Democratic lawmakers tend to favor, even as he has tried to plan for long-range population growth by supporting controversial projects such as high-speed rail that would eventually connect Sacramento to San Diego, currently estimated to cost between $70 and $100 billion.[18]

Brown has rebuilt himself into a trustworthy, practical "doer" who spurns the trappings of power. He has left behind the ascetic lifestyle of his "Governor Moonbeam" years when he shunned the governor's mansion for a sparsely furnished rented Sacramento apartment where it's said that he slept on a mattress on the floor, yet he still aims for efficiency. For example, he has trimmed the governor's staff to half the number that Governor Schwarzenegger had employed and moves about the capital without a large security detail. He prefers working from his Oakland office rather than the grandiose state capitol.

With a forceful style and thick eyebrows that are often furrowed, at times he appears the stern schoolmaster, holding the line against "unnecessary increases" in taxes and fines. In one veto message, he noted that doubling the penalty to $490 for drivers who fail to slow or move away from a stopped emergency vehicle seemed "more punitive than deterrent."[19] This role assumed greater importance in 2012 when Democrats achieved supermajority status for the first time since 1883 in both the Assembly and Senate, enabling them to approve tax and fee hikes without Republicans and to override gubernatorial (the governor's) vetoes. Through 2015, the legislature had not attempted to override any of Brown's vetoes. Education spending emerged as a priority in 2015 as sales and income tax revenue began to refill the state treasury, and Brown plunged into the predicaments of drought. He preached austerity, issued executive orders to restrict water consumption, and collaborated with other governing officials to untangle the complications of the Delta. Democrats lost their supermajority status in the legislature in 2014 but maintained a clear majority, and with Governor Brown they established the state's first-ever groundwater regulations, assembled a $7.5 billion bond to address drought-related needs that voters passed in 2014, banned single-use plastic grocery bags (a law that has been suspended, pending the outcome a referendum slated for 2016), imposed tighter regulations on assisted-living facilities, expanded "revenge porn" laws, initiated a phase-out of lead bullets, increased protections for transgender youth, mandated the tracking of chemicals used in "fracking" (hydraulic fracturing, an oil drilling method), wrote regulations on marijuana sales, and raised the minimum wage to $10 per hour as of July 2016. Lower signature requirements for ballot initiatives (based on votes cast for governor in 2014) will encourage many new agenda items, including 2016 ballot measures that would legalize recreational marijuana use—following the lead of Colorado, Alaska, Oregon, and Washington.

Conclusion: Political Earthquakes and Evolving Institutions

Like real seismic events, political earthquakes are difficult to predict. The tensions that produce them are ever present and recognizable in the fault lines that ripple the ground on which government is built. Periodic ruptures release some of that tension. Although political earthquakes may be triggered by conditions or events that are difficult to control—such as a weakening global economy, Supreme Court decisions, or wars—the shock waves that these events produce have the potential to effect transformations both large and small. They condition elected representatives' ability to govern successfully.

Throughout California's history, political earthquakes have reconfigured relationships between the elected and the governed, between citizens and their governing institutions, and among citizens. Each of these upheavals involved choices about who may use power and how they may do so legitimately. Rules have also mattered: in some cases, the shake-ups were about whether to change the rules themselves, whereas in other cases the rules shaped the alternatives available and determined who could choose among them. Many political events become supercharged emotionally because they raise questions about shared values and about the kind of social and political culture in which people will live. Finally, history also plays a role in creating opportunities for action or in creating conditions that shape alternatives. As this historical review demonstrates, California's past pulses in the political institutions, culture, rules, and choices of today.

Notes

1. Andrew Rolle, *California: A History,* 6th ed. (Wheeling, IL: Harlan Davidson, 2003), 174.
2. Quote is attributed to Robert G. Cleland in Evelyn Hazen, *Cross-Filing in Primary Elections* (Berkeley: University of California, Bureau of Public Administration, 1951), 9.
3. Arthur Samish and Robert Thomas, *The Secret Boss of California* (New York: Crown Books, 1971), 10.
4. *Silver v. Jordan,* 241 Fed. S. 576 (1965), and *Reynolds v. Sims,* 377 U.S. 533 (1964), following *Baker v. Carr,* 369 U.S. 186 (1962).
5. T. George Harris, "California's New Politics: Big Daddy's Big Drive," *Look Magazine* 26(20), September 25, 1962.
6. John Burns, *The Sometime Governments: A Critical Study of the 50 American Legislatures, by the Citizens Conference on State Legislatures* (New York: Bantam Books, 1971), 8.
7. Howard Jarvis and Paul Gann, "Arguments in Favor of Proposition 13," in *Primary Election Ballot Pamphlet* (Sacramento: California Secretary of State, 1978).
8. Proposition 13 limited property tax rates to 1 percent of a property's assessed value in 1975; for properties sold after 1975, the rate would be 1 percent of the property's sale price. These rates would not be allowed to increase more than 2 percent per year.
9. Dan Walters, "California Has by Far Nation's Largest Asian-American Population," *Sacramento Bee*, March 12, 2013, http://blogs.sacbee.com/capitolalertlatest/2012/03/california-has-by-far-nations-largest-asian-american-population.html, and "A Community of Contrasts: Asian Americans, Native Hawaiians and Pacific Islanders in Los Angeles County, 2013," Asian Americans Advancing Justice, 2013, http://advancingjustice-la.org/system/files/CommunityofContrasts_LACounty2013.pdf. See also, California Department of Finance Demographic Unit, "Report P-3: Total Population Projections by Race/Ethnicity and Age, 2010–2060," DOF, December 14, 2014, http://www.dof.ca.gov/research/demographic/reports/projections/P-3.
10. California Department of Finance Demographic Unit, "Report P-3: Total Population Projections by Race/Ethnicity and Age, 2010–2060," DOF, December 14, 2014, http://www.dof.ca.gov/research/demographic/reports/projections/P-3.
11. National Immigration Law Center, "Driver's Licenses Map," NILC, May 2015, http://www.nilc.org/driverlicensemap.html.
12. Esther Yu-Hsi Lee, "200,000 Undocumented Immigrants Now Have a California Driver's License," *ThinkProgress.com*, April 7, 2015, http://thinkprogress.org/immigration/2015/04/07/3643779/ca-drivers-license.
13. Edward "Ted" Costa, "Proponent's Statement of Reasons," and "Proponent's Recall Argument," California Statewide Special Election, Tuesday, October 7, 2003, Voter Information Guide for 2003, Special Election (2003), http://repository.uchastings.edu/ca_ballot_props/1215.

14. Proposition 23 in 2010 would have dismantled the law by suspending its implementation until unemployment dipped below 5.5 percent for four consecutive quarters, a phenomenon that last occurred in 2006–07.

15. Twenty-five same-party races in November 2014 included seven Congressional races (five featuring two Democrats and two featuring two Republicans); six state Senate races (five featuring two Democrats and one race featuring two Republicans); twelve Assembly races (seven featuring two Democrats and five featuring two Republicans). Among these, only nine were competitive as measured by the winner receiving less than 55 percent of the vote. Twenty-eight total same-party races in November 2012 included eight Congressional races (six races featuring two Democrats and two races featuring two Republicans); two state Senate races (both races involved Democrats only); and eighteen Assembly races (eleven featuring two Democrats and seven featuring two Republicans). Among these, only nine were competitive as measured by the winner receiving less than 55 percent of the vote. See the final official election results compiled by the Secretary of State (http://www.sos .ca.gov).

16. John Sides, "Can California's New Primary Reduce Polarization? Maybe Not," *The Monkey Cage*, March 27, 2013, http://themonkeycage.org/2013/03/27/can-californias-new-primary-reduce-polarization-maybe-not. See also Lucas Eaves, "Recent Study Misses Big Picture in Evaluation of Top-Two Primary," *Independent Voter Network*, May 22, 2013, http://ivn.us/2013/05/22/how-to-define-success-the-impact-of-the-top-two-primary-in-california.

17. Eaves points to the election of Democratic candidates who were not supported by Democratic leadership as evidence that the system is inducing intended change and, if only by implication, more moderation. He cites Eric Swalwell's victory over incumbent Pete Stark. Eaves, "Recent Study Misses Big Picture." In addition, the author has obtained data from the convener of the moderate caucus, a loosely affiliated group that assembles an agenda that tends to be pro-business. In 2015, there were over thirty Democratic members who could be counted on fairly regularly to cast what is considered to be the "moderate" vote on specific measures the caucus identified as priorities, in contrast to ten years ago when only six members associated with the "moderate caucus."

18. In 2008, voters approved Proposition 1A, which provides $9.95 billion in funding for high-speed rail. After a report in 2011 that revised the costs upward to nearly $98 billion, Governor Brown ordered redesigns that would bring costs down. In 2012, high-speed rail authorities reported new cost estimates to be closer to $68 billion, a figure that the state's General Accounting Office found to be "reasonable." "GAO: Calif. High-Speed Rail Estimates Reasonable," *CBS Sacramento Local*, March 28, 2013, http://sacramento.cbslocal.com/2013/03/28/gao-calif-high-speed-rail-estimates-reasonable. See also Ralph Vartabedian, Dan Weikel, and Richard Simon, "Bullet Train's $98-Billion Cost Could Be Its Biggest Obstacle," *Los Angeles Times,* November 2, 2011, http://articles.latimes.com/2011/nov/02/local/la-me-1102-bullet-train-20111102; and Mike Rosenberg, "High Speed Rail Chief: Bullet Train Won't Cost $100 Billion," *San Jose Mercury News,* March 14, 2012, http://www.mercurynews.com/california-high-speed-rail/ci_20168582/high-speed-rail-chief-bullet-train-wont-cost.

19. California Office of the Governor, Veto message regarding Assembly Bill 902, Governor Jerry Brown, September 9, 2013, http://gov.ca.gov/docs/AB_902_Veto_Message.pdf.

CHAPTER 3

Direct Democracy

Medical use of marijuana. No horsemeat to be sold for human consumption. Term limits for all state elected officials. Funding for stem cell research. Each of these measures became state law because citizens signed petitions to get them on the ballot and majorities of voters approved them. Neither the governor nor the legislature was involved in their creation or passage. For more than one hundred years California has had a "**hybrid**" government that is part representative, part direct democracy, a design that the nation's founders carefully avoided.[1]

Until 1911 California's government reflected the U.S. founders' belief that elected representatives working in separate departments—namely, the executive and legislative branches—would check each other with overlapping powers, filter the passions of their constituents through a deliberative process, find compromises, and create good public policy. Lawmakers and presidents would compete for power, and these arrangements would safely allow ambition to counteract ambition, as James Madison noted in the *Federalist Papers.* Spurning this logic, California Progressive reformers at the beginning of the twentieth century removed those checks by establishing the initiative, referendum, and recall, thereby creating a hybrid government in which the people can make laws without the help of representatives. What we might call the first branch of California government is the people's power to govern themselves through the instruments of direct democracy. Article II of the state constitution affirms this view: "All political power is inherent in the people . . . and they have the right to alter or reform it when the public good may require."

The Statewide Initiative Process

At the state level, the *direct initiative* gives Californians the power to propose constitutional amendments and laws that fellow citizens will vote on without the legislature's involvement. Twenty-three other states also have initiative processes, although each has different requirements for bringing measures to the voters; the indirect method allows legislatures to consider and sometimes amend citizen-initiated measures before they are presented to the public for a vote. The California legislature is barred from making changes of any kind to citizens' ballot propositions, either before or after an election (see Box 3.1), and it retains the power to propose constitutional amendments, bond measures, and changes in law for popular approval, all of which can appear as propositions in primary and general elections—so-called "legislatively referred" measures.

Prior to the "Prop 13 revolution" that emboldened Californians to use the initiative process, Oregon led the states with the most initiatives. Since then, Californians have produced more propositions: from 1979 to 2014, voters considered 195 different initiatives put forward by fellow citizens, compared to 153 in Oregon and 108 in Colorado.[2] Considering all types of measures, including bonds, referenda, and legislatively referred initiatives, California still leads the states with more than 425 measures having been put to voters between 1979 and 2014, and of these, they approved 123 measures.[3] Proposed laws typically fail even before they make it to the ballot because their sponsors fail to gather enough signatures in time or the secretary of state invalidates too many submitted signatures; in fact, 75 percent of proposed initiatives fail to qualify for the ballot.[4]

Initiatives cover all manner of subjects at the state level. Issues that surface frequently include taxation, welfare, public morality, immigration, education, criminal justice, and civil rights. Most prevalent are measures that focus on government and the political process—reforms intended to change the rules for political participation or control the behavior of elected officials—and it is no coincidence that term limits for statewide officials exist almost exclusively in states with the initiative process (Louisiana is the only exception). Requiring that two-thirds of all lawmakers agree to raise a tax or fee is another example of how Californians have played a vital role in setting the context for political decision making by imposing significant institutional controls on the legislative process. Without a doubt, initiatives have fundamentally altered California government and politics (see Table 3.1 and Figure 3.1).

Unfortunately, reforms are forced on government piecemeal, not according to any coherent plan, resulting in political rules that overlap unnecessarily and tend to encourage stalemate.[5] For example, Proposition 26 reclassifies almost all regulatory fees and charges as taxes so that they are subject to the two-thirds vote threshold that was originally imposed through Prop 13. While limitations such as these may be personally satisfying to anyone who despises taxes, generally supermajority rules privilege the "super-minority" (a few people) over the simple majority (that is, the most people) because no revenue-raising measures can succeed without the minority's consent. Historically in the state legislature, these rules have driven majority political party Democrats and minority political party Republicans into long standoffs over how to balance the state budget, regulate businesses, address public health issues, and clean up the environment. The bottom line is that the initiative process both directly and indirectly conditions the actions of all California elected officials, who work in fragmented institutions that are not systematically organized to encourage collective action. As a result, representative and direct democracy coexist uneasily.

Citizens can propose laws at the city, county, and state levels in California. Any registered voter may propose a law (an *initiative statute*) or a change to the state constitution (a *constitutional amendment*), and both types pass with simple majority approval. However, because most citizens cannot overcome the financial and time barriers associated with the initiative process, which hinges on

TABLE 3.1 Selected Landmark Initiatives in California, 1966–2014

Number	Description	Year
Proposition 1A	Constitutional reform, legislative professionalization	1966
Proposition 9	"Political Reform Act" (campaign finance reform)	1974
Proposition 13	Property tax limitation	1978
Proposition 98	Minimum annual funding levels for education	1988
Propositions 140, 28	Term limits for state officeholders; may spend twelve years total in either house	1990; 2012
Proposition 184	Three-strikes law	1994
Proposition 187	Ineligibility of illegal aliens for public services	1994
Proposition 209	Ending affirmative action in state institutions	1996
Proposition 215	Medical use of marijuana	1996
Proposition 5	Tribal state gaming compacts, tribal casinos	1998
Proposition 227	Elimination of bilingual education	1998
Propositions 11, 20	Citizens' redistricting commission to redraw state and congressional districts	2008, 2010
Proposition 8	Definition of marriage	2009
Proposition 14	Open primary elections (Top Two Primary)	2010
Proposition 30	Temporary taxes to fund education	2012

gathering hundreds of thousands of valid voter signatures for statewide propositions, well-funded interest groups now dominate a system that was intended to *reduce* their influence. In practice, nearly anyone who can spend about $2 to $3 million (but possibly less, now that the signature threshold has dropped) to hire a signature-gathering firm can qualify a measure for the ballot. Special interest groups, corporations, wealthy individuals, political parties, and even elected officials with such resources use the state's initiative process to circumvent regular lawmaking channels because it "is the only way for [them] to get the policy they want."[6] Large donors dominate the system: a mere forty-eight entities, from businesses to individuals to unions, contributed half of the approximately $2.3 billion spent on initiative campaigns from 2000 to mid-2012, while "small donors" who gave $1,000 or less accounted for just over *2 percent* of that total.[7] Although the process remains primarily a check against government unresponsiveness and corruption, Hiram Johnson's Progressives would probably be surprised at how the process works today.

Preparation Stage: Drafting, Public Review, and Titling

The first step in bringing an idea to the ballot is drafting, or writing, the text of the proposed law. Measures are worded carefully to fit the needs and goals of their sponsors, and it is the authors' responsibility to correct errors or ambiguities that may later provide opponents with a convenient excuse to challenge them in court. A proposed initiative must be submitted with $2,000 to the attorney general's office, where it will be posted online for a 30-day public review period. Authors may then change the wording before the attorney general assigns a title and summary of 100 words or fewer.[8] From that point on, the wording of the proposed law cannot be changed. The state also prepares a fiscal analysis of the proposed law if the attorney general requests one.

Qualification Stage: Circulating Petitions and Verifying Signatures

During the qualification stage, the initiative's proponents must circulate strictly formatted petitions containing the official title and summary and gather enough valid voter signatures to qualify the measure for the ballot. Signatures can come from anywhere in California because there are no specific quotas that must be met in each county, as some states require, but everyone who signs must be a registered voter in the county where the petition was signed. Signature requirements are based on a percentage of all votes cast for governor during the previous election: the requirement is 5 percent for an initiative (365,880 signatures) and 8 percent for a constitutional amendment (585,407 signatures). These totals dropped significantly in 2014 based on low voter turnout, a reduction that will lower costs of collecting signatures and probably raise the number of petitions in circulation—as well as the number of initiatives that qualify for the ballot.

Proponents have 180 days to collect signatures on their formal petitions. Usually a signature collection company is hired to coordinate and execute the statewide effort, and the rule of thumb is to gather almost twice as many signatures as required because up to 40 percent or so will likely be invalidated later.[9] In practice this means collecting about 700,000 signatures at an average cost of $2 to $3 per valid signature, and a last-minute scramble to meet a deadline can push the price up to more than $10 per signature.[10] Means of collecting signatures include in person in public places, such as in front of grocery stores or at churches using the "clipboard method" (by one person) or "table method" (one person sits at a table while a companion approaches passersby); direct mail (generally not cost-effective); and door-to-door (rare). Electronic signature gathering is not yet allowed.

Completed petitions must be submitted to the appropriate elections official (typically the county clerk or registrar of voters) in the county where each petition was filled out. County elections officials must receive and verify the signatures at least 131 days before the next general or special election, and they use a random sampling technique to determine how many signatures qualify. If the secretary of state concludes that enough registered voters signed the filed petitions, the measure is certified, given a number, and becomes known as "Proposition [number]."

Campaigning Stage: Persuading Potential Voters

Most initiative attempts fail during the qualification stage because insufficient signatures were gathered or because too many were found to be invalid, but for successful proponents, the campaigning stage begins the moment the secretary of state certifies their measure. In the coming months, they will usually raise and spend millions of dollars to mobilize or sway voters. A thriving political consulting industry has grown around the need to manage fund-raising, television and radio advertising, social media messages, and mass mailings. The price of initiative campaigns has skyrocketed in recent decades, and the most expensive in U.S. history have taken place in California (see Table 3.2). It is not uncommon for supporters and opponents to spend $100 million combined on highly controversial measures. Records were set in 2012 with Props 32 and 30. Prop 32 would

MAP 3.1 States with the Initiative Process, 2015

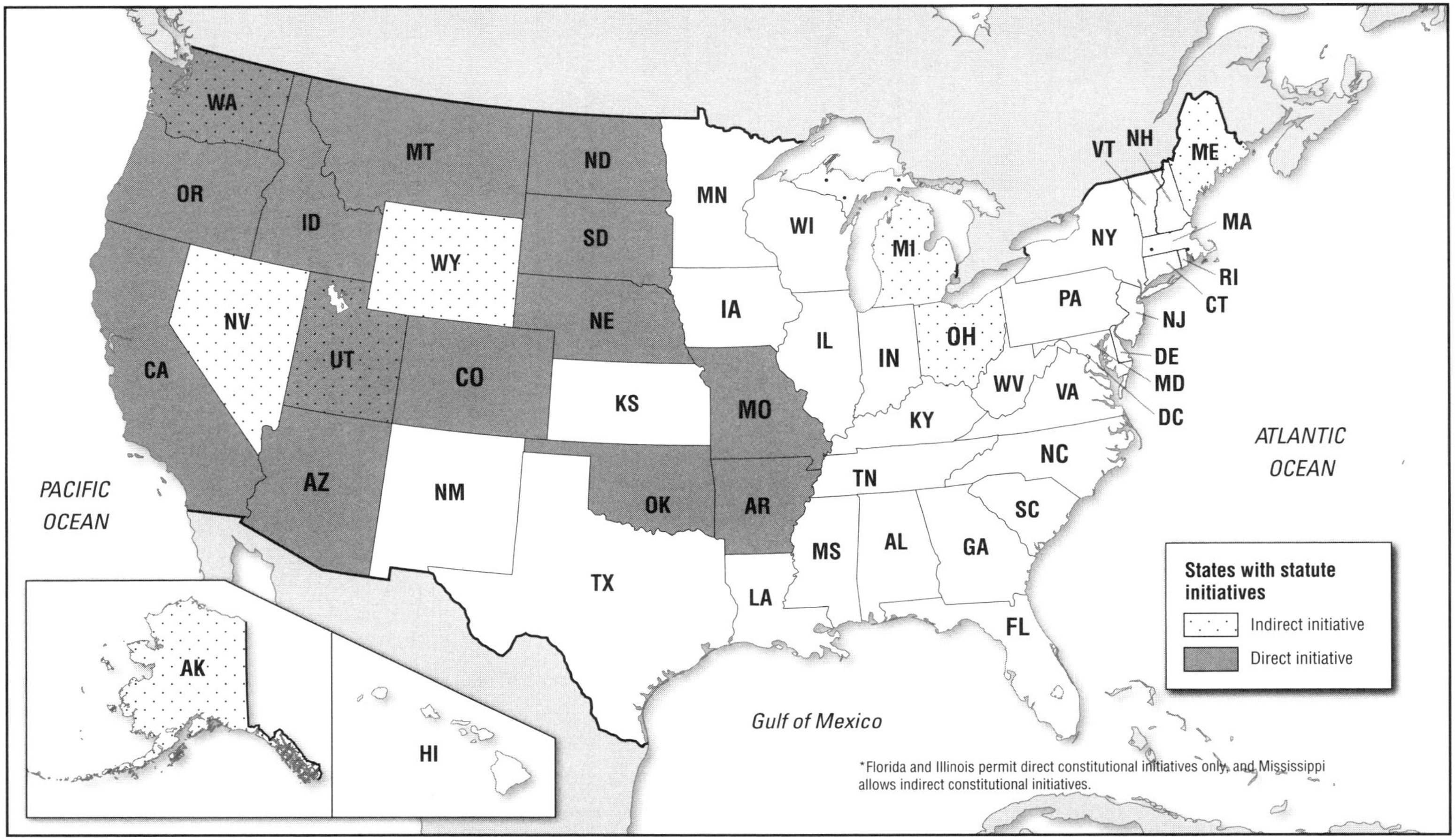

States with statute initiatives

- Indirect initiative
- Direct initiative

*Florida and Illinois permit direct constitutional initiatives only, and Mississippi allows indirect constitutional initiatives.

ATLANTIC OCEAN

Gulf of Mexico

PACIFIC OCEAN

MA
RI
CT
NJ
DE
MD
DC
ME
NH
VT
NY
PA
WV
VA
NC
SC
GA
FL
OH
KY
IN
TN
AL
MS
IL
MO
AR
LA
MI
WI
IA
OK
MN
KS
TX
ND
SD
NE
CO
NM
WY
MT
ID
UT
AZ
NV
OR
CA
WA
HI
AK

Source: National Conference of State Legislatures, "Initiative and Referendum States," http://www.ncsl.org/legislatures-elections/elections/chart-of-the-initiative-states.aspx.

FIGURE 3.1 Number of Statewide Initiatives that Qualified and Voters Approved in California, 1912–2014

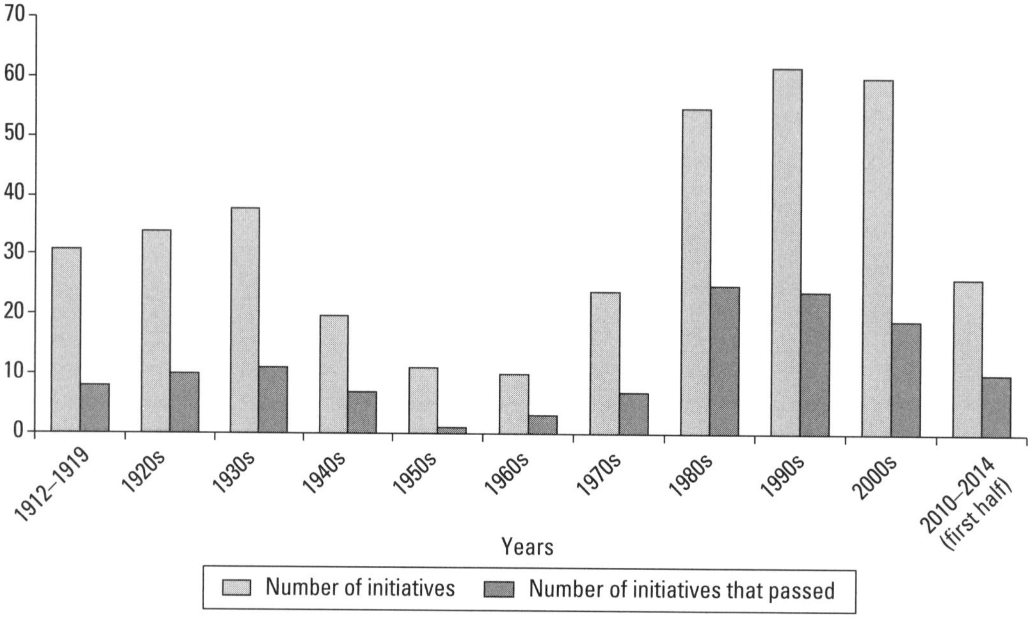

Sources: California Secretary of State, "Initiative Totals by Summary Year, 1912–January 2015," http://www.sos.ca.gov/elections/ballot-measures/pdf/initiative-totals-summary-year.pdf; Legislative Analyst's Office, "Ballot Measures by Type, 1974 to Present," accessed June 15, 2015, http://www.lao.ca.gov/BallotAnalysis/BallotByType.

Note: Excludes measures referred by legislature and referenda. Two initiatives in the 1980s and one initiative in 1999 qualified for the ballot but were removed from the ballot by court order.

have required that union members give permission annually for their dues to be deducted from their paychecks, the automatic deduction being an "injustice" fought by business interests and a "right" staunchly defended by unions. About $105.6 million was spent on that single ballot campaign. In the same election were dueling propositions concerning taxes for education, Governor Jerry Brown's Prop 30 and political activist Molly Munger's Prop 38, which topped the charts at $150.5 million spent either to promote or to defeat them. Not surprisingly, more money tends to be spent when industries are directly affected in some way, whereas uncontroversial measures tend to attract little or no spending.

Postelection Stage: Court Challenges and Implementation

Only a simple majority is needed to pass an initiative or recall an elected official, but a supermajority (two-thirds vote) is required for any general obligation bond and most school bonds (55 percent). Initiative laws generally take effect the day after they are approved, unlike bills, which normally go into effect on January 1 the following year. Election results don't always settle issues, however. Opponents often file lawsuits as soon as the votes are counted, triggering expensive court battles over a measure's constitutionality, meaning, or validity. These battles can last years and may result in partial

FIGURE 3.2 Sample Ballot with Initiatives

OFFICIAL BALLOT

SAN DIEGO COUNTY, CALIFORNIA
PRESIDENTIAL GENERAL ELECTION - November 4, 2008

MEASURES SUBMITTED TO THE VOTERS

STATE

PROP 8 ELIMINATES RIGHT OF SAME-SEX COUPLES TO MARRY. INITIATIVE CONSTITUTIONAL AMENDMENT. Changes California Constitution to eliminate the right of same-sex couples to marry. Provides that only marriage between a man and a women is valid or recognized in California. Fiscal Impact: Over next few years, potential revenue loss, mainly sales taxes, totaling in the several tens of millions of dollars, to state and local goverments. In the long run, likely little fiscal impact on state and local governments.

YES ◯

NO ◯

PROP 9 CRIMINAL JUSTICE SYSTEM. VICTIMS' RIGHTS. PAROLE INITIATIVE CONSTITUTIONAL AMENDMENT AND STATUTE. Requires notification to victim and opportunity for input during phases of criminal justice process,including bail, pleas, sentencing and parole. Establishes victim safety as consideration for bail or parole. Fiscal Impact: Potential loss of state savings on prison operations and increased county jail costs amounting to hundreds of millions of dollars annually. Potential net savings in the low tens of millions of dollars annually on parole procedures.

YES ◯

NO ◯

STATE

PROP 10 ALTERNATIVE FUEL VEHICLES AND RENEWABLE ENERGY BONDS. INITIATIVE STATUTE. Authorizes $5 billion in bonds paid from state's General Fund, to help consumers and others purchase certain vehicles, and to fund research in renewable energy and alternative fuel vehicles. Fiscal Impact: State cost of about $10 billion over 30 years to repay bonds. Increased state and local revenues, potentially totaling several tens of millions of dollars through 2019. Potential state administrative costs up to about $10 million annually.

YES ◯

NO ◯

PROP 11 REDISTRICTING. INITIATIVE CONSTITUTIONAL AMENDMENT AND STATUTE. Changes authority for establishing state office boundaries from elected representatives to commission. Establishes multilevel process to select commissioners from registered voter pool. Commission comprised of Democrats, Republicans, and representatives of neither party. Fiscal Impact: Potential increase in state redistricting costs once every ten years due to two entities performing redistricting. Any increase in costs probably would not be significant.

YES ◯

NO ◯

Emotions ran high on both sides as the vote on Proposition 8, a measure banning same-sex marriage, neared. Voters narrowly approved it in November 2008, 52.3 percent to 47.7 percent. The state supreme court upheld the measure, but a federal court later invalidated it. The U.S. Supreme Court ultimately dismissed a challenge to the lower court's ruling, and same-sex marriages resumed in California in summer 2013; full legalization occurred in June 2015.

or total invalidation of the measure. A court challenge to Proposition 8, the constitutional amendment defining marriage as between a man and a woman, was initiated shortly after the proposition's passage in 2008. The case twisted through the state courts, where it was eventually upheld by the California Supreme Court, and then was pushed through the federal courts, where it was struck down at the district court level as unconstitutional. The U.S. Supreme Court declined to hear the case in 2013, effectively allowing the lower court's ruling to stand, and same-sex marriages in California became legal in summer 2013. In June 2015 the U.S. Supreme Court effectively settled the issue by ruling that the Fourteenth Amendment requires all states to issue marriage licenses to same-sex couples and to recognize same-sex marriages performed by other states.

Public officials may also search for ways to get around laws they find objectionable, and there is always the likelihood that a contentious issue will be revisited in a future proposition, because new laws often have unintended consequences and because losers always have another chance to prevail. This is another reason that governing decisions seem prone to second-guessing in California, which feeds the perception that the state is governed ineffectively.

TABLE 3.2   Five Most Expensive Ballot Measure Campaigns (adjusted figures)

Proposition	Election year	Subject	Total spent	Spent by proponents	Spent by opponents	Pass/fail (% margin)
87	2006	Alternative energy	$174,931,000	$69,486,000	$105,445,000	F (45/55)
30, 38	2012	Taxes for education	$150,500,000	For 30: $58,400,000 For 38: $47,600,000	Against 30: $44,500,000 Against 38: $26,000	30: P (55/45) 38: F (29/71)
5	1998	Indian gaming	$129,341,000	$92,249,000	$37,092,000	P (62/38)
32	2012	Union dues	$105,600,000	$35,300,000	$70,300,000	F (43/57)
8	2008	Same-sex marriage ban	$94,352,000	$44,296,000	$50,056,000	P (52/48)

Sources: Figures for 2012 are from John Matsusaka, *Book of the States* (Lexington, KY: Council of State Governments, 2013). Proposition 8 figures are from "Proposition 8: Tracking the Money: Final Numbers," *Los Angeles Times,* February 3, 2009, http://www.latimes.com/local/la-moneymap-htmlstory.html. Figures for Props 87 and 5 from Center for Governmental Studies, *Democracy by Initiative: Shaping California's Fourth Branch of Government,* 2nd ed. (Los Angeles, CA: Center for Governmental Studies, 2008), http://policyarchive.org/handle/10207/bitstreams/5800.pdf.

Note: All figures have been adjusted to 2012 dollars and rounded.

The Power of the Initiative Process

Initiative use is robust for other reasons. Corporations and special interest groups find initiatives appealing because they know that successful measures can translate into financial gain or friendlier regulation. Aspiring politicians and lawmakers build their reputations by sponsoring propositions that can't get traction in the legislature. Competition also plays a role: at times adversaries take their fights to the ballot with dueling measures that propose very different solutions to a problem, as seen in the rival "taxation for education" measures proposed in 2012 (Props 30 and 38). It should be noted that if similar "rival measures" *both* receive enough votes to pass, the one attracting more votes goes into effect. (On a side note, in a move only the savviest of politicians might attempt, Brown signed a bill requiring that constitutional amendments be listed on the ballot first, thus ensuring that his measure, Prop 30, would appear at the top of the ballot. That rule will remain in effect for all future elections.[11]) Only rarely do genuine grassroots movements mushroom into initiative movements, and even those tend to be elite- or activist-driven efforts. Still, such movements can have enormous consequences for governing.

Today, the power of the average voter has been eclipsed by industry initiative activity and special interest group imperatives. There are no limits on contributions to ballot campaigns, and two-thirds of all donations are in amounts of $1 million or more.[12] The result: voters endure fanatical campaigns waged by organizations and corporations with deep pockets, their strategies packaged in media barrages containing oversimplified messages. Usually armed only with these biased accounts, voters must decide on complex policies frequently crafted without the benefit of compromise, and these policies may set rules that are difficult to amend later. Not surprisingly, confused voters tend to vote no, especially when the ramifications of voting yes are unclear. A recent survey revealed that less than 20 percent of adults think that the system is fine the way it is; three out of four people (76 percent) feel that minor or major changes are needed.[13] Given California's history, it is only a matter of time before citizens further reform the process (see Box 3.1). Representatives may also introduce reforms through regular lawmaking channels, as they did recently with SB 202, a law that ended the practice of voting on initiatives in primary elections. Now citizen-generated propositions will appear only in general elections or special elections called by the governor; the legislature may place initiatives, constitutional amendments, or bonds on any state election ballot.

Referendum

Citizens may also reject or approve recently signed laws or parts of laws, or redistricting maps, which are now drawn by the independent California Citizens Redistricting Commission. To prompt a referendum, petitioners must collect the same number of valid signatures required for an initiative (365,880) within 90 days after the scorned law goes into effect. If the referendum qualifies for the

WILLIS/San Jose Mercury News

ballot—since 2011, referenda may only appear on general election ballots—voters must choose to vote "yes" if they want to retain the law in question or "no" if they want to repeal it. Prompting referenda through petitions happens rarely: only forty-nine measures have qualified for the ballot since 1912, and voters have historically been more likely to repeal laws than to retain them (58.3 percent of laws were rejected through referenda; 41.7 percent were approved).[14] Gaming compacts negotiated between Native American tribes and the governor usually surface as referenda as well, and the people have approved all but one (rejected in 2014). Recently, plastic bag manufacturers recoiled from a new state law banning single-use plastic grocery bags and gathered enough signatures to trigger a referendum; that measure is included on the 2016 general election ballot.

A far more common type of referendum is a **bond measure,** first approved by the legislature and then passed along to voters for approval. The constitution requires that voters approve state borrowing above $300,000. Bond measures authorize the state treasurer to sell bonds on the open market, which essentially are promises to pay back with interest any amounts loaned to the state. Bonds are typically used to finance multimillion- or multibillion-dollar infrastructure projects ranging from water restoration to library renovation, and since 2000 the average bond has cost more than $5 billion (see chapter 8). During recent budget crises the state borrowed approximately $15 billion through the sale of bonds in order to close budget gaps, and in 2014 voters ratified Proposition 1, a $7,545,000,000 water bond intended to improve water reliability. Most bond measures generate little controversy, and around 60 percent pass, although some projects continue to generate conflict as they're implemented, such as a proposed $10 billion high-speed rail project that voters approved in 2008 (Prop 1A), now continually under fire as projected costs mount and plans are continually modified. Notably, financing state government projects with billion-dollar bonds involves substantial penalties and hidden costs: a sizable share of the state's annual budget each year is dedicated to paying interest, or "servicing the debt," and *taxpayers end up paying about twice the face amount of what is borrowed* after the interest and capital are repaid. Few voters are aware that a $10 billion bond will actually cost around $20 billion to pay off (the final pricetag depends on the interest rate).

Recall

California is one of nineteen states allowing voters to remove and replace *state* elected officials between regular elections, meaning that they can "recall" lawmakers, justices, and anyone serving in an elected executive capacity such as the governor or attorney general. It is one of at least twenty-nine states permitting the recall of *local* officials, including any person elected in a city or county, or to a court, school or community college board, or special district board.[15] It should be noted that citizens do not have the right to recall federal representatives, meaning U.S. House and Senate members.

A California recall election contains two parts: one, voters answer "yes" or "no" as to whether the representative in question should be removed from office; two, they may choose a replacement from anyone listed on the ballot, regardless of whether they voted to remove the official. This method of removing a politician before his or her term ends differs categorically from impeachment, whereby charges of misconduct in office are leveled, a trial is held by the state Senate and two-thirds vote to convict, and the Assembly votes to impeach. Nationwide, the majority of recall attempts are aimed at local officials such as judges, city council members, or school board members; recalls of state officials rarely triumph—although two state legislators in Colorado who had voted for stricter gun control legislation were singled out by the National Rifle Association and were successfully recalled by voters in September 2013.

Low recall success rates are partly ensured through fairly high signature requirements and relatively short deadlines. Signature thresholds vary with the office and size of the jurisdiction, or the area represented by the targeted official. For lawmakers and appeals court judges in California, for instance, petitioners have 160 days to meet the signature threshold, which is equal to 20 percent of the votes cast in the last election for the official being recalled. For mayors and other local officials, the number is based on registered voters: 30 percent if fewer than 1,000 people are registered, declining to 10 percent if over 100,000 are registered.[16] For statewide officials, signatures must be obtained from voters in at least five different counties, with minimums in each jurisdiction tied to the prior election results. These rules also apply to recalling the governor, and proponents have just over five months to submit valid signatures equal to 12 percent of the votes cast during the previous gubernatorial election (just over 878,000 signatures). In some states, the signature threshold to recall a governor looms as high as 40 percent of eligible voters.

No specific grounds for removal are needed to launch a recall in California, but proponents must state their reasons on the petitions they circulate. Since 1913, 160 recalls have been launched against state elected officials in California, but only nine of these qualified for the ballot, and only five ultimately succeeded.[17] Senator Richard Pan, the pediatrician who wrote the law requiring mandatory vaccinations for all public schoolchildren, has been targeted by opponents who must collect enough signatures to prompt a recall in 2016, but the odds are against them. By far, the most dramatic example was the 2003 recall of Governor Gray Davis, discussed in chapter 2. Ironically, it takes a majority vote to remove an incumbent, but the replacement wins by plurality vote (the most votes of all cast), so Arnold Schwarzenegger could have won with far less than the 48.7 percent he received in an election that featured 135 candidates.

Direct Democracy at the Local Level

It shouldn't be surprising that the three forms of direct democracy—the initiative, referendum, and recall—are available in every California county, city, and school district, and are used more frequently at the local level than at the state level. Voters are regularly invited to weigh in on changes to their city constitutions (charter amendments), local laws, bonds, citizen initiatives, and recalls of local officials. Local measures are adopted more often than state propositions, but the process seldom sparks a sensation unless scandals command local headlines, or personal vices (marijuana, sex-related issues) or money (land use, pension reform, or that of deep-pocketed interests) is at stake.

Controversial decisions on school boards lead to the most recalls—about 75 percent of all recalls are against elected school board members—yet they remain relatively rare events, and the same is true of local referenda. On the other hand, citizens have the power to generate ordinances through the local initiative process, and they do so with local flair and variable success. In 2011–12, about half of the 135 different petitions that were circulated in 537 city and county jurisdictions later qualified for the ballot, and more than half of them passed.[18] Most local initiatives relate to matters of growth and development, also known as land use; governance, or political reform; and taxation.[19] Recent initiatives have dealt with rezoning public property for private use, a process known as "eminent domain"; imposed term limits on city council members or county supervisors (a more common

BOX 3.1 Reforming the Initiative Process

Is the initiative process ripe for reform? Californians overwhelmingly support their right to make laws alongside the state legislature, but many acknowledge the process isn't perfect. Its built-in biases have long been recognized, and resource-rich special interests have advantages over average citizens at every stage, a situation that contradicts the original intent of empowering the many at the expense of the few. Fixing these problems and others will require balancing individual power and free-speech rights. Opinion is sharply divided over whether and how to address these complex issues and how effective any solutions would be.

Problems and Suggested Remedies

Problem: It is far easier for paid circulators to collect enough valid signatures than it is for volunteer-based groups; virtually anyone can qualify an initiative by paying a professional signature-gathering firm about $1 to $3 million (depending on number of signatures needed and proximity to deadlines).

Remedy: Ban paid signature gathering or require that a certain percentage of signatures be gathered by volunteers.

Problem: Big money dominates the initiative process.

Remedy: Because capping campaign donations violates free speech protections, disclose donor information immediately, and prominently display that information on initiative petitions and advertising throughout the campaign.

Problem: It is difficult to trace donors to ballot campaigns.

Remedy: Require in-ad disclosure of top donors to campaign committees; make online resources such as Cal-Access easier to navigate.

Problem: Ballot measures are confusing and complex.

Remedy: Make legislative hearings widely available to generate more substantive discussion about a measure's probable impacts. Broadcast hearings online and use traditional media to help voters find more comprehensive election resources and information. If two conflicting measures are being considered in the same election, place them together in the ballot pamphlet and explain which will prevail if both pass.

Problem: There are too many initiatives.

Remedy: Require the legislature to vote on proposed laws first. After a public hearing on a measure, the legislature could vote on passing it, with or without any changes that the initiative's authors may approve or reject. Courts could be given a role in verifying that the legislature's version respects the authors' intent.

Problem: It is too difficult to revise initiatives once they become law. They cannot be changed except through future ballot measures, even if flaws are discovered.

Remedy: Allow the legislature to amend measures after a certain amount of time, holding lawmakers to strict guidelines, special conditions, or further review.

Problem: The state constitution is cluttered with redundant and contradictory amendments.

Remedy: Enable more frequent, comprehensive reviews of the state constitution to weed out obsolete, unnecessary, or contradictory language. Alternatively, require a constitutional revision commission to meet periodically and make recommendations that voters or lawmakers may act upon.

Problem: Too many initiatives are declared unconstitutional.

Remedy: Although legislative hearings are now required, ensure that measures are reviewed by a panel of active or retired judges to determine whether the proposed law is consistent with the California state constitution. Inform voters of any conflicts, and give authors the option to withdraw their measures.

For further reading, see Center for Governmental Studies, *Democracy by Initiative: Shaping California's Fourth Branch of Government,* 2nd ed. (Los Angeles, CA: Center for Governmental Studies, 2008), http://policyarchive.org/handle/10207/bitstreams/5800.pdf.

reform in the past ten years); changed the manner and conduct of elections (for instance, San Francisco now allows Saturday voting); affected utility rates; altered the compensation packages for public employees (cutting or eliminating pensions, for example); and touched on every manner of civil rights, liberties, and public morals, such as regulating marijuana dispensaries, marriage, immigration, gambling, and alcohol. Pornographic film actors in Los Angeles County must wear condoms during filming thanks to Measure B, a county initiative.

When well-funded interests have a stake in the outcome, especially corporations or unions, campaign spending can quickly accelerate far beyond the reach of local citizens. In the city of Redlands, where voters in 2010 considered banning big-box retailers such as Wal-Mart from establishing new megastores within city limits, local activists raised and spent about $9,000 to support the ban but ultimately lost to the large retailer, which bankrolled $450,000 to defeat it. In Costa Mesa in 2012, labor unions spent $500,000 to defeat constitutional amendment Measure V, which would have eliminated prevailing wage requirements and forbade using union dues for political purposes, among other things; supporters spent $50,000 and lost.[20]

The procedures for circulating a petition for a city or county initiative are similar to those at the state level and are spelled out in the state's election codes: signature requirements, strict circulation guidelines, signature verification carried out by the county registrar of voters, and certification either by the registrar or the city clerk. Signature requirements vary among cities because they are based on prior turnout (for local laws, called ordinances) or voter registration (for charter amendments); thus, it takes about 43,750 signatures to qualify an initiative ordinance in San Francisco but only 15,250 in Bakersfield, for instance. In the city of Los Angeles, the threshold is just under 61,500 qualifying signatures based on turnout for the prior mayoral race, yet based on voter registration the *county* of

FIGURE 3.3 Municipal Ballot Measures in California: Subject Matter and Approval Rates, 1995-2012*

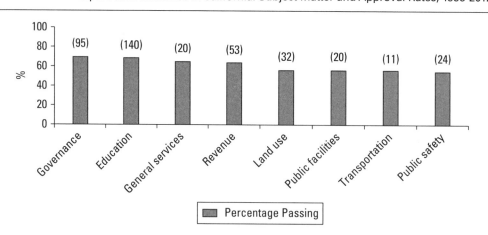

Source: Steve Boilard, David Barker, Valory Messier, and Sara Adan, "California County, City and School District Election Outcomes: Candidate and Ballot Measures, 2013 Outcomes," Institute for Social Research (Sacramento, CA) and Center for California Studies (Sacramento, CA), n.d., http://elections.cdn.sos.ca.gov/county-city-school-district-election-results/2013/city-report-2013.pdf.

*Numbers in parentheses represent the average number of local ballot measures per year.

Los Angeles requires 292,666 valid signatures (not less than 20 percent) for the Board of Supervisors either to adopt the ordinance at their next regular meeting or to call a special election for voters to consider it. Unlike the state process, citizens must first file a notice of intent to circulate a petition, and, depending on the number of valid signatures gathered, the local governing board (city council or county supervisors) may first consider and adopt a proposed measure without alteration before it is submitted to voters. This process is known as the *indirect initiative,* and if the local governing body approves a measure, then it becomes law without being put to a vote of the people. Local initiatives, or proposed ordinance, are placed on ballots as "Measure [letter]," such as "Measure U," as distinct from state propositions, which are assigned numbers. In 2011–12, approximately seventy-five cities considered one or more local ballot measures.

Conclusion: The Perils and Promises of Hybrid Democracy

The tools of direct democracy—the initiative, referendum, and recall—render California a hybrid government in which citizens possess the power to make or reject laws and elect or eject representatives. California's unique blend of representative and direct democracy gives the people tremendous power to govern themselves, but, ironically, citizens generally do not feel as if they are in control. In an outsized state with a sprawling population, money is a megaphone, and the initiative process favors the well-funded. Whether it's because of the money they can spend to spread their messages across major media markets, the blocs of voters they can mobilize, or the time they can dedicate to campaigning, resource-rich special interests overshadow a process that was established to give voice to the powerless.

The initiative process creates winners who use public authority to establish their version of reform and their vision of "better" policy that reflects their values and interests. It also produces losers who have the right to overcome their opponents by imposing their vision of good government through future ballots, should enough voters agree with them. This give-and-take over time is the essence of political struggle, but in a purely representative democracy, conflicts are harnessed by elected officials and saddled to a lawmaking institution where they are tamed through deliberation and compromise. The initiative process in California unleashes political conflicts to a diverse population where debate takes place, but bargaining and compromise are precluded. After all, initiatives offer one-size-fits-all solutions and are not open to amendment before passage. Unlike bills, which pass through many hands and many points where they can be challenged, tweaked, reconsidered, or adjusted to accommodate concerns, the referendum, recall, and initiative take one unchanging form that demands merely a yes or no response from voters at one point in time. Simple messages and emotional appeals are easier to broadcast across the expanse of California than the nuances and complexities normally associated with lawmaking and policycraft.

Furthermore, neither the initiative nor the referendum lends itself to an integrated set of laws or institutional rules. Thus, new reforms are layered upon prior reforms in California, and newer laws are imperfectly fitted to existing statutes, an incremental process that tends to breed a disordered system of governing. This is a key reason the Golden State's government appears illogical. In fact, state building through the ballot box has proceeded incoherently for decades, often in response to scandals and crises, but often because of voters' hopeful desire for better government.

Even though voters make far fewer decisions at the ballot box than legislators make in a typical morning at the capitol, the political, fiscal, and social impacts of initiatives and referenda can profoundly upset the status quo—frequently with unintended consequences. Yet direct democracy is sacred in California. Despite the systemic flaws that people see in the initiative process, at least six in ten citizens believe they make better public policy decisions than elected officials do,[21] and voters continually reshape their government with the goal of "making things work." California's hybrid democracy doesn't ensure that things will get better or that government will work more efficiently, but direct democracy feeds citizens' hopes that it will. For better or worse, Californians will continue to use direct democracy to restructure their relationships with their government and with each other.

Notes

1. The term *hybrid democracy* is attributed to Elizabeth Garrett, "Hybrid Democracy," *George Washington Law Review* 73 (2005): 1096–1130.

2. California Legislative Analyst's Office, "1974 to Present: Ballot Measures by Type," accessed June 14, 2015, http://www.lao.ca.gov/BallotAnalysis/BallotByType; Oregon Blue Book, "Initiative, Referendum, and Recall," accessed June 14, 2015, http://bluebook.state.or.us/state/elections/elections06.htm; Colorado State Legislature, "Ballot History by Year," accessed June 14, 2014, http://www.leg.state.co.us/lcs/ballothistory.nsf.

3. According to the California Legislative Analyst's Office, 426 measures were on ballots between 1979 and 2015. During the same period in Oregon, voters considered 294 measures, and between 1904 and 2015 approved 124 propositions, 23 referenda, and 254 of 430 legislatively referred measures (see Oregon Secretary of State, "Oregon Blue Book: Initiative, Recall, and Referendum Introduction," accessed June 14, 2015, http://bluebook.state.or.us/state/elections/elections09.htm). Colorado ballots have included 108 propositions and 65 referenda since 1979. These states represent the top three most active users of the initiative process.

4. The exact figure is 74.78%, or 1,367 out of 1,828 that were titled and summarized for circulation between 1912 and 2014. Source: Alex Padilla, "Summary of Data," Secretary of State, accessed June 15, 2015, http://elections.cdn.sos.ca.gov/ballot-measures/pdf/summary-data.pdf.

5. Prop 25 (passed in 2010) is a rare exception to these general historical patterns, as it lowered the vote requirement to pass the budget from a two-thirds supermajority to a simple majority. This modest change has resulted in budgets being passed on time and without the majority's having to "buy" minority party votes with budget favors. The law did, however, oblige legislators to forfeit their pay permanently if the budget is late, but in practice the "pay suspension" rule does not work as intended. In 2011, the Democratic-controlled legislature sent Governor Brown a budget just ahead of the June 15 deadline, but Brown and minority-party Republicans accused Democrats of submitting a budget filled with gimmicks and "questionable legal maneuvers." Brown promptly vetoed it (the first time a governor had done so since 1901), making the budget effectively late. In response, Controller John Chiang suspended the legislators' salary and per diem for 12 days (averaging about $4,800 per legislator), and Democrats sued to recover lost pay. On January 24, 2014, the Third District Court of Appeals in California upheld a lower court ruling that Controller Chiang had violated the separation of powers clause of the state constitution, agreeing that only the legislature may determine whether a budget is balanced (*Steinberg Perez v. Chiang* [2012], case C071498). See also Judy Lin, "Ruling Undermines Measure Blocking Lawmakers' Pay," *San Jose Mercury News*, April 25, 2012, http://www.mercurynews.com/news/ci_20478590/ruling-undermines-measure-blocking-lawmakers-pay; and Steven Harmon, "Brown Vetoes Budget, Criticizes 'Gimmicks,'" *Contra Costa Times*, June 16, 2011, http://www.mercurynews.com/california-budget/ci_18289420.

6. Elisabeth R. Gerber, Arthur Lupia, Mathew D. McCubbins, and D. Roderick Kiewiet, *Stealing the Initiative: How State Government Responds to Direct Democracy* (Upper Saddle River, NJ: Prentice Hall, 2001), 12.

7. Unadjusted dollars. The rest came from donations averaging over $10,000. The 48 big donors include nine labor groups, 15 businesses (led by PG&E), eight individuals, nine Native American tribes, the major political parties, two of Schwarzenegger's political committees, the League of Cities, one advocacy group, and

one PAC. See: Mike Polyakov, Peter Counts, Kevin Yin, "California's Initiative System: The Voice of the People Co-opted," *California Common Sense*, November 6, 2013, cacs.org/pdf/22.pdf.

8.   A filing fee of $200 was last set in 1943. Governor Brown agreed with arguments in favor of AB 1100 that the fee should be raised to reflect long-term inflation and to discourage the frivolous filing of initiatives. The increase took effect January 1, 2016. A public review period was also added in 2014 (AB 1253) to increase transparency in the process.

9.   Signature invalidation rates vary by county. The San Diego County registrar of voters reported that of the nine statewide petitions received in 2012, and of the 3 percent of the total signatures submitted (18,856 of 628,525), 17.5 percent were found to be invalid. One study published by the Center for Governmental Studies (CGS) reports that Los Angeles and Oakland have much higher invalidation rates (around 30 to 35 percent) due to duplicate signatures, signatures of unregistered voters, or names submitted in counties where they are not registered to vote. CGS estimates the average invalidation rate to be as high as 40 percent. See Center for Governmental Studies, *Democracy by Initiative: Shaping California's Fourth Branch of Government,* 2nd ed. (Los Angeles, CA: Center for Governmental Studies, 2008), http://policyarchive.org/handle/10207/bitstreams/5800.pdf.

10.   Ballotpedia calculates the average cost per required signature (CPRS) based on the amounts paid to the signature collection firms (publicly reported information) and the actual numbers of signatures needed. Based on figures for the 2014 election ballot measures, they calculate the highest average cost per signature at $5.22 (a referendum on a gaming compact); the other three were closer to $3.48 on average. Higher amounts were paid in 2012 with $10.86 (Prop 30) and $9.81 (Prop 38) CPRS. For all measures in 2012, the average cost per signature was $3.82. "California Ballot Initiative Petition Signature Costs," Ballotpedia, accessed June 15, 2015, http://ballotpedia.org/wiki/index.php/California_ballot_initiative_petition_signature_costs.

11.   Governor Brown was aware that many voters only vote for measures appearing at the top of a ballot. The "roll-off," or reduction in number of votes for down-ticket measures, in this case was about 1 percent, meaning that 12,667,751 people cast their votes for Brown's "top of the ticket" Prop 30, whereas 12,331,091 voted for Prop 38, a difference of 336,660 votes (or 0.97 percent). Ultimately, however, Brown's measure won by such a large margin that the roll-off did not matter to the election outcome.

12.   Center for Governmental Studies, *Democracy by Initiative,* 14. See also Polyakov, et al., 2013.

13.   Mark Baldassare, Dean Bonner, Sonja Petek, and Jui Shrestha, "California's Initiative Process: 100 Years Old," Public Policy Institute of California, September 2011, http://www.ppic.org/main/publication_show .asp?i=265. The polls were conducted in May 2011 (2,005 adults) and September 2011 (2,002 adults). Of those surveyed, 54 percent said that the initiative process in California today is controlled by special interests "a lot," 34 percent said "some," 6 percent said "not at all," and 6 percent responded that they didn't know. See also Mark Baldassare, Dean Bonner, Sonja Petek, and Jui Shrestha, "Californians and the Initiative Process," Public Policy Institute of California, November 2008, http://www.ppic.org/content/pubs/jtf/JTF_InitiativeJTF.pdf. In these earlier polls, conducted September 2008 (2,002 adults) and October 2008 (2,004 adults), 59 percent agreed with the statement "There are too many propositions on the state ballot," and 78 percent agreed that "ballot wording for citizens' initiatives is often too complicated and confusing for voters to understand what happens if the initiative passes." In 2008, a combined 64 percent believed that minor or major change was needed in the initiative process, compared to 76 percent in 2011.

14.   For a complete list of referenda that were circulated or qualified for the ballot, see "Referendum," California Secretary of State, accessed June 15, 2014, http://www.sos.ca.gov/elections/ballot-measures/referendum. "Summary of Referendum Data (1912 through February 2014)," California Secretary of State, Accessed June 10, 2015, http://www.sos.ca.gov/ballot-measures/pdf/referenda-data.pdf.

15.   According to the National Conference of State Legislatures, "at least 29 states" permit recall elections to be held in local jurisdictions, and "some sources place this number at 36." See NCSL, "Recall of State Officials," last modified September 11, 2013, http://www.ncsl.org/research/elections-and-campaigns/recall-of-state-officials.aspx.

16. For more details, see "Procedure for Recalling State and Local Officials," California Secretary of State, accessed June 10, 2015, http://www.sos.ca.gov/elections/recalls/procedure-recalling-state-and-local-officials.

17. Source: "Recall History in California, 1913-Present," California Secretary of State, accessed June 12, 2015, http://www.sos.ca.gov/elections/recalls/recall-history-california-1913-present.

18. California Secretary of State, "Report on County Initiative Measures during 2011–2012," http://www.sos.ca.gov/elections/ballot-measures/resources-and-historical-information/reports-county-and-municipal-initiative-measures. Note that some cities fail to report by the deadline, so figures may be slightly different than those reported in Steve Boilard, David Barker, Valory Messier, and Sara Adan, "California County, City and School District Election Outcomes: Candidate and Ballot Measures, 2013 Outcomes," Institute for Social Research (Sacramento, CA) and Center for California Studies (Sacramento, CA), n.d., http://elections.cdn.sos.ca.gov/county-city-school-district-election-results/2013/city-report-2013.pdf.

19. For a more comprehensive report, see Tracy M. Gordon, *The Local Initiative in California* (San Francisco: Public Policy Institute of California, 2004), http://www.ppic.org/content/pubs/report/R_904TGR.pdf.

20. See Calpensions, "Outsourcing Pension Costs: Costa Mesa Hits Snag," November 12, 2012, http://calpensions.com/2012/11/12/outsourcing-pension-costs-costa-mesa-hits-snag.

21. Mark Baldassare, Dean Bonner, Sonja Petek, Jui Shrestha, "The Initiative Process in California," Public Policy Institute of California, October 2013, www.ppic.org/main/publication_show.asp?i=1072.

CHAPTER 4

The State Legislature

Should unvaccinated children be prohibited from enrolling in public schools? Should college students be required to give "affirmative consent" to have sex, and how is that term defined? Should the importation and sale of shark fins be banned? Should affordable health and dental care be available to all Californians, regardless of citizenship status? Legislators answer just such questions. Throughout the lawmaking process, they are obligated to express the will of the citizens they represent, and they make decisions that touch almost every aspect of people's lives.

Design, Purpose, and Function of the Legislature

In California's system of separated powers, the legislature makes law or policy, the executive branch enforces or implements it, and the judicial branch interprets the other branches' actions and the laws they make. Chapters 2 and 3 discussed how the people also dabble in lawmaking through the initiative process, but primarily legislators are responsible for solving the state's problems. California's full-time lawmakers are far better suited to the task than are average citizens. They grapple with complex issues year round and are assisted by professional staff members who help assess anticipated and unanticipated outcomes, research the history of similar attempts, evaluate alternatives, and analyze costs of proposed laws.

California's legislature resembles the U.S. Congress in both structure and function. Like its federal counterpart, it is bicameral, meaning that it is divided into two houses that check each other. Legislators in both the state's eighty-member lower house, called the **Assembly**, and the forty-member upper house, the **Senate**, represent districts that are among the most populous in the nation: based on the 2010 census, Assembly districts average 465,600 people, and Senate districts are larger than U.S. House districts, averaging 931,350 residents.[1] Unlike members of the U.S.

Lower house:	Assembly, 80 members
Upper house:	Senate, 40 members
Term length:	Assembly, 2 years; Senate, 4 years
Term limits:	12 years (combined) in the Assembly and/or Senate
Majority party in Assembly and Senate:	Democratic
Leaders:	Speaker of the Assembly, president pro tem of the Senate, minority leaders of the Assembly and Senate
Leaders' salaries:	$111,776* annually plus a per diem of $168/day**
Legislators' salaries:	$97,197* annually plus a per diem of $168/day**

Source: California Citizens Compensation Commission, "Salaries of Elected Officials," effective December 1, 2014, http://www.calhr.ca.gov/cccc/pages/cccc-salaries.aspx. On June 20, 2014, commissioners voted to implement a 2 percent pay increase for all state elected officials.

*Legislators also receive a car allowance of $300 per month, which replaced the state-paid vehicle and gas card in 2011. Legislative salaries hit an all-time high in 2008 when regular members were paid $116,208 plus per diem.

**Per the Senate and Assembly rules committees, per diem amounts are set by the Victim Compensation and Government Claims Board and are intended to cover daily expenses associated with working away from home. Total amounts vary annually with the number of days in session and by chamber. On average in 2012, Assembly members collected a total of $28,656 in per diems, and senators collected $28,514.

Congress, however, California legislators are term limited. In 1990 voters adopted Proposition 140, an initiative that restricted the number of terms that Assembly members and senators could hold. In 2012 voters changed the rules through Prop 28, effectively reducing the total number of years that lawmakers can serve to twelve (from fourteen), but allowing them to serve those years in one house alone or to split their time between the two chambers. A lifetime ban means that lawmakers are prohibited from serving in those offices once they've reached the twelve-year limit. Although almost a third of the Assembly and senators took office as freshmen in December 2014, it's likely they will stay in office and help stabilize a legislature that has been wracked by membership turnover every two years.[2] Observers already note that new legislators are waiting longer to scout their next jobs, and are taking more time with long-term projects, rather than those designed for short-term gain. Overall, term limits have profoundly influenced individual representatives' perspectives and the way the legislature operates, a point revisited later in this chapter.

Legislators are elected from districts that are redrawn once per decade based on the U.S. Census. The task of redrawing district boundaries has traditionally rested with Senate and Assembly committees, but voters who were tired of hearing about gerrymandering and tricks to keep incumbents in office helped pass Proposition 11 (in 2008), transferring the mapmaking power over to a fourteen-member, independent citizens' commission. To be chosen once a decade through a multistage, public process, the politically balanced commission is charged with drawing districts based on "strict, nonpartisan rules designed to ensure fair representation."[3] In addition, "every aspect" of the process is open to the public and the press. The very first commission in 2012 created state district maps that survived judicial scrutiny and a statewide referendum, and they also recreated California's congressional districts. Their authority to redesign California's U.S. House districts was indirectly challenged in a recent federal court case against Arizona's citizen redistricting commission, and the U.S. Supreme Court upheld the principle that a citizen commission may help determine the "time, manner, and place" of Congressional elections through redistricting as it does for state government.[4]

Although a few high-profile criminal cases have been brought against California lawmakers over the past century, hundreds of public-spirited men and women have served and are serving resolutely and honorably as California state legislators. Yet a fervent antipolitician, antigovernment sentiment prevails among Californians, and the individuals whose job it is to sustain representative democracy are scorned rather than appreciated for the challenging work they do. As this chapter shows, lawmakers work hard to fulfill the expectations of their constituents and to meet the relentless demands of a state with a population of 39 million and counting.

California Representatives at Work

California's legislature has come a long way from the days when allegiances to the Southern Pacific Railroad earned it the nicknames "the legislature of a thousand steals" and "the legislature of a

AP Photo/Rich Pedroncelli

The Assembly floor is normally a beehive of activity when the house is in session. From the Speaker's view at the polished wood desk, the Democrats are seated to the left and Republicans to the right, reflecting their traditional ideological placement (Democrats appear on the right in the photo). Members cast votes by pressing buttons on their desks, and votes are registered on digital display boards at the front of the chamber.

thousand drinks." Today its full-time, professional members are the highest paid in the nation, earning more than $100,000 per year, including per diem payments intended to cover living costs. Special interests and their lobbyists still permeate Sacramento politics with their presence, money, and messages, but legislators' loyalties these days are splintered by district needs, statewide demands, and partisanship. Their crammed schedules are split between their home districts and Sacramento.

Nowadays, nearly everyone in the legislature is climbing the steep part of the learning curve. Term limits create large classes of freshman every two years, pushing others into campaigns for the next office and year-round fund-raising. Prop 28 will slow turnover rates somewhat, but legislators' desire to stay in politics will continue to keep rates relatively high. In past years, supermajority rules and rigid ideological positioning drove Democrats and Republicans to grid-lock over raising taxes and cutting social programs, key components of balancing the budget on time—particularly in tough economic times. Now that only a simple majority is needed to pass the budget, and healthier economic times have made tough trade-offs and cutbacks less likely, Republican representatives have fallen to new levels of irrelevance in most policy debates. How-ever, it may be surprising that day-to-day, legislators from both political parties work closely together in committees and other meetings, socialize outside the legislature occasionally, and

FIGURE 4.1   Profile of California's Population versus California State Legislature, 2015

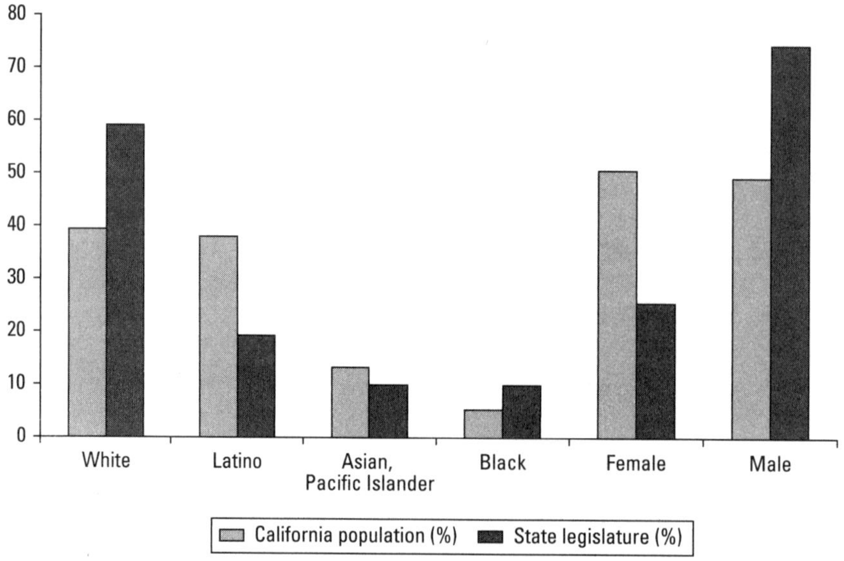

Sources: California Department of Finance, "Report P-3: Population Projections by Race/Ethnicity, Detailed Age, and Gender, 2010–2060," December 2014, http://www.dof.ca.gov/research/demographic/reports/projections/P-3; author's data, snapshot of legislature in August 2015.

BOX 4.2   **Term Limits: Political Earthquake**

Have term limits for legislators been good or bad? Both supporters and detractors can find ammunition in the findings. One thing neither side can deny, however, is that the reform has dramatically changed the rules of representation and the environment in which legislators work. Legislators elected in 2012 or after will help alter current understandings of the law's effects, because voters changed term limits (with Prop 28) to allow twelve years "in the Assembly, Senate, or both, in any combination of terms."

Prior to the passage of Prop 140 in 1990, state legislators were belittled as out-of-touch careerists who had developed cozy relationships with lobbyists and whose reelection seemed guaranteed. Their reputation sank after a Federal Bureau of Investigation (FBI) sting in 1988 netted fourteen state officials who were charged with bribery, including three legislators who went to jail.

AP Photo/Susan Ragan

Willie Brown, Speaker of the California state Assembly from 1980 to 1995, was an easy target of term limits supporters for his perceived abuses of power and flashy style.

The electorate was ready for change when an initiative modeled on one passed shortly before in Oklahoma qualified for the ballot. It restricted senators to two terms (a total of eight years) and Assembly members to three terms (six years) during their lifetimes. Echoes of the early California Progressives were heard in proponents' sweeping promises to restore a "government of citizens representing their fellow citizens."* The measure quickly gained momentum and passed with just over 52 percent of the vote. Since then, support for term limits among Californians has solidified and increased, and twenty other states subsequently adopted similar measures, although these were invalidated or repealed in six states, bringing the current total number of states with term limits to fifteen. In 2012, modifications to the term limits law were approved by 61 percent of California voters, who accepted arguments that politicians were "more focused on campaigning for their next office than doing their jobs."** Ever hopeful that tweaking the law could restore more accountability, voters will now allow lawmakers to stay up to twelve years in one chamber so they might "develop the expertise to get things done."

Term limits had immediate impacts in 1990. Long-term legislators were forced to campaign for other elected offices, and staff members were driven into private lobbying firms when Prop 140 slashed legislative budgets. Within a few years, long-standing speaker Willie Brown was mayor of San Francisco, Assembly careers were ending for good, and sitting senators were anticipating their next career moves. Overall, the wide-ranging effects of term limits have touched virtually every aspect of legislative life, and they have ranged from positive to negative.

Electoral Changes

- Competition has increased for political offices at all levels, from county boards of supervisors to the U.S. Congress, as more termed-out legislators seek them.

BOX 4.2 **(Continued)**

- Intraparty competition has risen as legislative members of the same party vie for the same seats—usually in the state Senate, but also in Congress, on county boards of supervisors and city councils, and as executive constitutional officers. This effect is exacerbated by the "Top Two Primary," which sometimes produces general election races in which each candidate squares off against other members of his or her own party in both the primary and/or general elections.
- Open-seat primary elections created through term limits are ferociously competitive, attracting millions in spending; open-seat general elections in a handful of districts are highly competitive as well.
- Incumbents still have huge advantages—about 96 percent are reelected. Many cruise to victory without serious challengers, and some face no challengers at all. Because individuals may be reelected five times to the Assembly, those incumbent-dominated contests reduce electoral competitiveness overall.
- For legislators elected under Prop 140 rules (elected prior to 2012), the Senate is a logical step up for members of the lower house; nearly all senators have been former state Assembly members. A few have returned or will return to the Assembly to finish serving out a final term before reaching *their* lifetime limit (fourteen years; their last term would be in 2024). This pattern is changing as new legislators seek reelection to spend up to twelve years in one place, rather than risk losing their seats to run for the other chamber. The Senate already contains more new legislators who have never had Assembly experience (five elected in 2014).

Membership Changes

- Far higher numbers of open seats have encouraged the candidacies and election of racial/ethnic minority members—higher than would be expected through redistricting alone. As of mid-2015, 40 percent of legislators were Latino, African American, Asian American, or other racial/ethnic minority.
- Higher turnover has led to record numbers of female candidates for office since 1990, although the total percentage of women in the legislature follows a longer historical upward trend unconnected to term limits.
- Women are occupying more leadership roles in both houses than before; these trends are more apparent among Democrats, in part because Democratic women have served as lawmakers in greater numbers than have Republican women.

Institutional Changes

- Newer legislators have recently experienced the effects of current laws in their districts and have fresh ideas about how to address problems arising from them.
- "Institutional memory" has drained away as career legislators and their staffs have left at regular intervals; members are less expert across a range of policy areas than in the past, and their knowledge of how state systems interrelate is poorer. As more legislators accumulate experience in one chamber under Prop 28, they should build expertise and gain longer-term perspectives.
- Under Prop 140, the average senator has had about two and a half times as much legislative experience as the average Assembly member. Under Prop 28, senators' and Assembly members' experience is expected to equalize.
- Senate staff members tend to be more experienced than Assembly staff members and consider the upper house the "watchdog" of the more turnover-prone Assembly. This "attitudinal" difference, shared by staff and senators alike, will probably persist because the Senate has half as many members as the Assembly, and senators enjoy four years between elections rather than two.
- Lobbyists who represent powerful groups, have experience, and are well connected can quickly establish relationships and exert undue influence over legislators. Lobbyists must work harder to get to know new legislators, however, as new members are likely to regard lobbyists with skepticism.
- Executive branch departments command informational resources and benefit from less frequent institutional turnover, rendering oversight by the legislature even more difficult than in the past.

BOX 4.2 **(Continued)**

Behavioral Changes

- "Lame duck" legislators (those in their last terms) lack electoral accountability to their current districts. Many look to their next possible constituency when considering how to vote; some feel less obligated to lobbyists in their last terms and more frequently feel free to "vote their conscience."
- Smaller, district-level projects delivering immediate results are more attractive to term-limited legislators. Longer tenures under Prop 28 may encourage longer-term, more comprehensive lawmaking that has suffered, as term-limited legislators lack the time and incentive to tackle many big projects or issues that will outlast their tenures. Changes to the term limits law were implemented because of a pervasive sense that "everyone is running for the next office." Term-limited legislators will still run for other offices (about two-thirds of legislators will do so within two years of their term limits), and most will find work in the public sector, but institutional turnover is expected to decrease as more legislators "play it safe" by staying in the same office until their twelve-year clocks run out.

Sources: Author's data. See also Thad Kousser, Bruce Cain, and Karl Kurtz, "The Legislature: Life under Term Limits," in *Governing California: Politics, Government, and Public Policy in the Golden State*, 3rd ed., ed. Ethan Rarick (Berkeley, CA: Public Policy Press, Institute of Governmental Studies, 2013); and Ava Alexandar, *Citizen Legislators or Political Musical Chairs? Term Limits in California* (Los Angeles: Center for Governmental Studies, 2011).

* California Secretary of State, "Argument in Favor of Proposition 140," November 1990 ballot pamphlet.

** Jennifer A. Waggoner, Kathay Feng, and Hank Lacayo, "Argument in Favor of Proposition 28," in *Presidential Primary Election Ballot Pamphlet* (Sacramento California Secretary of State, 2012), http://voterguide.sos.ca.gov/past/2012/primary/propositions/28/arguments-rebuttals.htm.

agree on many fixes for local and state problems. Every term hundreds of bills pass "on consent," or unanimously. They may disagree on fundamentals, and their core differences are exacerbated during economic downturns and highlighted by certain controversial issues such as providing health care or social services to undocumented immigrants—yet *members of the two parties work together often*, rather than rarely.

In many ways the legislature is a microcosm of California. More than ever before, the demographics of the Assembly and Senate resemble the state's population (see Figure 4.1). There are more women and a wider range of ages and backgrounds represented and 40 percent of Senate and Assembly members identify as racial or ethnic minorities.[5] The extent to which a legislature is, as U.S. founder John Adams put it, "an exact portrait, in miniature, of the people at large"[6] is a measure of **descriptive representation**. The extent to which members translate their values, backgrounds, and preferences into meaningful policies is **substantive representation**. Their work as representatives falls into several large categories: **policymaking and lawmaking**, **annual budgeting**, **constituency service**, and **oversight** of the executive branch.

Policymaking and Lawmaking

Assembly members and senators fulfill their representative functions chiefly through performing various aspects of lawmaking. To deal with approximately five thousand bills and measures introduced in a two-year session, they gather information through research generated by their staffs, pay attention to the cues given by their colleagues, hear arguments from hundreds of people—mostly lobbyists—about proposed laws, and visit sites such as schools and interact with community leaders and citizens to get a better sense of their districts. They introduce bills addressing problems that lobbyists or constituents bring to their attention. As members of committees (where the bulk of policymaking occurs), they help shape or amend legislation after fielding complaints, statements, and predictions from witnesses who will potentially be affected by proposed changes. They deliberate and vote both in committee and later on the Assembly or Senate floor, where every member has a chance to vote on every bill. Because all bills must be passed in identical form by both houses before they can be sent to the governor for a signature or veto, members also continue building support for, or opposition to, measures that are moving through the other house.

As in Congress, much of a legislator's workload is derived from membership on committees, the institution's powerhouses. The Assembly boasts thirty-one standing policy committees, plus six budget subcommittees and more than fifty "select" committees on issues ranging from agriculture to public safety—enough for each member of the majority party to become a chair if desired. Half as large, the Senate has twenty-two standing policy committees, fourteen subcommittees, and still more select, special, and joint committees (twenty-four in all; seven are shared "jointly" with the Assembly). In both chambers, committees are staffed by policy specialists whose intimate knowledge of past and present policy solutions allow them to play key roles in analyzing and shaping the bills referred to their committe.

In bygone eras, the committee chairmen would rule over their fiefdoms for decades, protecting pet projects, crushing bills at a whim, and blessing others before sending them to the Assembly or Senate floor for final consideration by all members. Power is no longer concentrated as it once was, because turnover leads to relatively less expert members and more competition for choice chairpersonships. Given that most senators are former Assembly members, they usually have at least four years of legislative experience when they are appointed as committee chairs. By contrast, many freshmen with no legislative experience have chaired Assembly committees under term limits, but that will change as Prop 28 takes full effect.

Each bill bears the imprint of a unique set of players, is shaped by the rules, and is affected by timing. More often than not, the concerns of important groups and "stakeholders" are gathered throughout the bill passage process and accommodated to some degree. Observers are often surprised at the overt influence that special interests wield in the process. When they raise objections to provisions in bills, legislators listen and respond. Lawmakers tend to be extrasensitive to the fears and threats expressed by well-financed, vocal, influential, and large organizations that support their political party or are active in their districts—as some say, "The squeaky wheels get the grease." For instance, if a bill to raise the minimum wage is being considered, then lobbyists for big retailers and restaurant chains will likely be arguing that it is a "job killer" in face-to-face meetings with lawmakers or their staff and will be forcefully presenting their cases in committee hearings, just as labor union lobbyists will be vigorously arguing that it creates more disposable income for workers. This scenario recently occurred when Governor Brown signed AB 10, a law that raised the minimum wage to $9.00 per hour in July 2014 and increases it to $10 per hour as of January 1, 2016.

Relationships also matter. Partisans tend to support fellow partisans, but legislators who get to know others "across the aisle" tend to be more willing to support them legislatively. Over time, representatives tend to develop what is commonly referred to as "social capital": a shared sense of norms, interpersonal networks, and trust among colleagues. Because in the final analysis compromise and bargaining are key, relationships among the players—from legislative staff to legislators to lobbyists to the governor's staff—help facilitate the necessary give-and-take to coconstruct workable policy solutions.

Bills vary in scope, cost, urgency, and significance and cover every imaginable topic. Most go no further than being referred to a committee, and not bringing up a bill in committee after it has been referred is the easiest way for a chair to kill it. Of lowest significance are simple **resolutions** passed to express the legislature's position on particular issues. For example, in April 2015, the state Senate and Assembly passed a joint resolution urging the U.S. Congress and president to recognize atrocities committed in Armenia 1915–1923 as *genocide*, a label they have carefully avoided.

Inexpensive **local bills**, which deal with such concerns as specific land uses, may matter a lot to the people directly affected by the legislation but usually have only minor impacts on state government. An example would be a 2015 bill authorizing Los Angeles County sanitation districts to partner with county flood control districts to manage stormwater and urban runoff.[7]

Many bills relate to the administration of government and make technical changes or amendments to existing state law. These proposed **statutes** might impose mandates, or obligations, on local governments or agencies, such as prohibiting state entities from displaying or selling items emblazoned with the Confederate flag, except where it has historical or educational value such as in books or museums. New laws (statutes) are also needed to authorize public agencies to take on new responsibilities or to collect fees, such as allowing cities to sponsor a local ballot measure asking for a $5 surcharge on car registrations so that bike trails can be developed. Other bills create new categories of crime, authorize studies, or set up programs. For example, it takes a law to set up a recovery program for unused paint or fluorescent lightbulbs that might otherwise be illegally dumped or to require that tattoo artists get annual permits from the state health department to operate legally.

Legislators also introduce bills that at first glance may appear to make small changes, but that, if enacted into law, would have tangible effects on Californians and their local governments. For instance, hydraulic fracturing, commonly known as "fracking," involves drilling horizontal wells deep into underground shale deposits and injecting chemical-laced water at high pressure to release trapped oil or natural gas. To grapple with the growing practice, lawmakers have introduced bills to temporarily halt fracking altogether, require pre- and postfracture groundwater testing, require regulation of hydraulic fluids as hazardous waste, commission studies of the environmental impacts, and demand that companies give thirty days' notice before commencing fracking activity. Most of these controversial bills have been defeated, then reintroduced in successive legislative sessions, and some provisions made it into law through SB 4. That new law requires the disclosure of chemicals used in fracking processes, demands oil and gas companies obtain special permits that take water usage into account, notify neighbors of operations, and monitor both air quality and well water. Local and/or state officials must figure out how to implement each new regulation, and each one could also have serious implications for property owners, oil and gas companies, and, ultimately, the prices consumers pay for energy.

Of major import are multimillion- or billion-dollar, long-range, intricate bills that affect many different groups and usually require years of preparation, study, and compromise. Examples include revising workers' compensation benefits and regulating ecosystems such as the Sacramento–San Joaquin River Delta and its related maze of waterways. Reshaping the state health care system to comply with federal regulations is another "big-ticket" item that lawmakers have spent years working on in anticipation of "Obamacare," the Affordable Care Act, which became operational in 2014. Several million residents now pay for health insurance either through a state-run plan called "Covered

California," or their health costs are covered through low- or no-cost Medi-Cal, the state's version of universal health insurance for poor and disabled people, including approximately 170,000 undocumented immigrant children.

Unfortunately, term-limited members lack incentive to unwind knotty problems that take years to understand and for which they will receive little credit, although this does not stop all legislators from trying to make a difference. Longer time in one house may counteract this tendency, and with the help of veteran committee staff and lobbyists, especially those who have greater longevity and knowledge than the legislators themselves, many members can work to craft solutions to problems that take time to understand well.

Given the scope and complexity of the state's ongoing issues, legislators need help. Thousands of staff members work directly for legislators in the capitol, in district offices, or for committees.

AP Photo/Rich Pedroncelli

Lawmakers translate the needs and concerns of their constituents into law. Under a new law (SB 277) authored by Sen. Richard Pan, a pediatrician and Democrat from Sacramento, almost without exception all schoolchildren must be vaccinated to attend California public schools. The bill was prompted by a 2014 measles outbreak, partly resulting from parents' choosing not to vaccinate their children. Governor Jerry Brown signed the bill in June 2015.

Inside each legislator's capitol and district office are **personal** staff: individuals hired to prepare bills their bosses will introduce, analyze the thousands of other bills that cross a legislator's desk during a two-year term, assist with scheduling, and perform constituent relations. **Committee** staff members manage all aspects of shepherding bills through a committee, from scheduling witnesses to writing analyses for each bill. The smaller Senate retained more veteran professional committee staff and more experienced legislators under the original term limits law and has tended to view itself collectively as having a stronger filter for "bad ideas." This may change as members accumulate a dozen years of experience in a single chamber, and they encourage personal and committee staff members to stay as well.

Legislators also heavily depend on institutional housekeepers like the Assembly chief clerk's staff or the Senate's secretary to ensure that legislators follow standing rules and parliamentary procedures. The nonpartisan **Legislative Analyst's Office (LAO)** has been the so-called conscience and eyes and ears of the legislature since 1941, providing professional analysis of the annual budget as well as fiscal and policy advice based on continuing, in-depth research of statewide programs. With analysts divided into eight subject areas, including education, housing, social service, health, and finance, the LAO remains one of the premier sources of information about state programs and the budget (http://www.lao.ca.gov). Similarly, since 1913 the nonpartisan **Legislative Counsel** has acted as an in-house law firm, crafting legislators' proposals into formal bills, rendering legal opinions, and making bill information available electronically (http://leginfo.legislature.ca.gov). Finally, staff members work for both political parties' leadership and routinely provide their own bill analyses and vote recommendations to their party members.

It should also be noted that the majority party controls the fate of nearly all bills because a simple majority vote (41 in the Assembly, 21 in the Senate) is all that's needed to pass most bills, although a good number of bills are noncontroversial and pass unanimously. With a simple majority also needed to pass the annual budget, the majority party can enact its agenda without being held hostage by a minority party trying to extract concessions in exchange for votes. The bottom line: today, minority-party Republicans are at the mercy of majority-party Democrats when it comes to lawmaking, and their bills rarely move out of committee—unless they are deemed "harmless" by the Democrats. Usually the majority party can safely ignore the minority unless votes are needed to pass urgency bills or fiscal measures such as new tax or fee hikes that require a two-thirds supermajority (54 in the Assembly, 27 in the Senate), a discouraging position for those in the minority. The 2012 elections laid a new milestone when, for the first time since 1883, Democrats secured a supermajority in both houses.[8] With fifty-five Democrats in the lower house and twenty-eight in the upper house (a threshold that was crossed and lost with several special elections in 2013), they enjoyed a "veto-proof" majority for several months, meaning that they could raise taxes or override a gubernatorial veto without relying on Republican votes. As Governor Brown opined in a 2013 interview, "The Republicans appear to have no power. . . . They aren't needed for any votes."[9] To be effective, Republicans contribute to the process in other ways. For instance, they keep the majority party accountable by raising pointed questions in committee hearings and voicing concerns during floor debates, by shaping their bills to attract consensus, and by trying to amend the Democratic majority's bills to soften potential impacts on their constituents.

FIGURE 4.2 How a Bill Becomes a Law

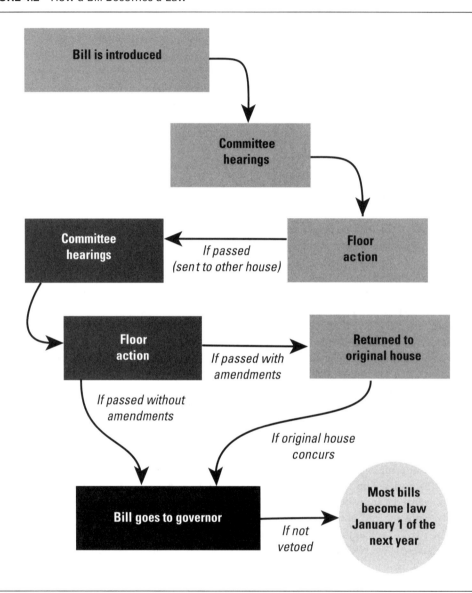

Annual Budgeting

It takes the legislature more than half the year to work out an annual budget for the fiscal year (FY) that starts July 1. The process formally begins on January 10 when the governor submits his version to the legislature, and it should end by June 15, when the budget is officially due—but long-overdue budgets had been the norm for decades. Delays ceased after voters passed Prop 25 in 2010, an initiative that lowered the vote threshold needed to enact the budget to a simple majority.

During the winter and spring of a normal fiscal year, the committees in both houses divvy up the work of determining how much money is needed to keep government programs running. They use the governor's budget as a benchmark for estimating costs and potential state revenues. Big-ticket items such as education are automatically funded, leaving a relatively small chunk of the budget pie for discretionary purposes; therefore, each legislator fights hard for the crumbs. The inherently partisan process becomes incendiary during tight budget years and is tempered when the economy is looking up and there is "unified government," meaning that both houses of the legislature and the governor's office are controlled by one party, as has been the case since Jerry Brown's election in 2010.

TABLE 4.1 A Day in the Life of Senator Connie Leyva

April 14, 2015 Tuesday	
7:30 a.m.–8:30 a.m.	Breakfast with California-Nevada Conference of Operating Engineers
8:30 a.m.–9:00 a.m. (note overlaps)	Meeting with Advocates at Chicory Coffee and Tea
9:00 a.m.–9:30 a.m.	Meeting with Advocates re: SB 364 Ellis Act (Capitol Office, Room 4061)
9:30 a.m.–10:00 a.m.	Meeting with State Building Trades Council & California Labor Federation (Room 2040)
10:00 a.m.–10:30 a.m.	Meeting with United Food & Commercial Workers 1428, Lobby Day (Room 4061)
10:30 a.m.–11:00 a.m.	Meeting with Transportation Workers Union of America, AFL-CIO (Room 4061)
11:30 a.m.–12:00 p.m.	Leadership Meeting
12:00 p.m.–1:30 p.m.	Democratic Caucus Lunch (Maddy Lounge)
1:30 p.m.–3:30 p.m. (overlaps)	Senate Veterans Affairs Committee; Present SB 384
1:30 p.m.–4:30 p.m. (overlaps)	Senate Transportation & Housing Committee Hearing (Room 4203)
4:00 p.m.–4:30 p.m.	Meeting with Los Angeles/Orange County Building Trades Council (Room 4023)
4:30 p.m.–5:00 p.m.	Capitol Office (Room 4061)
5:00 p.m.–6:30 p.m.	Time to "breathe"
6:30 p.m.–8:30 p.m.	Emerge California Reception (Citizen Hotel)
7:30 p.m.–8:30 p.m.	Dinner with Senators Carol Liu, Fran Pavley, Loni Hancock (Bistro Michael)

Constituency Service and Outreach

Constituency service entails "helping constituents navigate through the government system,"[10] particularly when their troubles stem from bureaucratic "red tape." Legislators hire caseworkers to help them respond quickly to requests, and these personal staff members, who typically work in district offices, spend their days tracking down answers from workers in state agencies like Caltrans and scheduling appointments at other state agencies for frustrated constituents, among other things. Legislators take constituency service seriously, although this part of the job is not mentioned in the state constitution. Many consider it "paramount to return every phone call, letter, and e-mail" and make government seem friendlier through personal contact.[11]

Most legislators try to communicate frequently with the residents of their districts through e-mail, Facebook, Twitter, official websites, or bulk-mail newsletters. Other activities include addressing select community groups, such as Rotary, or attending special public events (store openings, groundbreakings for public facilities, parades, and so forth). Through this kind of constituency service, or **public relations**, as some members call it, representatives educate those in the district about issues, get to know their constituents and what they care about, and reinforce their chances for reelection by enhancing their name recognition and reputation.

Executive Branch Oversight

Who monitors programs to ensure that a law is being carried out according to the legislature's intent? Ideally, Assembly members, senators, and their staff members should be systematically reviewing programs and questioning administrators by having them appear before committees, but term-limited legislators often don't have the time or staff resources to determine if the laws they have created are being faithfully executed. In practice, they rely on investigative reports in the media, lobbyists, citizens, and administrators to sound the alarm about needed fixes. Once a problem is identified, the Assembly and Senate can rescue legislative intent in a number of ways. For example, they might address the offending administrators personally or write a bill to clear up confusion over an existing statute. On the rare occasion when an issue grabs the media's attention, lawmakers might respond more dramatically, by interrogating uncooperative administrators in a public forum and then threatening to eliminate their positions, yank authority away from them, or reduce their program funding (a governor can also fire irresponsible administrators). In addition, senators influence programs through their power to confirm hundreds of gubernatorial appointees to the major executive departments and influential state boards and commissions, such as the seventeen-member California Community Colleges Board of Governors. Leaders in both houses also have the privilege of directly appointing some members of a few select boards, such as the twelve-member California Coastal Commission.

Leaders

Aside from the governor, the Speaker of the Assembly and the president pro tem of the Senate are among the most powerful figures in Sacramento. Along with the governor and the minority leaders of each house, these individuals form the "Big Five" of California government: the leaders who

The Senate Rules Committee, headed by the Senate president pro tem, holds hearings to confirm the governor's appointees. Where committee membership is concerned, the majority political party members (currently the Democrats) always outnumber those in the minority party.

speak for all their fellow party members in their respective houses and are ultimately responsible for cobbling together last-minute political bargains that clinch the budget or guarantee the signing of big bills. These days the "Big Three" Democratic leaders (the top two legislative leaders plus the governor) are most visible and central to the process.

A party leader's job is to keep his or her majority in power or to regain majority status. Nonstop fund-raising, policymaking, rule making, and deal making all serve that overarching objective. Leaders oversee their *party caucus* (all the members of a party in one house) and help shape the electorate's understanding of what it means to support a "Democratic" or "Republican" agenda. Still, institutional agendas are fluid, and they emerge from commonalities among legislators' individual efforts more often than they are imposed by elites at the top. However, the general rule is, what leadership wants, leadership gets. Leaders' ability to obtain desired results rests on many factors, including their wielding credible weapons such as the power to remove members from choice committees or kill their bills. Leaders may also endorse opponents, cut off campaign funds, reduce office budgets midyear, or move members out of offices or parking spaces to new and undesirable locations. For instance, Assemblyman Anthony Portantino's office budget was slashed in summer 2011 after he cast the only Democratic vote against the state budget bill.

The speaker is the most visible member of the Assembly and its spokesperson at-large. He or she negotiates budgets, bills, and policies on behalf of the entire membership; curries a high profile with the press; and cultivates a distinct culture of discipline and institutional independence through a unique and personal leadership style. The speaker actively fundraises in a manner that rewards his or her own faithful political party members and punishes traitors. The Senate's president pro tem plays these same roles, and as legislative experience has pooled in the upper house in a term-limited era, the Senate leader's visibility has increased relative to that of the speaker. Under Prop 28, it is likely that the two leaders will maintain rough parity as the years pass.

The speaker appoints chairs and members to all Assembly committees, as does the president pro tem in the Senate through his or her chairing of the all-powerful, five-member Rules Committee. The president pro tem also can use the Rules Committee's power over the governor's key administrative appointments as a bargaining chip in budget and bill negotiations—a tool the speaker lacks.

These days, neither the speaker nor the Senate president pro tem regularly leads floor sessions. Visitors catch glimpses of these leaders as they crisscross the floor to speak privately with members in an effort to find support for bills and negotiate deals while normal business proceeds. More often than not, a colleague acting as an assistant "pro tem" guides floor proceedings.

Leaders never forget that they are chosen by colleagues and stay only as long as they can maintain high levels of trust and confidence by meeting their colleagues' political needs. This was as true for flashy former speaker Willie Brown (1980–1995) as it is for speakers such as Toni Atkins (2014–2016) or her successor, Anthony Rendon (2016–) today. No tyrants can survive, if only because so many potential replacements impatiently wait in the wings—and under term limits, they needn't wait long before the next opportunity arises. Brown presided over the Assembly for almost fifteen years. In the span of fifteen years following his exit there were *ten* speakers.

Conclusion: Of the People, for the People

Although the legislature's basic framework has changed little since the constitutional revision of 1879, major changes in electoral law, campaign finance rules, ethics laws, redistricting rules, compensation levels, and terms of office have molded and remolded California's legislative environment. Initiatives continue to complicate the already difficult task of condensing a multitude of competing interests, opinions, backgrounds, values, expectations, and ideas into an effective decision-making body. Californians have been quick to alter the political rules in attempts to make their representatives resistant to what is generally regarded as the poisonous influence of partisanship, money, and power, yet these forces are inescapable.

Lawmaking is *supposed* to be hard, and conflict is inevitable in an institution brimming with ambitious officials who share similar powers and responsibilities. In California, the policymaking process is further complicated by direct democracy and hyperdiversity. Bills bear the imprints of competing interest groups, parties, leaders, funding sources, personal ambitions, rules, history, and a host of other factors that influence choice and impede the easy resolution of issues. The next election exerts gravitational pull on representatives as well. The lawmaking process is messy. Short of creating a tyranny, no reform will change that.

Spokesperson for both the lower chamber and her fellow majority party Democrats, Assembly Speaker Toni Atkins (2014–2016) shapes messages that affect how state government is perceived. The Senate president pro tem (Kevin DeLeón), pictured behind Atkins at left, does the same for the upper chamber.

Despite these various counterpressures, more often than not, Democrats and Republicans cooperate to enact policies that reflect the peoples' will and needs as they understand them. Their basic disagreements about how to govern effectively surface visibly in many areas of policymaking and state budgeting, but representatives also deal with countless issues that are not divisive. The ways in which they work together are often hidden from view, contributing to the public's sense that lawmakers are generally ineffective.

The California legislature comes closer to the U.S. Congress in form than any other state legislature in the nation. Perhaps that is one reason for its low approval ratings, but it also remains the best hope for each citizen to achieve a degree of representation that would be unimaginable under an unelected bureaucracy, a dictatorial governor, or even a part-time legislature responsible for helping to govern one of the largest "countries" on the globe. The lawmaking body is closer to the people than the other two branches could ever be: neither the elected executives nor judges can understand the needs and interests of California's communities as thoroughly as firmly anchored representatives can.

Notes

1. The U.S. Census 2010 apportionment population in congressional districts is 710,767; California contains fifty-three U.S. House districts. National Atlas of the United States, "Congressional Apportionment," accessed June 20, 2015, http://www.nationalatlas.gov/articles/boundaries/a_conApport.html#one.

2. It should be noted that although high turnover in 2012 was also prompted by redistricting, term limits have provided the impetus for high turnover in nonredistricting years since 1990. In 2012, turnover reached 47.5 percent.

3. Proposition 11, Section 2(d).

4. The case was *Arizona State Legislature v. Arizona Independent Redistricting Commission*, 576 U.S. ___ (2015).

5. Of the 120 legislators in office in August 2015, thirty-one were women. In terms of race and ethnicity, seventy-one were White, twelve were African American, twenty-three were Hispanic/Latino, twelve were Asian American or Pacific Islander, and two were of Middle Eastern descent (Jordanian and Armenian). In all, 49 of 120 (41 percent) were "nonwhite."

6. Quoted in Hannah Pitkin, *The Concept of Representation* (Berkeley: University of California Press, 1967), 60.

7. SB 485, authored by Senator Ed Hernandez, introduced February 26, 2015.

8. The Republican Party achieved supermajority status in both chambers at least a dozen times between 1891 and 1933.

9. James Fallows, "Jerry Brown's Political Reboot," *The Atlantic,* May 22, 2013, http://www.theatlantic.com/magazine/archive/2013/06/the-fixer/309324/?single_page=true.

10. Donald Lathbury, "Two-Thirds Majority Battle Still on Radar," California Majority Report, September 22, 2008, http://www.camajorityreport.com/index.php?module=articles&func=display&ptid=9&aid=3581.

11. Author's interview with freshman assembly member in Sacramento, California, in March 1999.

CHAPTER 5

The Executive Branch

Question: Who is in charge of California's K–12 education system?

Answer: Although the *governor* guides education policy through budgetary choices and is often held responsible for the overall state of education, it is the elected *state superintendent of public instruction* who heads the system by constitutional mandate, overseeing the *Department of Education,* the agency through which the public school system is regulated and controlled as required by law, taking cues from the administration's powerful *State Board of Education,* also appointed by the governor but technically administered by the superintendent, who in turn implements the educational regulations of the state board . . . not to mention the *Assembly* and *Senate education committees* that steer education bills into law, or the *local school district boards* that actually operate schools day to day.

Confusing? A case of checks and balances gone awry? Somewhere among the governor's need to obtain information and make recommendations, the legislature's regulatory imperative, and the people's desire to elect officers who can be held accountable, the system evolved into a tangled network of authority that even Department of Education employees have difficulty explaining.

California's Plural Executive

The founders of the United States rejected the notion that more than one person could effectively lead an executive branch. They argued that only a single individual, the president, could bring energy to an office that would otherwise be fractured by competing ambitions and differences of opinion. What then are we to make of California's plural executive, which comprises a whopping eight constitutional executive officers plus a five-member

BOX 5.1   FAST FACTS on California's Plural Executive

Number of executives:	8, plus the Board of Equalization (12 persons)
Elected executive offices:	Governor
	Lieutenant governor (LG)
	Attorney general (AG)
	Secretary of state
	Controller
	Treasurer
	Superintendent of public instruction
	Insurance commissioner
	Board of Equalization (4 of 5 members are elected)
Balance of political parties:	10 Democrats, 1 Republican, 1 nonpartisan (2014 elections)
Governor's salary:	$177,467*
Salary for AG and superintendent:	$154,150*
Salary for controller, treasurer, and insurance commissioner:	$141,973*
Salary for secretary of state, LG, and Board of Equalization members:	$133,100*
Terms of office:	Four years
Term limits:	Two terms (lifetime ban)**

Source: California Citizens Compensation Commission, "Salaries of Elected Officials," effective December 1, 2014, http://www.calhr.ca.gov/cccc/pages/cccc-salaries.aspx.

* Salary decreases totaling 20 percent went into effect between December 2009 and November 2013; the average decrease was around $40,000 per official from a peak in 2007 and 2008. Salary increases resumed in 2013.

**Once an executive has served two terms in a particular office, he or she may not run for that office again. Term limits took effect with Proposition 140 in 1990. Anyone who served prior to 1990 was not prevented from running again; this includes Governor Jerry Brown, who served two terms as governor from 1975 to 1983.

board—one of the biggest sets of officers among the states? Or the fact that these elected officials may be Republicans and Democrats who are ideologically opposed yet share responsibility for administering state government?

Term limits on each office—two four-year terms under Proposition 140—also dull executives' incentives to cooperate with one another. As ambitious, term-limited colleagues, they are potential or actual rivals for each others' seats, driven from one elected position to the next as in a game of musical chairs. Each must build his or her own name brand through independent actions that merit media attention. However, despite their towering list of responsibilities and industrious, collective efforts to lead the nation's most densely populated state, like most elected officials they remain obscure to average residents. Relative anonymity is one reason why Attorney General Kamala Harris announced her candidacy for U.S. Senate almost two years ahead of the 2016 election: even

FIGURE 5.1 California Executives and Musical Chairs

Under term limits that took effect in 1990, an individual may be elected to the same seat only twice. Elected officials are usually looking for their next jobs long before eight years are up, and open statewide offices are attractive options to those who have campaigned statewide and have run other aspects of state government. In a term-limited era, it's all about the "next" office.

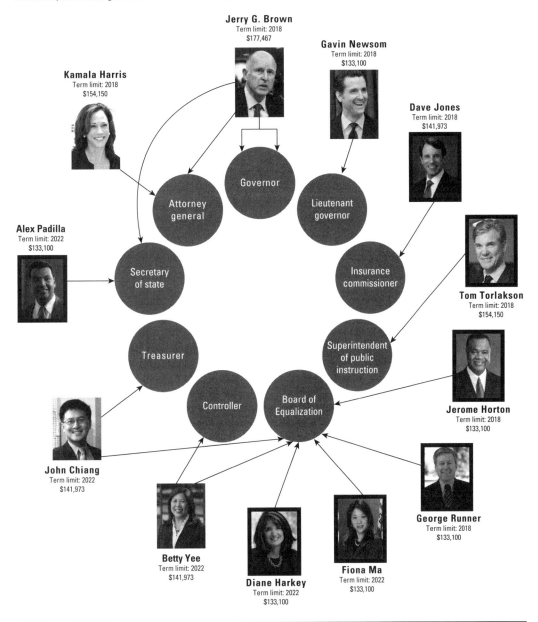

Notes: A **bold frame** indicates that the executive **served as an elected legislator** in the Assembly, the Senate, or both.

Photo credits, clockwise from top: Steve Granitz/WireImage; AP Photo/Paul Sakuma; Photo by Tia Gemmell, Riverview Media Photography; The California Department of Education; Courtesy of the California Board of Equalization; Courtesy of Senator George Runner (Ret.), Member of the California State Board of Equalization; Courtesy of the California Board of Equalization; AP Photo/Rich Pedroncelli; Courtesy of the Office of State Controller Yee AP Photo/John Chiang For State Controller; Brian Baer/Sacramento Bee/ZUMA Press; AP Photo/Rich Pedroncelli high-profile state executives need to create name recognition across a largely detached electorate. The story behind her candidacy also demonstrates the important dynamic of partisanship among state executives: working together—and not at cross-purposes—is easier when they represent the same party. Democrats were elected to fill all eight statewide offices in 2014 (one is nonpartisan but a Democrat occupies it), and Harris's chief potential rival, Lieutenant Governor Gavin Newsom, is aiming squarely for the governor's office in 2018—an arrangement that benefits both aspirants.

The duty of an executive is to carry out laws and policies. Whereas federal administrators direct agencies in their departments to implement a coherent presidential agenda, in California a wide assortment of departments, agencies, and commissions serve different masters: the governor, other California executives, the legislature, the entities they are supposed to regulate, or a combination of any of the above. Years of legislative and administrative turf battles, as well as popular initiatives, have produced a thicket of offices, boards, agencies, and commissions, some of which retain independent regulatory power and many more of which follow the governor's lead. In theory, the dispersion of power across several top offices inoculates government against the worst effects of a single, inept leader, but practically speaking, a fragmented power structure works against the production of consistent government policy and counteracts accountability.

California's Governor

According to the state constitution, "The supreme executive power of this State is vested in the Governor," which places him or her first among equals—for none of the elected executive officers answer directly to the governor. The most widely recognized and most powerful figure in California's state government possesses constitutional duties much like those of most other state governors; what distinguishes the office is both the size and hyperdiversity of the constituency (the entire state population) and the resulting volume of conflicts to be addressed.

TABLE 5.1 Modern-Era California Governors by Party Affiliation

Term (years)	Governor	Party affiliation
1943–1954 (12)	Earl Warren	Republican*
1955–1958 (4)	Goodwin Knight	Republican
1959–1966 (8)	Edmund "Pat" Brown	Democratic
1967–1974 (8)	Ronald Reagan	Republican
1975–1982 (8)	Edmund "Jerry" Brown Jr.	Democratic
1983–1990 (8)	George Deukmejian	Republican
1991–1998 (8)	Pete Wilson	Republican
1999–2003 (5)	Gray Davis	Democratic
2003–2010 (8)	Arnold Schwarzenegger	Republican
2011–present	Edmund "Jerry" Brown Jr.	Democratic

*Warren also received the nomination of the Democratic Party.

The usual route to office is through a battering election that commands national headlines. Only former governor Arnold Schwarzenegger initially escaped primary and general election contests, as well as an extended campaign, by winning office through a recall election in 2003, replacing the unpopular governor Gray Davis, who was only one year into his second term. Those with prior elected experience, strong partisans, and prodigious fund-raisers tend to survive the regular winnowing process—qualities that boosted Jerry Brown to victory over his recent Republican opponents: eBay cofounder Meg Whitman in 2010 and Neel Kashkari (a banker) in 2014. Brown regained the seat after having served two terms as governor (1975–1983, before term limits took effect), secretary of state, mayor of Oakland, and state attorney general.

Head of State

A governor has responsibilities both formal and informal. The role of **head of state** resonates with average citizens: the governor appears at official ceremonies and public events, summarizes California's outlook and his or her agenda in an annual "State of the State" address, receives and entertains foreign dignitaries, and speaks for Californians on both national and international political stages. He or she also functions as the state's official liaison to federal officials in Washington, D.C, and works with other state governors to advance causes nationally.

Chief Executive

The power to execute or carry out the law rests with the governor. Putting the law into practice is not something the governor can do alone, however. Brown employs 80 key "personal" staff to provide advice and assistance with research and communication (Schwarzenegger employed 202 at the end of his second term),[1] his cabinet secretaries, who oversee major departments containing scores of agencies, help implement mandated programs throughout the state, and coordinate the governor's policies. They are among the approximately 800 top-level appointees placed throughout the administration. Collectively, these appointees put into practice the governor's vision of good governance through the daily decisions they make about thousands of issues.

The governor also appoints members to approximately three hundred state boards and commissions with more than two thousand slots to be filled. Examples include advisory groups, boards that manage county fairs, professional licensing bureaus, and specialized councils that deal with everything from marine fisheries to the arts to sex offenders. Appointments to about one hundred full-time administrative positions and seventy-five boards and commissions require Senate approval, and overall only a fraction of appointees serve at the governor's pleasure—meaning that only a few can be let go for almost any reason. For instance, civil service laws protect virtually all state employees, and roughly 99 percent are hired based on merit rather than nepotism, favoritism, or patronage.[2] Outside of this, on rare occasion the governor may name a replacement to an open U.S. Senate seat or constitutional executive office. The governor also has the power to fill vacancies throughout the judiciary (superior, appellate, and supreme courts), although his appointees to appellate and supreme courts must first be reviewed and confirmed by two different judicial commissions and are later subject to voter approval at retention elections (see chapter 6). The governor may also issue **executive orders** directing state employees in how to implement the law, but the governor's power falls short of forcing all elected executives—constitutional partners such as the controller or attorney general—to do his or her bidding.

Legislative Powers

Legislatively, the governor plays a significant role by **setting policy priorities** for California not only through proposed laws but also through the budget. The power to **call special elections** and **legislative sessions** to deal with extraordinary matters, along with long-term, permanent staff members dedicated to research and program oversight, give the governor's office significant institutional advantages over the legislature. Governor Brown called two special sessions in 2015: one to mend how California funds roads,

Edmund Gerald Brown Jr., also known as Jerry Brown, first became governor at age thirty-six, was later reelected at age seventy-two, and was reelected to a fourth, final term at age seventy-six. He has also served as a community college board trustee, California secretary of state, mayor of Oakland, state Democratic Party chair, and state attorney general.

highways, and infrastructure, and the other to fix Medi-Cal, the main health care program for low-income and disabled Californians.

Aides monitor bills at all stages of the legislative process. They propose bills and participate in critical final negotiations over a bill's wording and price tag. They testify before Assembly or Senate committees about pending measures and help build coalitions of support or opposition among legislators, interest groups, and other stakeholders. They also advise the governor to **veto** or **sign** legislation, because a bill submitted to the governor by the legislature becomes law after twelve days without gubernatorial action. Like governors in four out of five states, the governor of California wields the **line-item veto,** the power to reduce or eliminate dollar amounts in bills or the budget. This is also called "blue pencil" authority, because in the 1960s governors actually used an editor's blue pencil to cross out items in print. In September 2014, for example, Governor Brown unleashed his power on a budget amendment, eliminating $100 million that had been intended for deferred maintenance at the California State University and the University of California (though it should be noted that he restored that funding in the 2015–16 budget). Veto overrides of such spending items or any bill passed by the legislature are rarely attempted or successful. In fact, the last recorded successful override occurred in response to one of "young" governor Jerry Brown's budget-related line-item vetoes in early 1980.[3]

Budgeting Power

Budgeting power arguably gives the administration a powerful advantage over the Assembly and Senate. On January 10 of each year, the governor submits to the legislature a proposed annual state budget for the upcoming fiscal year. The muscular **Department of Finance (DOF),** a permanent clearinghouse for state financial and demographic information, works in tandem with the governor, executive departments, and agencies to specify the initial budget in January, based on projections, and revises it in May based on actual tax receipts. The nearly 470 employees of this "superdepartment" work year-round to prepare the following year's budget and enact the previous year's financial plan, and they also analyze proposed laws that would have a fiscal impact on the state.[4]

Chief of Security

If the governor **calls a state of emergency** during a drought or after a natural disaster or terrorist act, he or she is authorized to suspend certain laws and use private property in the impacted area, and the locality becomes eligible for state emergency funds. The governor also promotes security as **commander in chief** of the state's National Guard, which may be called on at short notice to deliver, for example, emergency services to victims of natural disasters such as earthquakes or fires. The State Military Reserve is the defense force placed under exclusive control of the governor; the land-based California Army National Guard and the Air National Guard, dedicated to cyberspace, space, and air capabilities, provide support.

With few restraints, the governor also can reduce penalties associated with a crime by offering clemency; that is, he or she can pardon individuals or shorten sentences through commutation, even for death row inmates. Pardoning means that the offense stays on the individual's record, but no further penalties or restrictions will be imposed. The governor must report all acts of clemency and the reasons for them to the legislature annually. Governor Schwarzenegger granted a total of sixteen pardons and ten commutations of sentence—one of which was sharply, publicly criticized because it appeared to be done out of favoritism for the convicted son of close associate and former Assembly speaker Fabian Nuñez, a move that a state appeals court ultimately upheld as constitutional.[5] In contrast, after four and one-half years, Jerry Brown had pardoned 592 persons who had earned the privilege by demonstrating "exemplary behavior following their conviction" for at least ten years following their release.[6] (Incidentally, most of those convictions were drug-related offenses.) Finally, the governor has the authority to extradite fugitives from other states.

Sources of Power

The California governor's powers resemble those of U.S. presidents but with important exceptions. The state constitution spells out the governor's duties, but the constitutional blueprint for a plural executive limits a governor's ability to live up to citizens' expectations. For example, as the most visible and recognizable leader in state government, the governor sets policy priorities, yet he or she shares responsibility for day-to-day administration with almost a dozen other elected executive officers who may have their own agendas. The governor is held to account for actions that condition the overall state of affairs, even if they are outside his or her control. To overcome this structural disadvantage, the governor must draw on other sources of power to be an effective leader.

One source of power is *institutional*, such as whether the governor's party holds a majority in both the Assembly and the Senate, as well as the numerical advantage of the majority. Brown's own Democratic party has held the majority during all of his years as governor, and they even reached supermajority status during parts of his third term, meaning that they possessed the votes to override his vetoes (although they never attempted to do so). Another institutional factor is the cohesiveness of parties in the legislature, because the presence of many moderates may make the governor's job of reaching compromises much easier, whereas rigid or extreme partisans who are unwilling to budge from their positions can potentially thwart a more moderate governor's plans by obstructing specific bill language or foiling supermajority votes.

Power can also stem from a governor's *popularity*, *personal qualities*, and *style*. The governor's image as a loyal partisan friend or possibly as an untrustworthy party turncoat affects his or her ability to gather votes for preferred bills or provisions in them. For example, Governor Arnold Schwarzenegger alienated fellow Republicans by working with Democrats and championing policies that defied the state party's official platform. Jerry Brown (2011–present), despite having chaired the California Democratic Party at one time, has struck a note of practicality and toughness in his negotiations with Democratic leaders, disappointing them repeatedly with cuts to favored programs but earning him high marks from citizens. Aware of Brown's popularity and generally supportive of his ideological approach, Democratic legislators have had little choice but to back him, even if they cannot count on his unquestioning loyalty. Personal *charisma*, the *power to persuade*, the *perception of having a mandate*, and *strategic use of the media* can also go a long way in enhancing a governor's power base. Varied, lifelong *political experience* can also be a source of strength, as it has been for Governor Jerry Brown.

The Constitutional Executive Officers

Should the governor leave the state at any time, the **lieutenant governor** (LG) takes temporary control; should the governor resign, retire early, die, become disabled, or be impeached, the lieutenant governor takes the gubernatorial oath of office. Topping the LG's lackluster list of duties is presiding over the Senate, which in practice means exercising a rare tie-breaking vote. The "governor-in-waiting" is also a voting member of the California State University (CSU) Board of Trustees and the University of California Board of Regents and sits on several other regulatory and advisory state boards ex officio, or "automatically" by virtue of his or her position. The LG's staff includes only six people.

Second in power to the governor is actually the **attorney general** (AG), known as the state's chief law enforcement officer. Through the state's Department of Justice (DOJ), the AG employs deputy attorneys general to help represent the people of California in court cases, provides legal counsel to state officials, coordinates statewide narcotics enforcement efforts, enforces state firearms and gambling laws, fights fraud, assists with criminal investigations, provides forensic science services, and supervises all sheriffs, police chiefs, and state agencies to enforce the law adequately and uniformly. All told, approximately 4,850 people work for the DOJ. The office is inherently political not only because the state's lead lawyer is elected and may use the position as a stepping-stone to bigger and better offices (AG is also said to be shorthand for "aspiring governor") but also because he or she privileges some causes above others. For example, an AG might step up lawsuits against environmental polluters, forcefully prosecute financial crimes, or fight crimes against children—features of Kamala Harris's platform.

About five hundred employees assist the **secretary of state**, who acts as the chief elections officer and oversees all aspects of federal and state elections held within California. This includes registering voters, which can now be done online (http://registertovote.ca.gov), distributing ballot pamphlets in ten languages, printing ballots, certifying the integrity of voting machines, compiling election results, and certifying and publishing election results on the Web and in print. The Political Reform Division of the secretary of state's office implements rules relating to proper disclosure of lobbying and campaign finance activity and makes that information available electronically (http://cal-access.ss.ca.gov). As keeper of official historical records, the secretary of state also charters corporations and nonprofits, maintains business filings, stores complete records of official executive and legislative acts, and safeguards the state archives. All notaries public, persons authorized to formally certify signatures, are commissioned through this state office. The secretary also maintains several registries, including domestic partnerships, advanced health care directives, and "Safe at Home," a confidential address and name change program for victims of domestic violence and sexual assault, as well as reproductive health care workers and patients.

Fragmentation of authority is most evident in the three separate offices that regulate the flow of money through the state government. The prominent **controller** ("comptroller" in some states) is the chief fiscal officer who pays the state's bills and continually monitors the state's financial situation by keeping a tally of the state's accounts. State employees and vendors who sell services or goods to the state will see the controller's signature on their payment checks. As the state officer who is ultimately responsible for ensuring that certain moneys due to the state are collected fairly, the controller is the at-large member of the State Board of Equalization and sits on numerous advisory boards, including the Franchise Tax Board (which administers personal income and corporate tax laws) and more than sixty other commissions and organizations relating to state payouts for employee pensions, construction projects, and other large categories of expenses. The controller oversees a staff of almost 1,400 people.

The second money officer is the **treasurer**, the state's banker who manages the state's investments, assets, and bond debt. Every year the state borrows several billion dollars to finance huge infrastructure projects such as the rebuilding of bridges or schools, and this borrowing takes the form of bonds sold to investors. The treasurer manages the state's mountainous debt by selling and repaying bonds on an ongoing basis, trying to secure acceptable credit ratings that lead to lower loan interest rates, and maintaining the state's financial assets. About 230 persons run the treasurer's office. The treasurer also chairs or sits on almost sixty boards that are authorized to raise and spend money on huge infrastructure plans such as rail and road transportation, building and repairing schools, ensuring clean and available water, and housing.

The **Board of Equalization** (BOE) represents the third money office and consists of the state controller and four other regional officials elected from districts containing approximately 9.5 million Californians apiece. The board's job is to standardize the tax systems in the state, which bring in approximately $60 billion per year. The fee-based programs the board administers generate 30 percent of the state's annual revenues, and they funnel essential funding to counties, cities, and special districts.[7] The board helps collect local sales taxes and fees that provide more than $11 billion to local governments, and over 4,800 employees assist them with their tasks. Also aided by fifty-eight elected county tax assessors, the board ensures that residents pay fair rates on about 12 million properties within the state. BOE also collects state sales and use taxes; environmental fees on hazardous waste; and liquor, tobacco, and fuel excise taxes—all of which fund essential services, from transportation to cleaning up pollution. The board is the only one of its type elected in the fifty states and includes the only Republican executive and three Democrats after the 2014 elections.

In the same antitax spirit that led to the passage of Proposition 13, voters rebelled against spiraling auto insurance rates and elevated the Office of **Insurance Commissioner** from a governor-appointed subagency to a full-scale executive office in 1988. To protect consumers who participate in the world's sixth largest insurance market, the elected commissioner oversees the $123 billion-a-year insurance industry by reviewing and preapproving rates for car and home owners' (property and casualty) insurance, and is supported by 1,400 employees. The commissioner also makes sure that insurance companies are solvent, licenses agents and companies operating in California, investigates fraudulent practices in response to consumer complaints, and enforces rulings against violators. The department has taken a stronger role in reviewing health insurance rate increases as well, though the commissioner lacks authority both to force companies to reduce rates and to reject exorbitant rate increases. In 2014, health insurers and others spent over $57 million to defeat a ballot measure (Prop 45) that would have empowered the commissioner to authorize health rate increases; supporters raised and spent roughly $10 million.[8] It failed.

As noted in this chapter's opener, the **superintendent of public instruction** leads the Department of Education as well as the State Board of Education, advocating for student achievement as the state's only nonpartisan executive officer. The superintendent is the point person for statewide student testing and reporting, including implementation of the state's new standardized testing system (California Assessment of Student Performance and Progress, or CAASPP) as well as high school exit exams; data collection on a range of education-related issues such as dropout rates, yearly funding levels for K–12 and community college education, and student achievement levels; and implementation of education-related federal court opinions, the No Child Left Behind Act, and related U.S. education policy initiatives. Like other state constitutional officers tasked with coordinating policy among a snarl of governing bodies, the superintendent sits as an ex officio member on more than one hundred education-related boards and commissions.

Although these executive officers are free to consult each other and frequently find themselves in each other's company, at no point do they meet as a governing board, and no central mechanism exists to coordinate their work. Sometimes this arrangement makes for strange bedfellows, as Governor Schwarzenegger found in 2009 when he wrote an executive order closing state offices two Fridays per month, effectively furloughing all state workers, including the staff members of his fellow executives. However, his mandate legally could not apply to his colleagues, who promptly ignored the order. Sharp disagreements also surfaced between the legislature and the state's controller, John Chiang, with regard to the issue of temporary pay cuts for lawmakers who submitted a budget that "simply did not add up" in 2011.[9] Based on his interpretation of the recently passed Prop 25, Chiang refused to pay legislators after the governor's veto rendered the budget late. Legislators sued to recover lost wages, and a state appeals court ruled that only the legislature has the authority to control the budget process—thus preventing the controller from withholding disputed legislative paychecks during a budget delay and thwarting the people's will. One lesson to be gleaned from this example is that an organizational structure that allows Democrats and Republicans to share executive power virtually guarantees that differences in governing philosophies and approaches will exist, but it usually takes a crisis to make those differences visible and put them to the test.

Next to the governor, the most powerful executive officer in California is the attorney general. Here Attorney General Kamala Harris views firearms seized from persons possessing them illegally. In one six-week sweep, Department of Justice officers seized 1,200 guns. Some of these were taken from persons who had been determined to be mentally unstable or who had active restraining orders against them.

Administrators and Regulators

A great checkerboard of agencies, departments, administrative offices, and boards form the state's "bureaucracy," or bulk of the executive branch. Almost all are linked to the governor through secretaries whom he or she designates to head each agency or directors who head departments. Every organization within the executive branch is designed to help the governor execute state law faithfully, but bureaucratic reorganization is periodically needed to streamline operations and eliminate haphazard structures that have been added over the years. Citizens may not have noticed, but Governor Jerry Brown's overhaul of state government, approved by the legislature and implemented by 2013, reduced the size of government by consolidating several entities. Brown's plan aims to make government "easier to manage, and more coordinated and efficient" so that it can provide "better and more cost-effective service"—the object of all reorganization plans, to be sure.[10]

The "superagency" scheme of Governor Pat Brown—the late father of Governor Jerry Brown—has stuck since the 1970s, with alterations. The superagencies act as umbrella organizations for the

FIGURE 5.2 Organization Chart of California's Executive Branch

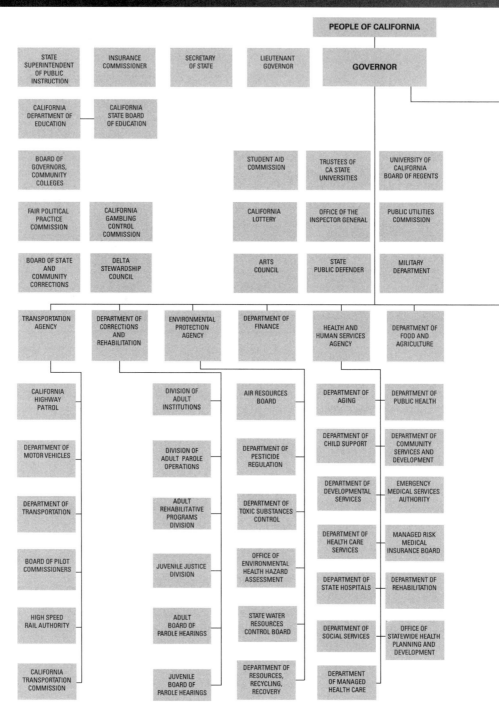

THE EXECUTIVE BRANCH

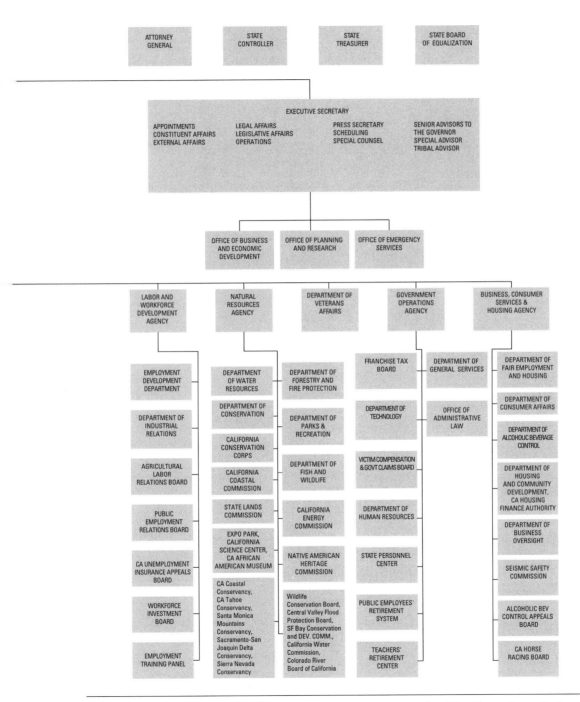

ATTORNEY GENERAL

STATE CONTROLLER

STATE TREASURER

STATE BOARD OF EQUALIZATION

EXECUTIVE SECRETARY

APPOINTMENTS CONSTITUENT AFFAIRS EXTERNAL AFFAIRS	LEGAL AFFAIRS LEGISLATIVE AFFAIRS OPERATIONS	PRESS SECRETARY SCHEDULING SPECIAL COUNSEL	SENIOR ADVISORS TO THE GOVERNOR SPECIAL ADVISOR TRIBAL ADVISOR

OFFICE OF BUSINESS AND ECONOMIC DEVELOPMENT

OFFICE OF PLANNING AND RESEARCH

OFFICE OF EMERGENCY SERVICES

LABOR AND WORKFORCE DEVELOPMENT AGENCY

NATURAL RESOURCES AGENCY

DEPARTMENT OF VETERANS AFFAIRS

GOVERNMENT OPERATIONS AGENCY

BUSINESS, CONSUMER SERVICES & HOUSING AGENCY

EMPLOYMENT DEVELOPMENT DEPARTMENT

DEPARTMENT OF WATER RESOURCES

DEPARTMENT OF FORESTRY AND FIRE PROTECTION

FRANCHISE TAX BOARD

DEPARTMENT OF GENERAL SERVICES

DEPARTMENT OF FAIR EMPLOYMENT AND HOUSING

DEPARTMENT OF INDUSTRIAL RELATIONS

DEPARTMENT OF CONSERVATION

DEPARTMENT OF PARKS & RECREATION

DEPARTMENT OF TECHNOLOGY

OFFICE OF ADMINISTRATIVE LAW

DEPARTMENT OF CONSUMER AFFAIRS

AGRICULTURAL LABOR RELATIONS BOARD

CALIFORNIA CONSERVATION CORPS

DEPARTMENT OF FISH AND WILDLIFE

VICTIM COMPENSATION & GOVT CLAIMS BOARD

DEPARTMENT OF ALCOHOLIC BEVERAGE CONTROL

PUBLIC EMPLOYMENT RELATIONS BOARD

CALIFORNIA COASTAL COMMISSION

CALIFORNIA ENERGY COMMISSION

DEPARTMENT OF HUMAN RESOURCES

DEPARTMENT OF HOUSING AND COMMUNITY DEVELOPMENT, CA HOUSING FINANCE AUTHORITY

CA UNEMPLOYMENT INSURANCE APPEALS BOARD

STATE LANDS COMMISSION

NATIVE AMERICAN HERITAGE COMMISSION

STATE PERSONNEL CENTER

DEPARTMENT OF BUSINESS OVERSIGHT

WORKFORCE INVESTMENT BOARD

EXPO PARK, CALIFORNIA SCIENCE CENTER, CA AFRICAN AMERICAN MUSEUM

Wildlife Conservation Board, Central Valley Flood Protection Board, SF Bay Conservation and DEV. COMM., California Water Commission, Colorado River Board of California

PUBLIC EMPLOYEES' RETIREMENT SYSTEM

SEISMIC SAFETY COMMISSION

EMPLOYMENT TRAINING PANEL

CA Coastal Conservancy, CA Tahoe Conservancy, Santa Monica Mountains Conservancy, Sacramento-San Joaquin Delta Conservancy, Sierra Nevada Conservancy

TEACHERS' RETIREMENT CENTER

ALCOHOLIC BEV CONTROL APPEALS BOARD

CA HORSE RACING BOARD

Source: Adapted from California Online Directory, "California State Government—the Executive Branch," http://www.cold.ca.gov/Ca_State_Gov_Orgchart.pdf. Updated August 3, 2015.

smaller departments, boards, and commissions nested within them. The seven superagencies are (1) Business, Consumer Services, and Housing; (2) Natural Resources; (3) Government Operations; (4) Transportation; (5) Health and Human Services; (6) Environmental Protection (EPA); and (7) Labor and Workforce Development. For example, the relatively new Transportation Agency houses six entities, including Caltrans, the Department of Motor Vehicles (DMV), and the state highway patrol. The state EPA oversees the State Water Resources Control Board, a headline-grabber during the drought; the Air Resources Board, tasked with implementing the state's carbon cap-and-trade program and other regulations related to AB 32; and four other major offices that regulate or assess pesticides, toxic substances, and other health hazards. Several "superdepartments" also house critical divisions and employ many specialists—Government Operations; Finance; Food and Agriculture; and Veterans Affairs (see Figure 5.2) lead the pack. In all, more than 204,000 full- and part-time public employees constitute the state administration or "state bureaucracy"—a workforce that decreased about 15 percent from 2009 to 2015.[11]

The governor's stamp is also seen in membership appointments to about three hundred commissions and boards that share some governing authority with him or her in advisory, regulatory, or administrative capacities. Among these are large entities such as the California Public Employees' Retirement System (CalPERS) and smaller ones such as the boards overseeing professional licensing for dentists, nurses, accountants, and so forth. Most boards consist of four or five members, and some meet only twice a year. Full membership turnover of a board rarely occurs during a governor's term; thus, competing ideological viewpoints are often represented on boards depending on who appointed whom. In addition, many organizations operate autonomously, meaning that they don't need to consult the governor or other elected executives before taking independent action on an issue, although state elected officials are ultimately responsible for the actions state boards and commissions might take. Together, these unelected authorities make rules affecting Californians in virtually every imaginable way, from making beaches accessible to determining where waste can be dumped.

Conclusion: Competition for Power

The Progressives' lack of faith in political parties and mistrust of elected officials have left a legacy of many individuals at the top both sharing and competing for power. Ironically, although no single person is in charge, most Californians believe the governor is and blame him or her when things go awry. Perhaps not surprisingly, then, citizens are also unwilling to vest more power in that office and have, for example, rejected proposals to allow the governor to cut the budget more easily.[12]

What are we to make, then, of California's plural executive? In the first place, the division of labor among high-profile officials can mean that each brings a different kind of energy and focus to his or her specialized role. The splintering of authority among many offices also provides checks against the concentration of authority, but, perversely, this arrangement also obscures accountability. Decentralized decision making means that voters cannot hold anyone but the governor accountable for decisions produced at the state level, even though he or she may not be the source of their discontent.

In the second place, no one is truly "in charge" of the state. The governor may be vested with supreme administrative authority by the constitution, but he or she can no more tell the controller what to do than the secretary of state can. Fragmented authority limits the governor's ability to coordinate a political agenda, because his or her fellow state executives are entitled to their own approaches, initiatives, and budgets, and they use them to defend their individual reputations and, indirectly, in pursuit of other offices. Thus, Republicans and Democrats may be elected to share responsibility for governing through a branch that lacks the means to build consistent, integrated policies, but it should be noted that an organic division of labor means that they don't often need to coordinate their work. Shared partisanship also certainly helps smooth out their differences, which the 2010 and 2014 elections facilitated when Democrats captured all eight top offices (excluding the Board of Equalization).

All in all, California's executive officers coexist in pursuit of the same basic goal: to allow the state to prosper. The ship of state is piloted by a governor who has access to more levers of government than any other executive officer, and the extent to which he or she successfully uses instruments of power such as the signing of legislation, vetoes, executive branch reorganization, appointments, and annual budgeting to coordinate "the big picture" is a measure of California's governability, and ultimately, state government's effectiveness.

Notes

1. In the previous edition of this book, the numbers reported were 120 and 230 respectively, numbers supplied by the governor's offices. The numbers here are actual positions authorized in the annual budget (ebudget.ca.gov) for years 2015–16 (approved by Brown) and 2010–11 (approved by Schwarzenegger).

2. Most state workers are members of the powerful union known as the California State Employees Association.

3. According to the Assembly Clerk's Office (personal correspondence with author, June 2013), there was a series of veto overrides in 1979 to 1980, but the last occurred when the Senate overrode a gubernatorial budget line-item veto on September 5, 1979 (Senate Journal, p. 7174). The Assembly overrode this line-item veto on February 4, 1980 (by a vote of fifty-five to twelve), but a motion to reconsider was noticed. The motion to reconsider lapsed on February 5, 1980, so the override took effect on that day (Assembly Journal, p. 11086).

4. According to the Human Resources Department at the Department of Finance, the actual number of employees in June 2015 was 467.

5. Christopher Goffard, "Appeals Court Upholds Schwarzenegger's Clemency for Nunez's Son," *Los Angeles Times*, June 3, 2015, http://www.latimes.com/local/lanow/la-me-ln-esteban-nunez-sentence-reduction-upheld-20150602-story.html.

6. Brown typically grants pardons on the eve of Christmas and Easter; he pardoned eighty-three persons in April 2015. State of California, "Governor Brown Grants Pardons," press release, April 5, 2015, http://www.gov.ca.gov/news.php?id=18914. For the reasons behind Brown's decisions, see *Executive Report on Pardons, Commutations of Sentence, and Reprieves,* issued annually by the governor's office under statutory order.

7. California State Board of Equalization, "The Agency and Its History," accessed August 30, 2013, http://www.boe.ca.gov/info/agency_history.htm.

8. Based on Secretary of State final campaign finance filings, the National Institute on Money in State Politics reports that $10,641,103 was raised in support, and $56,967,052 was spent in opposition (see: http://www.followthemoney.org/entity-details?eid=24717484&default=ballot).

9. John Chiang is quoted in the Sacramento superior court judge's opinion in *Steinberg Perez v. Chiang* (2011), filed January 1, 2012, Introduction, Section 2, supra 12.

10. Governor Edmund G. Brown, "Government Reorganization Plan," March 30, 2012, http://gov.ca.gov/docs/Cover_Letter_and_Summary.pdf.

11. The total number was 204,049 as of May 2015, including full-time and part-time workers and excluding 22,592 intermittent employees and employees of the California State University system. In June 2009, the comparable state employee workforce numbered 244,061. California State Controller's Office, "State Employee Demographics," May 2015, http://www.sco.ca.gov/ppsd_empinfo_demo.html.

12. The most recent examples are Proposition 76 in January 2006 and Proposition 1A in May 2009, both of which were resoundingly defeated.

CHAPTER 6

The Court System

A victim of domestic abuse finally decides to seek a restraining order against her abusive boyfriend, but the nearest court is a three-hour drive away, the victim doesn't own a car, and she can't miss more than a couple hours of work on a weekday. A landlord refuses to fix a moldy ceiling or replace a broken heater, but the tenants are unaware of their rights, and in any case lack the money to hire a lawyer who could help them navigate the legal system to obtain the repairs or sue for damages.

Lack of ready access to courts and legal representation costs Californians more than just time and money; as retired California Chief Justice Ronald M. George phrased it, "Access and fairness in the courts are not abstract philosophical principles; they are basic to preserving the rule of law."[1] This precept has been tested through budget cuts that have forced court closures, reduced court operations, and led to a significant decline in court filings, as millions have reconsidered their chances of finding a just resolution to their issues in the California justice system.

Fundamentally, the state courts' place in a separated system of powers is to provide "fair and equal access to justice for all Californians." Judges also verify that the rules, laws, and policies that the executive and legislative branches produce and the initiatives that the voters approve are lawful. In one of the largest court systems in the world (and certainly the largest in the United States), over 2,000 judicial officers and 19,000 court employees handle about *7.5 million* cases annually.[2] Chances are good that every Californian at some point in his or her life will engage the justice system directly as a juror, to resolve family matters resulting from divorce or child custody disputes, or because of a traffic violation—the top reasons people connect to California's courts.

California's constitution guarantees citizens the right to a jury trial for both criminal and civil cases, but chronic underfunding has led to shortages of judges, employee layoffs, huge trial backlogs, and long delays for those involved in lawsuits—not to mention severe jail overcrowding.

The judicial branch is still recovering from the largest reduction in funding in state history—$1 billion over five years.[3] Waits for regular trials and adjudications in family court can seem everlasting, and rural residents must travel hours to a courthouse because of unprecedented court closures: 52 courthouses and 202 courtrooms in all. Court reporters have been eliminated for civil and family matters. Fewer employees at every level means that what used to take a few minutes to resolve now takes hours, and what took days now takes weeks. The courts' operating expenses represent merely 1.4 percent of the state's general fund expenses, and the "incremental" additional money for courts that was included in the 2015–16 state budget will not revive the system completely. For millions of people who rely on the courts to deliver justice, it will be many years before they find that the system has regained full capacity.

The Three-Tiered Court System

As in the federal judicial system, California courts are organized into three tiers, and the legislature controls the number of judgeships. At the lowest level are trial courts, which are also known as superior courts, located in each of California's fifty-eight counties. In a trial court, a judge or jury decides a case by applying the law to evidence and testimony presented. Working at this level are more than 1,600 judges and 360 subordinate judicial officers such as commissioners, and they deal with virtually all 7.5 million civil and criminal cases that begin here. Most citizens who use the courts are involved in resolving minor *infractions* for which a fine rather than jail time is imposed, including traffic violations such as texting while driving. Infractions, which are heard by a judge only, make up about 65 percent of the superior courts' docket. A recent rule change allows traffic violators who challenge their tickets to avoid paying their fines until a trial is held. The next-higher level is a category of crime called *misdemeanors,* for which the maximum punishment is a $1,000 fine and up to one year in a county jail. Examples include drunk driving, vandalism, and petty theft. Finally, an accused criminal may be charged with a *felony,* which is a serious and possibly violent offense, punishable by a state prison sentence or possibly death. Examples of felonies include murder, robbery, rape, and burglary of a residence. County district attorneys (DAs) bring cases against the accused, and anyone who cannot afford to pay for his or her own legal defense is entitled to help from a public defender. California's DAs have a conviction success rate of around 80 percent.[4] Sentencing outcomes depend on the severity of the crime, the offender's criminal history, and the court's discretion.

Civil suits, on the other hand, usually involve disputes between individuals or organizations seeking monetary compensation for damages, usually incurred through injuries, breaches of contract, or defective products. A *small claims* case is filed by a person seeking $10,000 or less, and attorneys are not allowed to be present at the court hearing. *Limited* civil cases involve damages valued at less than $25,000, and *unlimited* civil matters exceed that threshold. The huge number of civil lawsuits in the state, nearly 850,000 annually,[5] reflects a general acceptance of litigation as a "normal" way to resolve problems. The state attorney general can also bring civil cases against companies that break environmental, employment, or other types of state laws. Civil suits typically result in monetary judgments. Unlike criminal defense, the state does not supply legal representation for citizens who are involved in civil cases.

Juvenile, family, and probate cases are specific types of civil cases that are also heard in superior court. Family matters typically involve divorces, marital separations, and child custody cases. Parties might also ask a judge to rule on a family member's mental competence, settle an inheritance dispute, or legally change a name. A single judge or a trial jury may decide a case at this level.

Building on the work of her predecessor, current Chief Justice Tani Cantil-Sakauye has focused on improving access to justice for at-risk populations, repeat offenders, and low-income defendants who represent themselves in court. Online "self-help" resources are available on the *http://www.courts.ca.gov* website to inform citizens about obtaining legal aid, to research the law, prepare them for court appearances, or avoid going to court altogether. Alternative dispute resolution (ADR), also known as mediation or legally binding arbitration, offers a quicker way to decide cases and avoid the pricier option of hiring a private attorney. *Collaborative courts* have also become an important component in dealing with repeat offenders. Known as "problem-solving courts" that operate through superior courts, they combine judicial case processing, drug and alcohol treatment services, and monitoring to help individuals rebuild their lives and avoid recidivism. Among the 374 collaborative courts in California are combat veterans' courts, mental health courts, homeless courts, drug courts, and domestic violence courts. When a veteran of the Iraq War pleads guilty to driving under the influence (DUI), for instance, in a veterans' court he may be placed on parole and ordered to enroll in a program to treat alcoholism or possibly be treated for PTSD (posttraumatic stress disorder) while being monitored closely, in lieu of paying a fine or serving jail time.

If the losing party in a case believes the law was not applied properly, he or she may ask the next-higher district **court of appeal** to hear the case. There are no trials in district appellate courts, although three-judge panels commonly hear lawyers argue cases. Spread across six different geographical areas in nine court locations are 105 appellate justices who review approximately 22,000 cases for errors, improprieties, or technicalities that could lead to reversals of the lower courts' judgments; they dispose of more than half these cases without issuing written opinions. On the whole, appellate court decisions clarify and actually establish government policy, as the state supreme court allows the great majority of these decisions to stand.

The highest judicial authority is vested in a seven-member **supreme court**, whose decisions are binding on all California courts. Headquartered in San Francisco, the justices of the supreme court also hear oral arguments in Los Angeles and Sacramento for cases appealed from the intermediate-level district courts throughout the year, but they automatically review death row cases and exercise original jurisdiction over a few other types. Of roughly eight thousand cases appealed to it in 2013–14, the court issued a mere eighty-five written opinions, made available to the public on the court's website (http://www.courts.ca.gov) and through published official reports. The justices are not required to review all cases and therefore have wide discretion over case selection, concentrating mostly on those that either address important questions of law or promote uniform judgments across the system. They must, however, analyze thick and complex death penalty case records to generate internal memoranda that can exceed one hundred pages apiece, even when they issue no written opinion in those instances; thus, death penalty cases demand significant court resources. The court acted on twenty-six such cases in the 2013–14 term.

Automatic appeals aside, justices spend considerable time choosing cases, and each justice employs support staff and permanent staff attorneys to assist him or her. Their interpretations of the law define the boundaries of acceptable behavior for businesses, government, and citizens. As the principal supervisor of the lower courts, the chief justice shoulders more responsibility than the other justices. As spokesperson for the judicial branch, Chief Justice Cantil-Sakauye delivers the

Courtesy of the Supreme Court of California.
Photo by Bob Knapik.

Consisting of six associate justices and one chief justice, California's Supreme Court is one of the most racially/ethnically diverse in the nation. The supreme court building is located in San Francisco. From left to right: Mariano-Florentino Cuéllar (confirmed 2015), Kathryn Werdegar, Carol Corrigan, Chief Justice Tani Cantil-Sakauye, Goodwin Liu, Ming Chin, and Leondra Kruger (confirmed 2015).

"state of the judiciary" address annually to the legislature and has become the "chief lobbyist" for restoring state funding to the court system. The court's reputation at any given time reflects its collective policy decisions, both in the questions the justices choose to address or ignore and in their interpretation of the wording and intent of specific laws.

Controversy often stems from the supreme court's review of ballot initiatives, political measures that can only be ruled on *after* passage and are often overturned in whole or in part for violating the state constitution. Proposition 8, a constitutional amendment that eliminated same-sex marriage by defining marriage as between a man and a woman only, became a hot potato in 2009 for the justices, who were threatened with recall if they overturned it. (They didn't, although three supreme court justices in Iowa did legalize same-sex marriages and were ousted by that state's voters in 2010.)

On and Off the Court

An attorney who has practiced law in California for at least ten years may become a judge, but individuals usually enter the position through gubernatorial appointment rather than by first running for office. Those who are interested in becoming judges may apply through the governor's office. The

FIGURE 6.1   California Court System

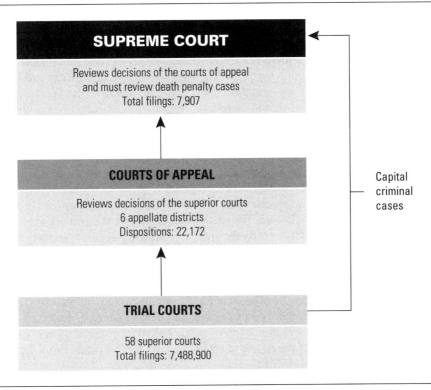

Sources: Judicial Council of California, *2015 Court Statistics Report: Statewide Caseload Trends, 2003–2004 through 2013–2014* (San Francisco: Judicial Council of California, 2015), http://www.courts.ca.gov/documents/2015-Court-Statistics-Report.pdf.

Note: Missing and/or incomplete data from six courts affects these totals.

combination of a recent state supreme court ruling and a new law known as AB 1024 now allows undocumented immigrants to gain admittance to the state bar and practice law in California.

A governor has ample opportunity to shape the long-term ideological bent of the judiciary by selecting individuals whose partisanship and political principles are reflected in their judicial philosophies. When then-attorney general George Deukmejian (1982–1991) was asked why he was running for governor, he replied, "Attorney generals don't appoint judges. Governors do."[6] Governor Arnold Schwarzenegger was perhaps the least partisan in his judicial appointments than any governor in recent times: about 40 percent of his appointees were Democrats, whereas Jerry Brown has appointed fewer than 10 percent Republicans.[7] Governors also directly affect the demographic composition of the bench, which today remains disproportionately male, middle-class, and White—in contrast to the state's heavily racial/ethnic prison population (see Table 6.1 and Box 6.1). However,

Brown has taken the lead in appointing minorities throughout his tenure, boosting gender equality with appointees who have been 40 percent female, over 15 percent Latino, 11 percent Black, and almost 10 percent Asian. Vacancies are unpredictable. In the seven years between November 2003 and December 2010, Governor Schwarzenegger made 627 appointments to the bench. Between January 2011 and June 2015, Governor Brown appointed 252.

Supreme court replacements seldom occur, but coincidentally, several retirements opened up spots for Schwarzenegger, who appointed two of the seven supreme court justices and fortified the conservative court with his selections, and three spots for Jerry Brown, whose appointments eventually may tilt the court in the opposite ideological direction. Interestingly, none of Brown's three appointees have prior judicial experience, although all three graduated from Yale law school, excelled as attorneys, have worked in U.S. presidential administrations, and are prolific scholars. Goodwin Liu was born to Taiwanese immigrant parents; Mariano-Florentino Cuéllar is a naturalized citizen of Mexican parentage; and Leondra Kruger is an African American woman who was age 38 when selected (in 2014).

Superior court justices serve for six years without term limitations, and if they were first appointed to office and not elected, they must become nonpartisan candidates for their offices when their terms expire. Longer terms are intended to increase the judiciary's independence and stability over time by reducing the frequency of distracting campaigns that can create potential conflicts of interest with campaign contributors. Contested elections are rare, and unopposed judges usually win.

Appointees to the six appellate courts and the supreme court also require the governor's nomination, but they must first be screened by the State Bar's Commission on Judicial Nominees, a state agency whose members represent the legal profession, and then be confirmed by the Commission on Judicial Appointments. Members of the latter include the attorney general, chief justice of the supreme court, presiding judge of the courts of appeal, and at-large members of the legal community; together, they evaluate appointees' fitness for office. Confirmation allows a justice to fulfill the remainder of his or her predecessor's twelve-year term, but the judge must participate in a nonpartisan "retention election" at the next gubernatorial election, at which time voters are asked to vote yes or no on whether he or she should remain in office. The judge may seek unlimited terms thereafter.

Voters rarely reject judges. Defeat requires public outrage fueled by provocative, media-driven campaigns, as three supreme court justices discovered in 1986. Having earned reputations for being "soft on crime" at a time when rising crime rates were rattling the public, Chief Justice Rose Bird and two of her colleagues were targeted for their opposition to the death penalty. For the first time in California history, three justices lost their retention bids, and Governor George Deukmejian replaced them with conservative justices.

Although judges rarely lose elections, they are not immune to campaign or interest group pressures. Progressives realized this when they established nonpartisan elections for judges in 1911, but many judges must run retention campaigns in which outspoken donors or independent "super spenders" try to influence election outcomes. In their primary role as defenders of law and order, judges are expected to be independent arbiters of justice, but elections can jeopardize their impartiality. In the thirty-three states that directly elect judges, the price of judicial campaigns—even for retention elections—is rising, a trend that alarms court observers. Nationwide in 2011 to 2012, special interest groups and political parties reportedly spent "an unprecedented $24.1 million" on state court races.[8] In 2010, an outspoken Christian conservative group tried to unseat four superior

TABLE 6.1 Diversity of California's Justices and Judges (in percentages)

Court (persons reporting)	Female (N = 534)	Male (N = 1,122)	Black or African American (N = 109)	Hispanic or Latino (N = 156)	Asian (N = 100)/ Pacific Islander (N = 4)	White (N = 1,156)	Native American (N = 8)/ Other/ More than one (N = 77)	Information not provided (N = 46)
Supreme court (7)	57.1%	42.9%	14.3%	14.3%	28.6%	28.6%	14.3%	0
Court of appeal (98)	31.6	68.4	7.1	6.1	1.0	76.5	8.1	1.0
Trial court (1,551)	32.2	67.8	6.5	9.6	6.6	69.6	4.9	2.9
Total	32.2	67.8	6.6	9.4	6.3	69.8	5.1	2.8

Source: California Courts, "Demographic Data Provided by Justices and Judges Relative to Gender, Race/Ethnicity, and Gender Identity/Sexual Orientation," December 31, 2014, http://www.courts.ca.gov/documents/2015-Demographic-Report.pdf.

court judges in San Diego by promoting its own candidates, sparking a larger debate over the integrity of California's court system. (All four judges managed to keep their jobs, despite relatively low voter turnout.)

Judges can also be dismissed for improper conduct or incompetence arising from a range of activities, among them bias, inappropriate humor, and substance abuse. Hundreds of complaints are filed each year with the Commission on Judicial Performance, the independent state agency that investigates allegations of judicial misconduct. The commission does not review a justice's record but focuses instead on personal behavior that may warrant a warning letter, formal censure, removal, or forced retirement. Only a tiny fraction of judges face disciplinary action; the great majority have internalized the norms of judicial propriety that are imparted through law school and the legal community.

Court Administration

Like the U.S. federal court system, the state judicial branch is headed by a chief justice. However, a formal organization, the **Judicial Council of California**, which the chief justice chairs, sets policy for the state's court system. The twenty-one voting members (plus eleven advisors, bringing the total to thirty-two members) of this public agency are tasked with policymaking, establishing rules and procedures in accordance with ever-changing state law, making sure the court is accessible to citizens with diverse needs, and recommending improvements to the system. The council also controls the judiciary's annual budget and reports to the legislature and responds to its mandates. A subagency of the Judicial Council, the Administrative Office of the Court(AOC), is made up of staff members who actively implement the council's policy decisions. Administrative officers throughout the state manage the court system by supervising a supporting cast of thousands who help run the court system day to day. Among many other activities, they keep records, hire interpreters, schedule hearings, and, when times are prosperous, create task forces to study and find ways to address issues that affect court caseloads and court operations, such as foster care or domestic violence.

Juries

Barring a traffic violation, jury duty tends to be the average citizen's most direct link to the court system, and roughly 9,900 juries will sit in judgment at trial every year.[9] Names of prospective jurors are randomly drawn from lists of registered voters and names provided by the Department of Motor Vehicles. Under the "one day or one trial" program, prospective jurors are excused from service at the end of a single day if they have not been assigned to a trial, and they only need to respond to a summons to serve once a year. If assigned to a trial, jurors consider questions of fact and weigh evidence to determine whether an accused person is guilty or not guilty. Convincing citizens to fulfill their duty to serve as jurors isn't easy, and juries tend to overrepresent those who have relatively more time on their hands, such as the elderly, the unemployed, and the wealthy. About 8 million people are summoned to serve on juries each year in California, although only about 3 million of them are eligible and able to sit on a trial; in all about 150,000 people serve as jurors annually.[10] All jurors are compensated $15 per day starting with the second day of service plus thirty-four cents for mileage one way. There are no plans to raise this rate, although it is well below the national average of approximately $19 for the first day and $25 for the second day of service.[11]

Grand juries are impaneled every year in every county to investigate the conduct of city and county government and their agencies. Each contains nineteen members, except for Los Angeles's grand jury, which has twenty-three members due to the city's large population. During their one-year terms, grand jurors research claims of improper or wasteful practices, issue reports, recommend improvements to local programs, and sometimes indict political figures for misconduct, meaning they uncover sufficient evidence to warrant a trial.

Criminal Justice and Its Costs

About 90 percent of cases never make it to trial. High costs and delays associated with discovery, investigations, filings, and courtroom defense encourage out-of-court settlements and mediation, and the chance to receive a lesser sentence for pleading guilty results in plea bargains that suppress prison crowding. Although California's crime rates have declined over the past two decades, the state's prisons have been bursting at the seams for years. With 163,000 inmates in facilities designed to hold about 85,000, by the Department of Corrections and Rehabilitation's own admission the state's prisons were 185 percent above capacity in early 2011.[12] "Bad beds" have been crammed into prison libraries, gymnasiums, day rooms, and other areas not intended for sleeping bunks. By June 2015, the inmate population had been reduced to 111,250—under the federally mandated cap, which will be 116,988 beds in 2016, equating to 137.5 percent of capacity.[13]

The "three strikes" initiative is largely to blame for the blistering growth of the prison population. In 1994, voters were horror-struck at the abduction and murder of twelve-year-old Polly Klaas, a crime perpetrated by a man with a long and violent record. Klaas's family and others lobbied vigorously for tougher sentencing of repeat offenders, and their efforts culminated in the "three strikes and you're out" law: anyone convicted of a third felony is sentenced to a mandatory prison term of twenty-five years to life without the possibility of parole, with enhanced penalties for second-strikers. In 2013, approximately 42,500 inmates were serving time for second and third strikes, most of which were nonviolent offenses. Those convictions either have been or will be reconsidered because of two recent ballot initiatives: Prop 36 revises the law to impose a life sentence only when a new third felony conviction is serious or violent, and authorizes resentencing for current inmates if they were imprisoned for nonviolent offenses; and Prop 47 reclassifies some drug-related crimes as misdemeanors rather than felonies. Together these new laws will further draw down the prison population, although they will put more pressure on other parts of the system, such as parole programs and county jails.

Longer sentences translate into an aging prison population with expensive health care issues, and under the Eighth Amendment's prohibition against cruel and unusual punishment, inmates are the only population in the United States guaranteed the constitutional right to receive adequate health care—although the quality of that care is often in doubt. Prompted by a class-action lawsuit in 2001 alleging dire conditions and the state's slowness to reform, a federal court removed control of prison health care from the state and appointed a federal receiver to help raise standards to an acceptable level. Immediately, the receiver demanded that at least $8 billion more be invested in upgrades to compensate for historically insufficient funding.

Underfunding of the correctional system has been the default option for state lawmakers because prisoners are esteemed by no one: spending cuts to prisons represent a rare convergence point for those on the left, who would prefer more spending on rehabilitation and crime prevention programs, and those on the right, who tend to equate spending with unfair comforts for criminals who deserve to pay for their crimes. In fact, cuts to prisons and corrections are the only ones that citizens consistently say they would make in order to balance the annual budget: 62 percent supported this choice in a May 2011 poll.[14] This attitude may also be attributed to a popular misconception that prisons and corrections are *the* top spending category in the state budget, but at 7.6 percent of general fund spending, this area is the fourth largest item in the state budget, well below health and human services (31.2 percent) and K–12 and higher education combined (38.9 percent).[15] The receiver has remained in charge since 2005, and with lawmakers' authorization, major improvements to on-site medical facilities have been made, including a new $839 million inmate medical complex in Stockton, which costs approximately $295 million annually to run.[16] Despite those investments, deliberate cuts over the years have led to deteriorating facilities, and the state has failed to build more penitentiaries; the result is a prison population that remains dangerously dense.

Skyrocketing costs are also connected to overcrowding. In 1980, the total prison population was 22,500, and in 1985 it cost less than $100 million to run the entire correctional system. Today the system devours $13.538 billion (from all sources, 2015–16). At a projected yearly cost of about $66,000 *per inmate,* California pays far more than other states, where the costs are closer to $30,000 per offender.[17] The comparatively higher costs are attributable mainly to expenses for security personnel and medical care. For each inmate approximately $19,000 is spent on pharmaceuticals and medical, mental, and dental care; in 2015–16 the general fund costs for treating inmates with hepatitis-C alone were $60.6 million. About $31,000 per inmate goes to staff salaries and benefits, and the remainder covers

BOX 6.1   FAST FACTS on California's Criminal Justice System

Enacted budget 2015–16:	$10 billion (general fund), $13.54 billion (total)
Cost per inmate, 2015–16 (estimated):	$66,000*
Staff, 2015–16:	61,500
Total number of inmates (estimated):	112,500 (February 2015)
Lifer (parole poss.) + Life without parole:	30,800
Prisoners on death row:	750 (including 21 women)
Parolees:	44,200 (September 2015)
Most common crime:	Property crime (86% of reported crimes)
Number of prisons:	34, minimum to maximum security, and including 1 new medical prison, plus 42 adult firefighting camps, 1 community prisoner mother facility, and 1 female rehabilitative correctional center
Mean age:	39 (male), 38 (female)
Gender of inmates:	95.3% male, 4.7% female

Racial composition of inmate population:

Category	Inmate population
White, non-Hispanic	23.0%
Hispanic/Latino	41.3%
Black	29.4%
Other	6.3%

Sources: Larger figures have been rounded. California Department of Corrections and Rehabilitation, Offender Information Services Branch, Estimates and Statistical Analysis Section, Data Analysis Unit, "Weekly Report of Population as of June 17, 2015," http://www.cdcr.ca.gov/Reports_Research/Offender_Information_Services_Branch/WeeklyWed/TPOP1A/TPOP1Ad150617.pdf; California Department of Corrections and Rehabilitation, Offender Information Services Branch, Estimates and Statistical Analysis Section, Data Analysis Unit, "Prison Census Data as of June 30, 2013," September 2013, http://www.cdcr.ca.gov/Reports_Research/Offender_Information_Services_Branch/Annual/Census/CENSUSd1306.pdf (most recent available as of September 2015). Budget statistics from California Department of Finance, "Governor's Budget 2015–16," http://www.ebudget.ca.gov.

*Figure calculated by the Legislative Analyst's Office ("How Will Prop 47 Affect State Corrections?" March, 2015).

facilities, food, record keeping, rehabilitation, administration, and educational and drug treatment programs—associated costs that generally do not shrink as the prison population declines. It costs less to send California prisoners to out-of-state facilities in Arizona, Mississippi, and Oklahoma, where approximately 6,500 prisoners are incarcerated, although Governor Brown's goal is to slice that number by at least half by 2017. In addition, felons who are not legal U.S. residents impose direct costs on the state of at least $500 million per year because the federal government only reimburses less than 10 percent of the costs associated with their incarceration.[18] Costs are also driven by housing and managing approximately 650 juveniles residing in three facilities and a conservation camp and supervising and treating about 44,000 adult parolees who need to be apprehended if they commit new offenses.[19]

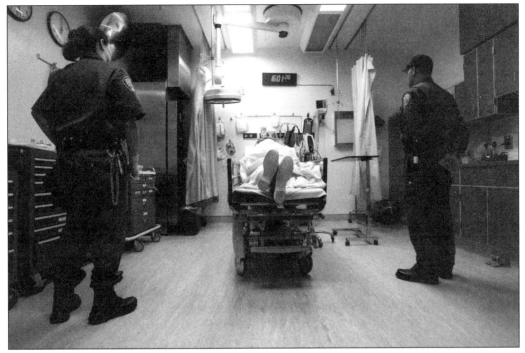

An aging inmate population has made prison medical care a costly business; the average annual cost per person is $19,000, with much higher price tags for specialized care—for example, it costs close to $1 million a year to care for and guard a prisoner lying in a vegetative state not only because of necessary medical equipment and round-the-clock care, but also because of the high-security environment.

Indefensible overcrowding resulted in a federal court order for the state to cap the prison population at 137.5 percent of capacity, to which Governor Brown responded by signing AB 109 in 2011, the "Public Safety Realignment" law. Realignment policy shifts the responsibility for locking up low-level non-serious, non-violent, non-sex (so-called *triple-non*) offender adult felons to county governments, and thousands of state parolees have also been transferred to county probation departments. County jail systems were not originally intended to hold convicts sentenced for longer than one year, many have population caps that are being exceeded, and almost half of all facilities were built before 1980.[20] Even as counties receive more state funding to defray the cost of expanded jail services and construction ($2.3 billion statewide so far), they will inherit demands that they were not designed to meet, including the burdens of providing adequate health care facilities, space and beds to house inmates, and personnel to supervise and help rehabilitate those on probation. State money ($3 billion already and billions more to come) will offset these costs in the coming years, but varying economic environments, local policies, and politics across fifty-eight counties will inevitably translate into differences in the ways that inmates are treated, raising further questions about fairness and equality.

One consequence of realignment is that state prisons are now packed with the most violent, most serious offenders (about 90 percent mid-2013). Recidivism rates do not appear to have changed much—the state already had one of the highest recidivism rates for a decade—and while 18,000 more offenders on the streets have been linked to a rise in auto thefts, violent crime rates have not escalated, in line with national trends.[21]

In fact, crime rates in California are at their lowest in almost fifty years, having fallen from a peak in 1992, and many point to the three-strikes law as the reason. Crime rates and imprisonment trends in states that lack three-strikes penalties are similar to California's, however, and researchers have shown the cause-and-effect relationship to be complicated by other variables. Yet voters believe it works. Until 2012 they were unwilling to soften the law, but enough voters changed their minds as the costs of overcrowding became apparent. Because voters approved Prop 36 in 2012, three-strikes sentencing is now restricted to those who commit violent and serious offenses.

Conclusion: Access to Justice

How much access to justice can Californians count on? Chief Justice Cantil-Sakauye has stated that current funding for the judicial branch has helped raise baseline services incrementally but "won't be enough to provide the kind of access to justice the public deserves."[22] The cumulative impacts of budget cuts have been spread broadly, and they fall especially hard on Californians who already have difficulty accessing the courts because they live far from an operating courthouse, or who have little daytime to spare outside their jobs, or who require interpreters, or who don't have the money to hire lawyers to defend themselves in civil suits. Year after year, budget reductions have forced those who run the courts to make unsatisfactory decisions that inevitably cause certain subpopulations to suffer more than others. It will take years for the court system to dig out of the fiscal hole that the legislature has created for it, and years to achieve the "fair and equal access to justice" guaranteed by the state constitution.

Chronic underfunding has also beleaguered the correctional department, which suffers from deteriorating infrastructure. In 2015, it remained under federal court order to cap the prison population, and its health care system is recuperating under the treatment of a federal receiver through higher injections of state cash and the opening of a state-of-the-art medical prison. Although crime rates have declined steeply since the 1990s, an aging prison population with increasing medical needs and high personnel expenses including employee benefits have driven up costs that California taxpayers find difficult to stomach. Voters find it hard to justify spending more on prisons when the maximum Cal-Grant (state money to cover tuition and fees) is $12,240 (University of California) or $5,472 at a California State University campus, yet it costs over $66,000 to house one inmate for a year. Where the courts and prison populations are concerned, the lack of lobbying on behalf of inmates—the kind perfected by most special interest groups—and virtual absence of public sympathy are problematic in a political system that is responsive to such pressures.

Impartiality forms the judicial system's core, but the branch is political nevertheless—and it fights to suppress the forces that politicize it. Judicial branch politics and flaws in the correctional system also shed light on the complexity of governing. Prison overcrowding, an inmate population that is about three-quarters ethnic minority, and crowded court dockets are outcomes of other political and social issues that require legislators' attention, namely, poverty, lack of education, racism, unemployment, access to mental health care, and homelessness. Such social problems are manifest in crimes ranging from minor to serious and are inherent indicators of Californians' quality of life. Only a governing approach that comprehensively addresses the relationships among these issues can bring about fair, equitable, and accessible justice for all Californians—a daunting responsibility indeed.

Notes

1. Excerpted from Ronald George's address to the state bar in 2000, quoted in: California Commission on Access to Justice, "The Path to Equal Justice," October 2002, http://www.calbar.ca.gov/LinkClick.aspx?fileticket=QhMjgCPh4gg%3d&tabid=224&mid=1534.

2. Judicial Council of California, "California Judicial Branch," January 2015, http://www.courts.ca.gov/documents/Calif_Judicial_Branch.pdf.

3. Five years refers to the number of budget cycles from 2008 through 2012, as reported on the official website of the California courts. California Courts, "InFocus: Judicial Branch Budget Crisis," http://www.courts.ca.gov/partners/courtsbudget.htm#ad-image-0.

4. Mac Taylor, *California's Criminal Justice System: A Primer* (Sacramento: California Legislative Analyst's Office, January 2013), http://www.lao.ca.gov/reports/2013/crim/criminal-justice-primer/criminal-justice-primer-011713.pdf.

5. Judicial Council of California, Administrative Office of the Courts, *2015 Court Statistics Report: Statewide Caseload Trends, 2003–2004 through 2013–2014* (San Francisco: Judicial Council of California, 2015), http://www.courts.ca.gov/documents/2015-Court-Statistics-Report.pdf.

6. Governors' Gallery, "George Deukmejian," http://governors.library.ca.gov/35-deukmejian.html.

7. Julie Patel, "Forum Sheds Light on How Judges Are Screened, Chosen," *San Jose Mercury News,* June 4, 2006; Howard Mintz, "Gov. Jerry Brown Puts Deep Imprint on California Judiciary," *San Jose Mercury News,* February 16, 2014.

8. For more about the politics and costs of judicial elections, see James Sample, Adam Skaggs, Alicia Bannon, and Lianna Reagan, *The New Politics of Judicial Elections 2011–2012: Decade of Change* (Washington, DC: Justice at Stake Campaign, Brennan Center for Justice at NYU School of Law, October 23, 2013), http://www.brennancenter.org/publication/new-politics-judicial-elections-2011-12.

9. The number was 9,900 jury trials in 2013–2014. See California Judicial Council, *2015 Court Statistics Report.*

10. California Judicial Council, Juror Improvement Program. Approximately 9.4 million persons completed jury service in 2008; the number was 8.67 million in 2010–11 (see "About California Courts," 2012). "Completed service" means the individual appeared at the court on the appointed day, although he or she may not have been assigned to a trial and was dismissed at the end of the day.

11. According to data collected by the National Center for State Courts in 2007, the average compensation rate was $18.75 (plus mileage) for the first day of service and $25.30 for the second day (assuming the juror was sworn in by day two). Data for some states were incomplete. See Gregory E. Mize, Paula Hannaford-Agor, and Nicole L. Waters, *The State-of-the-States Survey of Jury Improvement Efforts: A Compendium Report* (Williamsburg, VA: National Center for State Courts, April 2007), http://cdm16501.contentdm.oclc.org/cdm/ref/collection/juries/id/112.

12. California Department of Corrections and Rehabilitation, Offender Information Services Branch, Estimates and Statistical Analysis Section, Data Analysis Unit, "Weekly Report of Population as of Midnight June 17, 2015," June 17, 2015, http://www.cdcr.ca.gov/Reports_Research/Offender_Information_Services_Branch/WeeklyWed/TPOP1A/TPOP1Ad150617.pdf.

13. Legislative Analyst's Office, "Impact of Prop 47 on State Corrections," March 5, 2015, http://www.lao.ca.gov/handouts/crimjust/2015/Impact-of-Proposition-47-on-State-Corrections-030515.pdf.

14. Mark Baldassare, Dean Bonner, Sonja Petek, and Jui Shrestha, "Californians and Their Government" (San Francisco: Public Policy Institute of California, May 2011), http://www.ppic.org/content/pubs/survey/S_511MBS.pdf.

15. In a January 2015 PPIC poll, 42 percent of adults and 42 percent of likely voters (incorrectly) named prisons and corrections as the largest area for spending in the state budget. See Mark Baldassare, Dean Bonner, Renatta DeFever, Lunna Lopes, and Jui Shrestha, "Statewide Survey: Californians and Their Government," PPIC, January 2015, http://www.ppic.org/content/pubs/survey/S_115MBS.pdf.

16. According to Taylor: "The federal court stipulated that the transition from the receivership back to state control will begin when the administration can demonstrate both (1) the ability to maintain an inmate medical care system that provides care as good as or better than that being delivered under the Receiver and (2) that any outstanding construction or information technology projects initiated by the Receiver would not be jeopardized. Likewise, the federal court overseeing inmate mental health care recently expressed satisfaction with progress made to date by the department towards a constitutional level of mental health care." Taylor, *California's Criminal Justice System,* 66. Costs cited in governor's budget summary (June 2015), http://www.ebudget.ca.gov/FullBudgetSummary.pdf.

17. Data provided by the Legislative Analyst's Office, June 2015. These numbers are based on actual per capita expenditures of $51,889 in 2011–2012, $60,723 per inmate in 2013–2014, and current policy and budget allocations of $66,294 for 2015–2016. The costs quoted have been rounded and are based on estimations for 2014–2015 and projections for 2015–2016.

18. Cost estimates vary widely. According to the Legislative Analyst's Office (LAO; communication with author, September 2015) the average cost to house nonlegal inmates would be calculated on a "marginal cost" basis, which excludes fixed costs and includes marginal costs such as food. Using that formula, the cost is about $28,000 per inmate per year per contract bed. The precise number of nonlegal inmates is also elusive, because many of them lack a social security number. Current estimates of the nonlegal U.S. felon population are between 18,000 and 20,000 (source: LAO, communication with author, September 2015). Other reports that include fixed costs place the total closer to $1 billion per year.

19. Legislative Analyst's Office, "The 2015-16 Budget: Governor's Criminal Justice Proposals," February 20, 2015, http://www.lao.ca.gov/reports/2015/budget/Criminal-Justice/cj-budget-analysis-022015.aspx#Criminal_Justice_Budget_Overview. See also Division of Juvenile Justice, "Population Estimates as of December 31, 2014," California Department of Corrections and Rehabilitation, http://www.cdcr.ca.gov/Reports_Research/docs/research/Population_Overview/POPOVER2014.pdf.

20. Magnus Lofstrom and Brandon Martin, "Just the Facts: California's County Jails," PPIC, April 2015, http://www.ppic.org/main/publication_show.asp?i=1061.

21. Magnus Lofstrom and Brandon Martin, "Realignment, Incarceration, and Crime Trends in California," PPIC, May 2015, http://www.ppic.org/main/publication_quick.asp?i=1151; Magnus Loftstrom, Steven Raphael, and Ryken Grattet, "Is Public Safety Realignment Reducing Recidivism in California?" PPIC, June 2014.

22. California Courts, "Chief Justice Issues Statement in Response to 2013–14 Budget," press release, June 27, 2013, http://www.courts.ca.gov/22629.htm.

Other Governments

Not just one, but *thousands* of governments operate within California's borders. Counties, cities, special districts, and regional governments share responsibility for delivering essential services that both protect and enhance residents' quality of life—from maintaining police forces to making sure clean water flows beneath paved streets and from every tap. These many governing bodies do their work in plain sight and are almost entirely unnoticed, stretching scarce taxpayer dollars across a huge range of services that residents mostly take for granted. Regular trash pickup, bus routes, sewage treatment, street lighting, cemeteries: these are the type of services either provided, managed, or contracted out to private companies by a patchwork of subgovernments in California. In cases where one entity, such as a city, cannot or will not deliver a service, new districts or governing boards have been created without regard to centralized planning. Their abundance reflects historically high demands for services, citizens' general unwillingness to pay higher taxes for them, and strong desires to maintain control over local matters, or what's known as self-rule. Bottom-up solutions are thus joined to state and federal mandates in a functionally segmented system—one that works with surprising efficiency considering the enormous number and scope of issues encompassed and the limited budgets available to local governments today.

County Government

Almost half of California's fifty-eight counties were created in the constitution of 1850, and, in 1907, a portion of San Diego County was cleaved off to form Imperial County, the last county added to the list. County boundaries have remained static for about a hundred years while their populations have changed dramatically. All carry out programs authorized by the state government and provide critical services to Californians. The relationship

MAP 7.1   California, 2010 Population by County

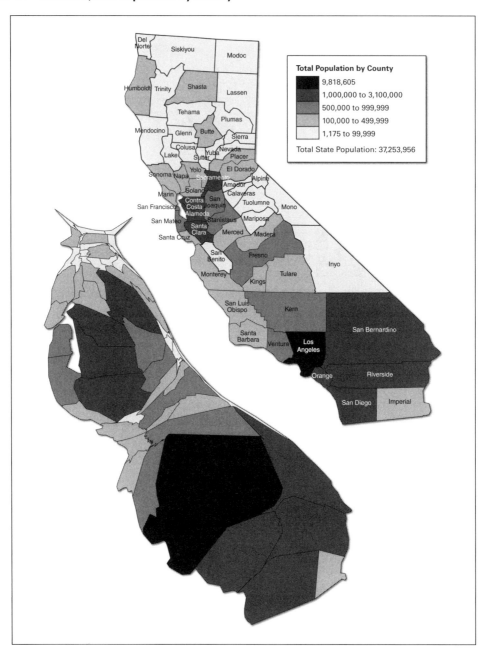

Total Population by County

■ 9,818,605
■ 1,000,000 to 3,100,000
■ 500,000 to 999,999
■ 100,000 to 499,999
□ 1,175 to 99,999

Total State Population: 37,253,956

Source: U.S. Census Bureau, 2010 census, http://www.census.gov.

Notes: Geographic area and population are two variables used to measure the size of California's fifty-eight counties. Geographic boundaries are shown in the top map with shadings for population density, and the lower "cartogram" illustrates the relative distribution of population by county.

BOX 7.1 **FAST FACTS on California's Other Governments**

Number of counties:	58
Number of cities:	482
Number of federally recognized tribes:	110
Number of school districts:	1,030
Number of special districts:	4,700*
Five largest cities by population:	Los Angeles, 3,957,022
	San Diego, 1,368,061
	San Jose, 1,016,479
	San Francisco, 845,602
	Fresno, 520,159
Largest county by area:	San Bernardino, 20,052 square miles
Smallest county by area:	San Francisco, 47 square miles
	(10,000 people per square mile)
Largest county by population:	Los Angeles, 9,958,091
Smallest county by population:	Alpine, 1,121
Number of chartered cities:	121 (25%)
Number of general law cities:	361 (75%)
Number of cities with directly elected mayors:	149 (30%)

*Note: Numbers vary depending on what kinds of districts are counted. These actively report to the State Controller's Office yearly. More than 5,100 were listed in their online database as of September 2015, including an unknown number of inactive entities. The number in the table was reported in the State Controller's "Special Districts Annual Report, 2011-12," Appendix B, http://www.sco.ca.gov/ard_locarep_districts.html (the most current report available as of September 2015).

Sources: State of California, Department of Finance, "E-1 Population Estimates for Cities, Counties and the State with Annual Percent Change—January 1, 2014 and 2015." Sacramento, California, May 2015; California League of Cities, "Learn about Cities," http://www.cacities.org/Resources/Learn-About-Cities; California Department of Education, "Demographics" (statistics for 2013–2014), http://www.ed-data.org/state/CA; California Charter Schools Association, "2014-15 Fact Sheet," November 2014, http://www.calcharters.org/blog/2014-15New_Charter_Schools_Fact_Sheet.pdf.

between the state and counties is like that of a restaurant owner (the state) who creates a master menu, gives its fifty-eight "top chefs" (boards of county supervisors) a wad of cash, directs them to buy the right ingredients and to prepare the meals according to the plan, and then makes them serve the finished dishes to their customers (California residents).

Each county can be pictured as a partially finished jigsaw puzzle, with a defined boundary and solid portions taking up most of the space inside, empty spaces interrupting the picture. The completed areas represent cities, and counties are filled with them: some almost completely, some only partially, and three without any (Alpine, Mariposa, and Trinity Counties do not contain cities). San Francisco is the only combination city/county, having consolidated the functions of both into one government. The blank spaces are considered "unincorporated" because they fall outside city boundaries, and all counties contain large swaths of unincorporated areas, where more than 20 percent of Californians live. County governments directly provide services and local political representation to those residents.

Original county lines bear no relation to population density or economic activity today, and all counties are expected to provide the same kinds of services to their constituents regardless of population size or geographic area. This means that the largest county by population, Los Angeles, with 10 million people, maintains the same baseline political departments, elected officials, and responsibilities as tiny Alpine, population 1,121. The legislature endows each county with the responsibility to provide for residents' health and welfare and can either delegate state functions to the counties or revoke them.

The constitution permits general law and charter counties, with the main difference lying in how officers are selected and organized. All counties are governed by five-member *boards of supervisors* (San Francisco's board has eleven members and a mayor). Supervisors face nonpartisan elections every four years, and most are reelected overwhelmingly unless they cannot run due to term limits, and that depends on whether voters in a specific county have enacted such limits via local initiative. Many termed-out state lawmakers are prolonging their political careers as county supervisors, putting their knowledge and "institutional memory" about state issues and systems to good use by helping run the state's largest subgovernments. Forty-four counties are the **general law** variety, organized according to state statute. Each county must elect a sheriff, district attorney, and assessor and may appoint or elect a variety of other officers, such as a medical examiner and public defender. Fourteen counties are organized under **charters** that allow flexibility in governing structure: apart from elected supervisors and the above-named officials, they can determine the other types of offices, whether they will be combined (will they have an assessor/recorder/clerk or a recorder/clerk?), whether they will be appointed or elected, and if they will be elected at-large or by district.

County officials such as the sheriff and assessor help the board of supervisors supply basic but vital social and political services in many areas:

- *Public safety:* courts, jails, probation, public defense, juvenile detention, sheriff, fire, emergency services, animal services
- *Public assistance:* housing, services for the homeless, food stamps, state welfare programs
- *Elections and voting:* voting processes, voter registration, signature verification
- *Tax collection:* county, city, special districts, schools
- *Environment and recreation:* parks, sports, and entertainment facilities; open space; waste removal and recycling; air quality; land-use policy; water
- *Public health:* hospitals, mental health clinics, drug rehabilitation programs
- *Education:* libraries, schools
- *Social services:* adoptions, children's foster care
- *Transit:* airports, bus and rail systems, bridges, road maintenance
- *Vital records:* birth, death, marriage certificates

Counties finance these operations by levying sales taxes and user fees, and through state government funding, property taxes, and federal grants. They spend the most on public safety and public assistance (see Figures 7.1 and 7.2). When state budget crises stem the flow of revenue, counties must lay off employees, cut services, and raise fees to make ends meet. Even when economies are in recovery mode, it takes years before the state restores funding to previous levels, and counties continually struggle to fulfill their state-mandated obligations—from preventing disease to ensuring foster children's safety—with relatively meager funding. Some of their financial struggles today stem from their payment obligations to employees and future retirees for salaries and benefits, which are consuming more of their budgets over time.

Municipal Governments

Communities in unincorporated areas of a county may want more control over land use in their neighborhoods, better services, or a formal identity. They can petition their state-chartered local agency formation commission, or LAFCO, to incorporate as a city or municipality if the residents generate enough tax revenues to support a local government. The average population of a California city is 65,000, with a huge span between the smallest (Vernon, population 123) and the largest (Los Angeles, population 3.9 million).

Much like counties, cities provide essential public services in the areas of public safety and emergency services; sewage and sanitation; public health; public works, including street maintenance; parks and recreation; libraries and schools; and land-use planning. Sometimes these overlap or supplement county programs: for example, a city might maintain its own library and also contain two or three county library branches. If lacking their own facilities, cities can contract with counties for services, pool their resources in a joint-powers agreement, or contract with private firms. A new trend among cities, especially as residents have refused to pay higher taxes to cover expanding public employee pension obligations, has been to cut personnel, benefits, and public works costs through outsourcing. One such "contract city" is the town of Half Moon Bay, which since 2011 has outsourced recreation services, engineering, legal services, code enforcement, and police protection, mostly to private contractors, the neighboring city of San Carlos, and San Mateo County. Similarly, as cities in Orange County (OC) have multiplied, the OC Fire Authority has continued to provide critical fire services to them under contract, and contracted county sheriffs patrol municipalities that cannot afford their own police forces.

More than 75 percent of California's 482 cities are incorporated under **general law,** meaning they follow state law in form and function. The remaining **charter cities** are creatures of local habits, formed through city constitutions that grant local government supreme authority over municipal affairs. This **"home rule" principle** permits municipal law to trump similar state laws. The city of Bell in the Los Angeles area serves as an uncomfortable reminder of this fact: using home rule to evade salary limitations that are set by state law, Bell's city leaders voted themselves exorbitant pay raises that technically were legal. When finally exposed, the city manager was raking in $1.5 million a year in total compensation—about nine times the governor's salary. In all, they stole more than $10 million from one of the state's poorest cities.[1]

Virtually every city is governed by a five-member **city council** that concentrates on passing and implementing local laws, called **ordinances**. Thus, unlike how state and federal governments separate powers among different branches to ensure checks and balances, legislating *and* executing local law blends in city councils. City councils rely heavily on small **boards** and **commissions** filled by local volunteers or appointees to help recommend and set policy relating to the special needs of citizens and businesses. For example, the city of Oakland has more than forty, including a Citizens' Police Review Board and a Youth Advisory Commission that is tasked with creating appealing community programs for kids and youth. To facilitate public participation in these and other public-planning bodies, as at the state level, all city and county governing institutions must abide by the **Ralph M. Brown Act**, which mandates advance notice of all meetings, "open" meetings that do not take place in secret, and full public disclosure of the proceedings.

City council members are reelected every four years in nonpartisan elections, usually by the entire city's electorate in an **at-large election** rather than by voters separated into **districts** or **wards**. Many city councils are now subject to local voter-imposed term limits, and the list of term-limited cities grows each year. If the **mayor** is not elected at-large (meaning that the whole city votes for mayor), council members designate one among them to act as a ceremonial mayor, typically on a rotating basis, for one or two years at a time. Each city makes its own rules regarding how long and how often

FIGURE 7.1 County Revenues and Expenses, 2013

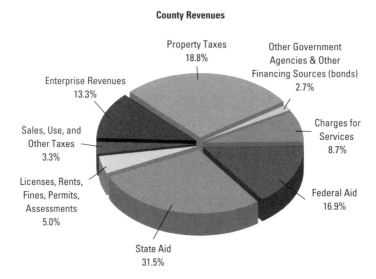

County Revenues

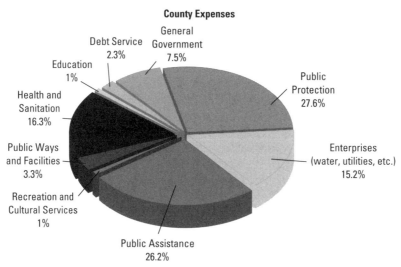

County Expenses

Source: California State Controller's Office, https://bythenumbers.sco.ca.gov.

Notes: Includes the city/county of San Francisco. Figures may not add to 100 percent due to rounding. In 2013, total county revenues were $60.95 billion and expenses totaled $58.96 billion.

city council members can act as mayor and whether the appointment will be automatic, by acclamation, or by election. Automatic rotation creates opportunities for many young council members to assume the role of mayor, and mayors in their twenties are not altogether uncommon. Ceremonial mayors lack veto power, and their vote on the council is equal to the votes of their colleagues. In place of an elected mayor, the council hires a manager to run city operations.

If the mayor proposes the city budget, has the power to veto city council actions, and can hire and fire high-profile appointees to help run city operations, then a **strong mayor** form of government is in place. Some 30 percent of California cities maintain this form of municipal government, partly because a sole individual can offer a clear agenda and be held accountable as the city's "chief executive officer" (CEO) for its success or failure. The far more popular **council-manager system** exists in nearly 70 percent of cities, an institutional legacy of Progressives who believed that efficient city management required technical expertise because "there is no partisan way to pave a street." In most cities, then, a council retains a ceremonial mayor but hires a professional **city manager** to budget for, manage, and oversee the day-to-day operations of a city. As a city's CEO, the city manager is authorized to make decisions independent of the council and thus wields great power behind the scenes. The office handles hiring and firing decisions and supervises all city departments. Most city managers possess a master's degree in public administration and have experience managing local government departments. Typically, the highest-paid city employee is the city manager, who earns more than $175,000 per year on average—although again the numbers vary widely, with some making little (less than $20,000) and others making a lot (more than $300,000). The average annual wage for all types of California city employees is $61,500, but the pay scales vary immensely and so do the numbers of city employees, resident-to-employee ratios, and the types of professionals in any given municipality.[2] Those earning over $300,000 a year tend to be police or fire chiefs or city attorneys working for large cities.

Cities depend heavily on taxes and fees to finance operations. Prior to Proposition 13, property taxes constituted 57 percent of combined city and county revenues annually; in 2011–12 property taxes represented only 8 percent of the average aggregate city budget. The bulk of funding now comes from service charges for public utilities and transit; sales taxes; property taxes; a variety of taxes and fees on hotels, developers, other businesses, and property use; and state and federal agencies. Bond money also enlarges budgets.

Assembly members and senators perform economic gymnastics to balance the state budget during hard times, and their routine includes yanking property taxes and other fees previously committed to cities to backfill the state's budget hole. In an effort to stop such state "raiding" of local funds, cities and counties sponsored a constitutional amendment (Proposition 1A in 2004) to prevent state legislators from transferring locally generated property taxes, vehicle license fees, and sales taxes into the state's general fund. The state, however, can override some of those restrictions during fiscal crises, effectively diverting millions of dollars away from the cities and counties in which they were generated; some funds are "borrowed" by the state with the promise to repay the debt when the state's fiscal outlook improves.

In the absence of a steady stream of property tax revenue, local governments hunt for substitute sources continually. For instance, it's common to charge developers heavy fees for new construction projects or saddle them with the costs of constructing new streets, schools, lighting, sewers, or any infrastructure improvements related to population growth. These fees are then imposed on home buyers. Mello-Roos fees, for example, can amount to thousands of dollars a

City councils make local laws (their legislative function includes passing *ordinances*) and also execute laws by implementing city plans or programs. The San Bernardino city council meets twice weekly, compared to Los Angeles's city council, which meets three times a week, and the councils of smaller cities, which commonly meet twice a month. At a typical meeting, council members might listen to citizens' concerns, discuss pending regulations, decide land-use matters, pay tribute to community heroes, approve expenses and payments for city services, and/or vote on contracts for city services.

year for home owners who live in houses constructed in previously undeveloped areas. Assessed as a special lien against each property that will be in effect for as long as forty years, the annual charges can vary dramatically from area to area and even house to house. In counties such as San Diego, the average home owner in a Mello-Roos-related district pays an additional $1,826 per year on top of property taxes, with these fees totaling $195 million in San Diego County in 2012 alone.[3] Another strategy is to base land-use decisions on a project's net fiscal impact, a phenomenon known as the **fiscalization of land use.** In practical terms, this means that cities today have incentives to entice and keep retail businesses that can generate substantial sales taxes, as local governments receive 1 percent of state sales taxes collected in their jurisdictions. Auto dealerships, shopping malls, and big-box retailers like Home Depot are therefore favored over low-income housing for people who will further stress city resources, or service-based industries that will not generate tax revenue—in other words, decisions are made without regard to the intrinsic value of, or need for, a project.

FIGURE 7.2 City Revenues and Expenses, 2013

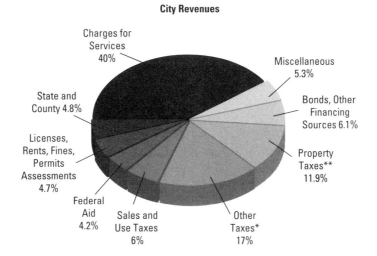

City Revenues

Charges for
Services
40%

Miscellaneous
5.3%

Bonds, Other
Financing
Sources 6.1%

Property
Taxes**
11.9%

State and
County 4.8%

Licenses,
Rents, Fines,
Permits
Assessments
4.7%

Federal
Aid
4.2%

Sales and
Use Taxes
6%

Other
Taxes*
17%

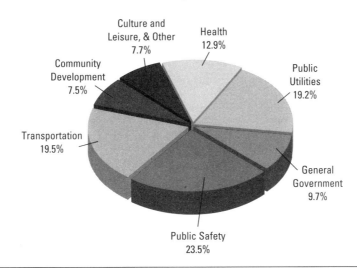

City Expenses

Culture and
Leisure, & Other
7.7%

Health
12.9%

Community
Development
7.5%

Public
Utilities
19.2%

Transportation
19.5%

General
Government
9.7%

Public Safety
23.5%

Source: California State Controller's Office, https://bythenumbers.sco.ca.gov.

Notes: Includes the city/county of San Francisco. Figures may not add to 100 percent due to rounding. In 2013, total city revenues were $68.64 billion and expenses totaled $67.81 billion.

*Includes transportation, transient lodging, franchise, business license, real property transfer, utility user, and other nonproperty taxes.

**Includes property tax in-lieu of vehicle license fees.

Borrowing large sums to upgrade city services with better technology, to build new sports facilities, or to rebuild schools, for example, has also become a favored tool for local governments of all types, especially school districts. Debt typically takes the form of a voter-approved **bond**, which can range into the hundreds of millions of dollars. Taxpayers "issue" (sell) bonds to lenders and commit to repay them, with interest, after twenty or thirty years, for example. Bonds are also used to cover financial obligations such as long-term leases. One source estimates that California city and county bond debt is over $90 billion, and school district debt is around $150 billion.[4]

Debt can also take shape in long-term commitments to pay for hefty projects that may or may not generate income, such as a water treatment plant that local citizens pay for through higher sewage bills. So-called **unfunded liabilities** probably constitute the most hazardous type of debt; this catchphrase refers to whatever a city or county legally owes in future payments but does not yet have the financial reserves to cover. Historically, California's cities and counties have negotiated retirement and health care benefits in contracts with public employees, such as firefighters and police, but some of those commitments have drained—and continue to threaten—public treasuries to the point of bankruptcy. Generous employee labor contracts have been based on optimistic projections of tax receipts and returns on investments, but those investments tanked along with the economy. Even if rates of return improve, municipalities and counties owe no less than an estimated $20 billion in pension payments—*plus* health care benefits (which are likely to *triple* those outlays).[5] How will local governments fulfill these colossal pension obligations without going broke? Residents in some cities, as in San Diego, have passed local initiatives eliminating pensions and switching to 401(k) plans for new city employees. Other cities simply can't avoid running out of money. Following Vallejo's lead, the cities of San Bernardino, Mammoth Lakes, and Stockton filed for Chapter 9 **bankruptcy** protection in 2012 in hopes of erasing soaring debt loads that have been pushed into the stratosphere by employee compensation and pensions, bond repayments for ill-advised infrastructure projects, and general financial mismanagement by city officials. City payouts have shot up while tax receipts have plummeted. To recover, a bankrupt local government must raise taxes to pay its bills and curtail virtually every service it provides to citizens as it charges higher fees. Crime rises as the police force dwindles, the city's ability to borrow vanishes along with its good credit ratings, the roads become gutted with potholes, and tourism evaporates. Creditors are repaid pennies on the dollar, and the city's long-term debt is reduced through the renegotiation of current labor contracts—yet huge pension obligations remain.

To date, the courts have treated retirees' pensions (earned retirement benefits, with interest) as ironclad contractual obligations, and labor unions have fiercely defended them as vested rights. If judges decide that pension systems can be treated as all other creditors and these contracts can be broken, then cities will have a greater incentive to bargain for lesser payments or to declare bankruptcy, and retirees will see drastic changes in their long-anticipated retirement incomes. Municipalities now considered financially vulnerable by big credit-rating agencies, including Los Angeles and San Jose, which spend tens of millions of dollars (roughly 20 percent of their annual budgets) on these expenses, would find this option irresistible. In 2014, a federal bankruptcy judge issued a landmark opinion that under U.S. law, pensioners are not entitled to unequal protections compared to other creditors in a bankruptcy, giving municipalities a weapon to use in future bankruptcy fights. So far the full impact of the ruling remains untested, as Stockton and San Bernardino have agreed to follow through on their pension obligations.

Special Districts

A **special district** is a geographic area governed by an autonomous board for a single purpose, such as running an airport or providing a community with street lighting or a cemetery. Arguably the most abundant power centers in California, but virtually invisible to the average citizen, special districts proliferate because they are created to meet critical needs that cities and counties lack the will or capacity to address. Like regular governments, they can sue and be sued, charge users for their services, and exercise the right to *eminent domain* (the taking of property for public use). Unlike most governments, however, they may cover only a portion of a city or stretch across several cities or counties.

Close to 4,700 special districts operate in the state, about two-thirds independently with their own boards of governors chosen by voters in low-profile elections; the remainder are controlled by counties or cities through appointments. About 2,700 special districts independently generate their own revenue as enterprises through fees or by providing services and charging their customers, while the remainder are funded by counties and cities. The majority of special district services are paid for through property-related service charges or special assessments that initially require a two-thirds majority vote. In other words, property owners pay a fee based on a percentage of their own property's assessed value, so neighbors might pay different rates for the same services. Hospital, rat and mosquito control, trash disposal, fire protection, irrigation and water delivery, bus and rail transit, and utility districts are a few types. The Southern California Metropolitan Water District (MWD) epitomizes this type of fee-based service organization: created by the legislature in 1928, its mission is to provide adequate, reliable supplies of high-quality water to current and future residents in Southern California. A water wholesaler, it owns and operates major infrastructure, including the Colorado River aqueduct, hydroelectric plants, pipes, and water treatment facilities. Twenty-six cities and water districts buy more than 1.7 billion gallons of drinking water from MWD every day, supplying 19 million residents in six counties. In addition to paying their local water district for the water they use, Southern California residents see charges listed on their annual property tax bills for MWD operations. In response to the drought and Governor Brown's edict to slash water use by 25 percent starting spring 2015, MWD cut back by 15 percent the amounts of water supplied to its member agencies, with stiff penalties for overuse.

School Districts

School districts constitute a separate but most familiar category of special district: more than a thousand provide K–12 education for about 6.2 million students attending almost ten thousand different schools; an additional 72 districts encompass 112 community colleges.[6] Created by state law, nonpartisan five-member boards of education (Los Angeles's board has seven) govern their school districts by following the detailed operating instructions of the state's education code and heeding the State Board of Education's mandates. A superintendent manages the local system, which may be responsible for more than 653,000 students—as is the case in the gargantuan Los Angeles Unified School District—or fewer than twenty students. School boards handle issues relating to nearly every aspect of student life, from regulating students' cell phone use to defining nutritional standards to designing appropriate curricula, and they must weigh the concerns of vocal parents and special interests trying to influence their decisions along with the concerns of those who do not speak up so forcefully.

State-funded, K–12 public **charter schools** operate outside the jurisdiction of the local school board; these are organized by parents, teachers, and/or community groups to provide specialized education programs that may have a particular emphasis in the performing arts, sciences, languages, or college preparation, for example. The school's mission is spelled out in its charter, or contract. Since a 1992 state law enabled charter schools to form, their number has increased annually, reaching 1,184 in 2015.[7] Charter schools are free and open to all students, and if a school receives more requests to attend than it has spots available, it must hold a blind lottery to determine which students can attend.

Proposition 98 dedicates approximately 40 percent of the state's general fund budget to K–14 education, yet schools receive funding from a variety of sources. Using the 2012–13 fiscal year as a point of reference, just over 70 percent of K–12 public school funding is sourced through Prop 98 with general fund money and local property tax revenue. The rest comes from a variety of sources: approximately 10 percent from federal dollars, and miscellaneous sources supply the remaining 20 percent, including bond payments, the state lottery (a mere 1.5 percent), special local parcel taxes, and donations funneled through private foundations that have been formed to supplement operations by buying equipment or hiring specialized teachers (music or arts instructors) that districts cannot afford.

Don Bartletti/Los Angeles Times via Getty Images

Public water agencies are tasked with providing clean, reliable water to the cities, farms, and businesses within the special districts they govern. The San Diego County Water Authority diversified its supplies with a $1 billion desalination plant in Carlsbad that will filter 50 million gallons of sea water daily for 300,000 San Diegans by the end of 2016. More desalination plants are in the works (Huntington Beach and Monterey; reviving one in Santa Barbara), but the large plants occupy prime real estate, and high-pressure pumps needed for reverse osmosis consume tremendous energy, a costly process.

Regional Governments

Unlike governments that make and enforce binding laws, **regional governments** provide permanent forums in which local elected officials can exchange ideas and information, plan, and coordinate their policies across county and city boundaries, usually for land-use and development-related activities arising from population growth and change. State law allows for the creation of a variety of regional governments with joint powers authority (JPA), and these **councils of government** (COGs) plan for future populations by addressing common issues that encompass a wide spectrum of infrastructure-related needs, including housing and transportation, water and food availability, toxic waste disposal, and environmental quality. COGs in California, therefore, are a collection of local officials and agencies that voluntarily agree to share responsibility for solving collective problems. At least forty-three major COGs operate in California and have formed joint-powers agreements, plus there are many localized JPAs.[8]

COGs coordinate rather than dictate because they cannot force decisions on local governments. Their governing boards are composed of mayors, city council members, and county supervisors, making them *intergovernmental* entities. In these collaborative forums to promote regional planning, they receive input from research specialists and advisers from federal departments, special districts, state agencies, and even sovereign nations such as California Native American tribes and Mexico. Their planning activities include reviewing federal grants-in-aid and proposing legislation. They do not deliver public services.

COGs can take the form of *transportation planning agencies* or *commissions,* such as the Contra Costa County Transportation Authority, which coordinates freeway expansions and improvements, maintains emergency roadside call boxes, helps fund bus transit, oversees bicycle paths, and encourages ridesharing. Nineteen COGs are also federally designated *metropolitan planning organizations* (MPOs), legally responsible for researching, designing, and finding funding for regional transportation plans for areas with more than fifty thousand people. MPOs include associations like the San Joaquin COG (SJCOG) and the Santa Barbara County Association of Governments (SBCAG). Other COGs are *planning councils* with wider scope, like the Tahoe Regional Planning Agency, through which elected officials from surrounding areas create overarching plans that have vital impacts on construction, recreation, water quality, and the environment around Lake Tahoe. Their boundaries can be extensive: for example, the Association of Bay Area Governments (ABAG) unites local elected officials from nine counties and 101 cities to deal with housing, open space, employment, waste, transportation, recreation, and equity challenges posed by a population that is seven million and growing.

Regional government may also take the form of regulatory entities that set rules for environmentally sensitive activities. These bodies are authorized by state law to set rules and enforce them. For instance, California's thirty-five "air districts" are dedicated to controlling pollution from stationary sources (Air Pollution Control Districts, or APCDs) and promoting air quality (Air Quality Management Districts, or AQMDs) through comprehensive planning programs that include the setting of compulsory rules for residents and the enforcement of those rules, air quality monitoring, research, public education, and the issuing of special business permits.

Federalism

Whereas the state authorizes county governments, local jurisdictions, and special districts to perform necessary functions, the U.S. Constitution guarantees that states share governing power with the national government, although states' authority has diminished as both the federal purse and federal capacity have grown. The U.S. Congress discovered long ago that **funding** is a convenient instrument for enticing states to adopt federal goals by granting or withholding moneys in exchange for new state policy. In this way, highway funds have been exchanged for lower speed limits and a minimum drinking age of twenty-one—issues that only the states can legislate.

California is also subject to **unfunded mandates**. These are federal laws that require the states to provide services, but no federal funds are supplied to implement them. Such mandates amount to hundreds of millions of dollars in various areas, including social services, transportation, education, health care, and environmental cleanup. For example, the Legislative Analyst's Office estimates that holding undocumented immigrants in correctional facilities costs at least half a billion dollars per year (other estimates place the number at $1 billion). In 2015, the federal government's State Criminal Alien Assistance Program (SCAAP) provided counties only $55 million to cover correctional officer costs related to 72,275 persons who had committed a felony or two misdemeanors—about 10 percent of the average cost to house inmates.[9] Mandates also can take the form of **preemptive legislation,** which prohibits a state from passing certain laws; the federal government has used legislation of this kind to prevent some of California's progressive environmental rules and legislation from taking effect, such as a ban on ride-on lawn mowers—a move that would negatively affect workers in states where the mowers are manufactured.

California remains dependent on the federal government to balance its ledgers, receiving billions for major programs such as welfare and health coverage. Federal money flows to individuals in the form of Social Security checks, for example, to counties and cities as grants, and also through the state budget. For instance, the U.S. government supplements schools for the cost of educating low-income students and students with disabilities, and about a quarter of all transportation funds are generated through federal taxes on diesel and gasoline. Money that went straight to the state amounted to $100 billion for fiscal year 2015–16, or 37 percent of total state spending, which topped $267.5 billion. Given California's staggeringly high population, position as a military gateway to the Pacific, and importance to the nation as an agricultural hub and economic powerhouse, federal dollars will continue to backfill permanent and growing needs.

Tribal Governments

An often-overlooked class of government functions alongside state and local entities and also under the thumb of the federal government: that of sovereign tribal nations. Tribal governments operated in relative obscurity until recently. Isolated on one hundred thousand acres of mostly remote and frequently inhospitable reservations throughout California, the state's 110 federally recognized tribes had minimal impact on neighboring cities or state government. Native groups were defined politically by their interaction with the U.S. Congress and federal agencies such as the Bureau of Indian Affairs, as well as by prior case law that treated them as wards of the federal government rather than as fully sovereign nations. In the main, California governments could ignore them.

Gaming changed all that. As bingo halls flourished in the 1970s and blossomed into full-scale gambling enterprises by the late 1980s, states began looking for ways to limit, eliminate, tax, influence, or otherwise control this new growth industry, one whose environmental and social effects on surrounding communities were proving significant.

BOX 7.2 California's Landmark Climate Change Law: AB 32

California set itself apart yet again when the state's majority-Democratic legislature joined Governor Arnold Schwarzenegger in crafting the Global Warming Solutions Act of 2006, otherwise known as Assembly Bill 32 (AB 32), the world's first law establishing a program of regulatory and market mechanisms to curb emissions of greenhouse gases. Voters beat back an initiative to rescind it in 2010 (Proposition 23), but businesses and antiregulatory interests continue to oppose the law strongly, anticipating higher costs. The law aims to promote a low-carbon, sustainable economy by encouraging jobs that promote more efficient, renewable energy sources that improve air quality, and it authorizes the state's Air Resources Board (ARB) to set new fuel efficiency standards for new vehicles sold in California; establish a statewide plan to reach an emissions cap in 2020 based on 1990 emissions levels; require mandatory reporting of greenhouse gas outputs; create advisory boards; and collect fees from significant sources of greenhouse gases.

Most notably, ARB has enacted the nation's first **cap-and-trade program** for greenhouse gas (GHG) emissions. Modeled on other successful market-based pollution reduction programs, California's version is designed to reduce the overall amount of GHGs by setting an upper limit, or cap, on the aggregate amount of statewide emissions from 85 percent of GHG sources. About 360 "polluters" (businesses creating carbon and other gases linked to climate change, representing six hundred facilities) were initially given trading credits, or allowances, for the normal amount of GHGs they produce. Chevron's Richmond refinery is the biggest source, producing 4.5 million metric tons of an overall estimated 447 million metric tons in the state yearly; the University of California is another large emitter. Every year the total cap on statewide emissions will decline by 2 to 3 percent (the total number of allowances will decline), providing incentives for polluters to invest in more efficient technologies or fuels that will reduce their own emissions, thereby creating for them a surplus of carbon trading credits that they can sell at a quarterly online auction, which commenced November 2012. Companies in capped industries must register and report their emissions annually (also subject to independent verification), a requirement imposed in 2008, and ARB has designed the process to protect against collusion, cheating, and price manipulation. Advocates of the cap-and-trade approach tout the facts that no new taxes are directly assessed, businesses have flexibility to alter their practices to be compliant, and revenues support "green" initiatives. Opponents bemoan the new layer of regulations and paperwork and costs of compliance, and equate new costs with indirect taxes, dubbing them "carbon taxes" that they promise to pass along to consumers. California and Quebec, Canada, linked their cap-and-trade auctions on January 1, 2014.

2013 Emissions by Sector

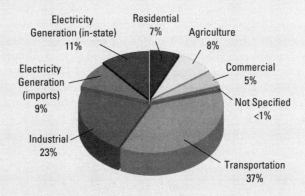

Source: California Environmental Protection Agency, Air Resources Board, "California Greenhouse Gas Emission Inventory," http://www.arb .ca.gov/cc/inventory/data/data.htm.

Note: Total California emissions for 2013: 459.3 million metric tons of carbon dioxide equivalent.

(Continued)

BOX 7.2 **(Continued)**

Initially the act was fiercely opposed by a tight coalition of automobile, manufacturing, and energy industries, which challenged the new law as going "too far" by setting stricter standards than the federal government—despite the fact that the federal Environmental Protection Agency (EPA) had never set a greenhouse gas emissions standard. Ruling that AB 32 superseded federal authority to maintain clean air standards, the EPA under the George W. Bush administration denied California a waiver from adhering to clean air standards lower than those set in the Federal Clean Air Act. On June 30, 2009, the EPA under the Barack Obama administration reversed the ruling, giving California and thirteen other states the green light to proceed with implementation and enforcement of laws like AB 32. Governor Schwarzenegger crowed: "After being asleep at the wheel for over two decades, the federal government has finally stepped up and granted California its nation-leading tailpipe emissions waiver. . . . A greener, cleaner future has finally arrived."* According to a U.S. Energy Information Administration report in 2013, however, California remains the second-highest producer of carbon dioxide, behind Texas and ahead of Pennsylvania.

Source: California Environmental Protection Agency, Air Resources Board, "About the ARB," last reviewed April 26, 2012, http://www.arb.ca.gov/html/aboutarb.htm.

*California Governor's Office, "Governor Applauds EPA Decision Granting California Authority to Reduce Greenhouse Gas Emissions," June 30, 2009, http://gov.ca.gov/issue/energy-environment.

After the U.S. Supreme Court ruled in 1987 that tribes do indeed have the right to run gambling enterprises on their lands, Congress exercised its supreme lawmaking authority (to which tribes are subject) and wrote the **Indian Gaming Regulatory Act (IGRA)**, a law that restricts the scope of gaming and defers regulatory authority to the states. The IGRA also stipulates that tribes within a state and the state itself must enter into compacts to permit certain forms of gaming irrespective of tribal sovereignty. In California, casinos with 350 or more slot machines are considered Class III gaming operations and are subject to compacts. Class II gaming includes card rooms and bingo played for monetary prizes.

No state can tax a tribal nation, a law that California governor Gray Davis kept in mind during contract negotiations with sixty-one tribes in the late 1990s. The final compact specified that in exchange for permitting Las Vegas–style gambling, tribes would participate in revenue sharing with nongaming tribes and also contribute to a fund for reimbursing casino-related costs to cities and counties, such as those stemming from traffic congestion, public safety concerns, and gambling addiction. California voters overwhelmingly approved this first compact as Proposition 5, which was superseded two years later by constitutional amendment Proposition 1A in 2000. Gaming compacts that are renegotiated must be ratified by the legislature and may be challenged through referenda, subject to the voters' will. This occurred when several Southern California tribes arranged a deal to add thousands of slot machines in exchange for millions more paid annually into the state's general fund. Native American groups then spent a combined $108.4 million to convince voters to approve four referenda on their amended gaming compacts in 2008 (Propositions 94 through 97), and each passed by at least 55.5 percent.[10] Today, the state's casino industry is exceeded in size only by that of Nevada, and more than half of the state's slot machines are located in three Southern California counties: San Diego, Riverside, and San Bernardino. Eleven Native American casinos were expanded or renovated before 2010, and a few more have been authorized since then, bringing the total number of authorized gaming machines to more than 72,000.

FIGURE 7.4 Tribes Are Recognized Sovereigns

The U.S. Constitution explicitly recognizes four sovereigns:

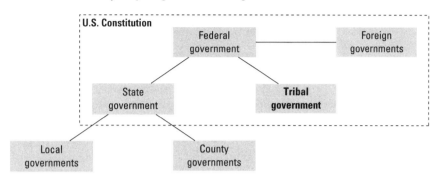

Source: K. A. Spilde, J. B. Taylor, and K. W. Grant, II, "Social and Economic Analysis of Tribal Government Gaming in Oklahoma" (Cambridge, MA: Harvard Project on American Indian Economic Development, 2002). Reprinted with permission of the authors.

Sensing opportunity, a few smaller, more remotely located tribes have recently angled into the gaming business. As of 2015, California had ratified gaming compacts with seventy-two tribes, and a total of sixty casinos were in operation (sixty-seven if all casino floors are counted), plus eighty-eight card rooms and a smattering of satellite slot arcades, which do not require compacts. The fact that casinos must be located on existing tribal lands limits their proliferation, but a few tribes have successfully taken additional land into trust with the consent of the federal government, enabling them to erect casinos in higher-trafficked areas. Voters rejected a proposed compact in 2014 that would have allowed the North Fork Rancheria of Mono Indians and Wiyot Tribe to build a casino on new land they acquired for that purpose in Madera County some thirty-eight miles from the North Fork reservation. Recent rule changes implemented by the federal government's Bureau of Indian Affairs make it more likely that casinos will crop up in urban centers as 34 additional tribes petition for federal recognition, 22 of which plan to build casinos in places like San Francisco, Los Angeles, Orange County, and Kern County, should they acquire the land. Seventy-three tribes without casino operations receive an annual payout from the Indian Gaming Revenue Sharing Trust Fund (to which large gaming tribes contribute) amounting to $1.1 million per tribe annually.

Clearly, "tribal sovereignty" has limits with regard to both federal and state law. Tribes retain control over political activities within their reservations' borders, and their governments usually take the form of all-powerful tribal councils vested with executive, legislative, and judicial powers. Councils have full control over tribal membership, which numbers more than fifty thousand registered individuals in California alone, and they implement federal assistance and grants covering health care, education, and other social needs, which amounted to about $278 million in direct payments and grants in 2009.[11] Gaming operations have laid the foundation for socioeconomic and political development in and around tribal territories. Relative prosperity has transformed tribal governments into fully staffed operations that have increasing institutional capacity to provide services that the state

The Morongo Casino Resort and Spa rises above the desert floor near the San Jacinto Mountains. The Morongo Band of Mission Indians in Cabazon, California, operates one of sixty Class III tribal gaming enterprises in the state; California has ratified compacts with seventy-two tribes.

can't or won't provide; however, local governments are obligated to provide services such as law enforcement, road access and repairs, and emergency services. Tribes are now important participants in regional planning, and cities, counties, and local communities benefit from their charitable donations as well as from the jobs and tax revenues the casinos generate. Additionally, the state benefits from the tribes' ability to obtain federal dollars for improvement projects such as widening roads and building bridges, especially when such upgrades are otherwise unaffordable. Fourteen California tribes also make annual payments to the state's general fund, amounting to approximately $330 million out of a total estimated $7 billion in casino revenues in fiscal year 2014–15.[12]

Gaming enterprises have transformed tribal governments into major players at both the state and national levels, enabling them to lobby for or against policies of interest to them and to donate heavily to campaigns. Tribes nationwide contributed approximately $14 million to federal candidates, parties, and outside groups in the 2013–14 election cycle and spent another $25 million on lobbying activities.[13] California tribes constituted four of the top ten donors at the national level, and among them were Southern California's San Manuel, Pechanga, and Morongo bands. The Table Mountain Tribe alone spent over $12 million in support of the tribal gaming compact referendum discussed above (Prop 48, which failed), helping to bring the spending among the top ten heaviest spending tribes to $20 million in the 2014 off-year election cycle.[14] Like many other special interests, Native American tribes have "found a voice" in the political system through the power of money.

Conclusion: The State's Interlocking Systems

California's state government is much more than a mega-institution with a few major components. The "big" institutions that include direct democracy, the legislature, state executive offices, and the courts may generally set overarching policies for the state, but they tend to obscure the importance of the thousands of local and regional entities responsible for countless directives that have immediate impacts on everyday life—laws and rules that are crafted by thousands of people working in elected and unelected capacities across county, city, special district, and regional governments, as well as in tribal nations. In ways both small and large, their decisions directly condition the health and livelihoods of communities throughout the state. These entities safely dispose of millions of cubic feet of trash daily, kill mosquitoes that spread disease, hire more than 300,000 teachers across the state, and assume responsibility for solving these and other significant collective action problems that transcend boundaries but require local input and cooperation to solve.

The state's government should therefore be viewed as a complex organism, with approximately six thousand identifiable working parts that have specialized and localized functions. Each part contributes to the welfare of the whole, either singly or in conjunction with others, but never in isolation. When dissected, the system appears as a bewildering mess of overlapping boundary lines, yet with remarkable success, these interlocking systems provide essential services that citizens need and will continue to demand. Operating mostly out of sight, their day-to-day work attracts little attention from either the public or the media, yet they play key roles in governing the state effectively.

Notes

1. The *Los Angeles Times* broke the story in 2010 (for which they won two Pulitzer Prizes). Archives of their investigative stories can be found on their website: http://www.latimes.com/local/bell.

2. California State Controller's Office, "Government Compensation in California, California Cities 2011," http://publicpay.ca.gov/Reports/Cities/Cities.aspx. The posting includes reported information for 462 cities.

3. Kevin Crowe and Joanne Faryon, "Do You Pay Extra Property Taxes? Mello-Roos: Who's Paying What," KPBS News, inewsource, May 29, 2013, http://www.kpbs.org/news/2013/may/29/mello-roos-taxes-vary-dramatically-whos-paying-wha.

4. California Public Policy Center, "Calculating California's Total State and Local Government Debt," Spring 2013, and Kevin Dayton, "Unrecognized Legacy of Prop 39," California Public Policy Center, April 2015, who estimates that the debt service on borrowing for public schools between 2000 and 2015 was $137 billion. See also California State Treasurer's Office, "Debt Issuance Data Summary Tables," http://www.treasurer.ca.gov/cdiac/debtdata/debtdata.asp.

5. Ed Ring, "Calculating California's Total State and Local Government Debt." California Public Policy Center, April 26, 2013. Health care costs are notoriously difficult to estimate; these are based on reports issued by the State Controller's and Treasurer's Offices.

6. These statistics are for the 2013–14 school year, published by the California Department of Education on their data website: www.ed-data.org.

7. Total number reported by the California Charter Schools Association, "2014–15 New California Charter Schools Fact Sheet," November 2014, http://www.ccsa.org/blog/2014-15New_Charter_Schools_Fact_Sheet.pdf.

8. The exact number of COGs is difficult to calculate because a number of transportation planning commissions, planning councils, and other more localized (but intergovernmental) organizations qualify as COGs. The California Association of Councils of Government listed forty-three member organizations in 2015,

including major transportation authorities or commissions. CALCOG, "Find Your COG," http://www.calcog .org/index.aspx?nid=45.

9. The 2015 SCAAP per capita reimbursement rate was $41.26 (only for eligible inmates), based on correctional officer salary costs; food, housing, medical care, administrative costs (etc.) are not reimbursable. U.S. Department of Justice, Bureau of Justice Statistics, "State Criminal Alien Assistance Program, FY2015," https:// www.bja.gov/ProgramDetails.aspx?Program_ID=86#horizontalTab8.

10. Vote results supplied by California Secretary of State. Data from ballot measure summaries for Propositions 94–97 are from Follow the Money, "Ballot Measures," accessed September 17, 2013, http://www .followthemoney.org/database/StateGlance/ballot.phtml?m=493.

11. Data from U.S. Census Bureau, *Consolidated Federal Funds Report for Fiscal Year 2009: State and County Areas* (Washington, DC: U.S. Census Bureau, August 2010), http://www.census.gov/prod/2010pubs/cffr-09.pdf.

12. Legislative Analyst's Office, "Overview of Gambling in California," May 20, 2015, http://www.lao. ca.gov/handouts/crimjust/2015/Gambling-Overview-052015.pdf. The National Indian Gaming Commission reported that total revenues for sixty-six gaming operations in California and northern Nevada tribes were $6.993 billion in FY 2013. National Indian Gaming Commission, "Tribal Gaming Revenues by Region, Fiscal Year 2012 and 2013," http://www.nigc.gov/Gaming_Revenue_Reports.aspx.

13. Kent Cooper, "Indian Tribes Gave Record Amount," *Roll Call,* Political MoneyLine blog, March 1, 2013, http://blogs.rollcall.com/moneyline/indian-tribes-gave-record-amount. See also, Opensecrets, "Indian Gaming," accessed June 25, 2015, http://www.opensecrets.org/industries/summary.php?cycle=2010&ind=G6550.

14. Author's calculations based on lobbying reports for 2013–14, California secretary of state's campaign finance database: http://cal-access.sos.ca.gov. See also, California Fair Political Practices Commission, "Top Contributors to State Ballot Measure Committees Raising at Least $1 Million: November 2014 Election," http:// fppc.ca.gov/topcontributors/past_elections/nov2014/index.html.

CHAPTER 8

The California Budget Process

The best evidence of the fairness of any settlement is the fact that it fully satisfies neither party.

—Winston Churchill, 1926

Annual budgeting at the state level is a grueling process of translating social and political values into dollars, a set of interrelated decisions that creates winners and losers. A budget is a statement of priorities, the result of intense bargaining, and the product of a sophisticated guessing game about future income and economic trends that provides risk-averse politicians with incentives to respond to the most vocal and powerful interests participating in the political system. All the while, larger economic conditions provide a context for decision making that can set the stage for massive heart attacks (from ballooning deficits that require terrifying cuts, for instance) or just mild heartburn (from conflicts over how best to spend unexpected revenues).

California's annual budget, around $100 billion, represents a temporary answer to the state's infinite needs and wants and, despite its enormous scale, still makes many Californians wonder, "Why do we pay so much in taxes, but the state never has enough?" This chapter examines the budgeting process and explores the reasons for California's budgetary dilemmas that, more often than not, force representatives to make painful choices among alternatives.

California Budgeting 101

California's fiscal year begins July 1 and ends June 30. By law, a new budget must be passed by June 15 or lawmakers are supposed to forfeit their pay.

The governor must then sign the budget by July 1, or the state cannot write checks for services or goods in the new cycle. In past years, the budget was routinely completed late, triggering more uncertainty and panic for Californians dependent on state services, but the on-time budget five years in a row (2011–15) attests to the power of unified government (that is, when one party dominates both the legislative and executive branches), as well as rules (the budget now passes with a simple majority—rather than a two-thirds—vote).

Advance work begins in the governor's **Department of Finance (DOF)**, which is staffed by professional analysts who continuously collect data about state operations. Each branch of government and executive department itemizes its own programmatic budget needs, from personnel to project costs, including items such as habitat restoration (Department of Fish and Game), in-home care for people with disabilities (Department of Health and Human Services), and trial court funding (judicial branch)—merely a sampling from among thousands of state government activities. The DOF's projections about how much money will be available through taxes and fees provide baselines for estimating how much *must* be spent on major existing programs and how much *can* be spent on new desired programs or services. **Mandatory spending** already committed through existing laws, such as Medi-Cal and debt payments, absorbs most of the approximately $100 billion annual budget, leaving limited room for legislators to duke it out for the **discretionary funds** used to cover all other state services, from monitoring the safety of amusement park rides to sheltering victims of domestic violence.

Guided by the governor's initiatives, political values, and stated objectives, the DOF prepares a budget by assigning dollar amounts to state programs and services. The governor submits his or her budget to the legislature by January 10, whereupon it is routed to the legislature's own **legislative analyst** for scrutiny. Heeding recommendations from the Legislative Analyst's Office and anticipating the governor's updated version that accounts for actual tax receipts (the **May Revision or "May Revise"**), throughout the spring, Assembly and Senate budget committees and subcommittees construct their own version of the budget. State analysts testify before the committees, as do officials, lobbyists, and citizens representing every sector of society and local government as they seek protection for existing benefits or beg for more.

Once the budget committees finalize their work, and the legislature resolves its differences into a comprehensive budget bill (usually through the help of a conference committee made up of three members from each house), legislative leaders and their staff members begin negotiating with the governor and his or her staff to reach compromises. Will tuition at state universities and colleges remain flat, be lowered, or increase? If lowered, will it be paid for through cuts to mental health programs or after-school care? Will reentry programs for former prison inmates be enhanced? Hundreds of decisions like these play into negotiations both at the committee level and in high-level negotiations that routinely included the party leaders from both houses (along with the governor, they constitute the "**Big Five**") until the primary responsibility for passing the budget was shifted to the majority party (according to Proposition 25 in 2010, only a simple majority is sufficient to pass it). When the same party controls the governorship and both legislative chambers, minority-party leaders will ultimately be excluded from the top-level negotiations if they refuse to compromise on issues the majority party considers fundamental, and if the minority's votes are not ultimately necessary for passing the budget. Thus, the "**Big Three**" (the governor, the Speaker, and the Senate president pro tem, all Democrats) have been the key negotiators since 2011.

Final agreements also hinge on the governor's line-item veto power (see chapter 5). In 2015, the governor excised only $1.3 million from the budget with this authority. Eventually, often after

Budget committees in both the Assembly and Senate chisel the governor's budget into shape throughout the months of spring, in advance of a June 15 deadline. Democrat Shirley Weber chaired the Assembly Budget Committee in 2015; here she is trailed by fellow Assembly members as they leave the Assembly floor after a vote on the $117.5 billion budget plan for 2015. The budget bill must also go through the Senate Budget Committee, be approved by the Senate, and signed by the governor to become enacted.

considerable debate and struggle, the budget is passed and signed into law, as are "**trailer bills**"—a package of omnibus or large bills that make the necessary policy changes to the state laws and codes outlined in the budget plan.

Mechanics of Budgeting: Revenue

A budget reflects the governor's and legislature's educated guesses about how much money the state will collect in taxes, fees, and federal grants during the coming year, as well as the state's commitments to spending or saving what it collects. All budgets are built on economic data, assumptions, and formulas designed to produce accurate forecasts about dollar amounts and the numbers of people who will demand the services and products these dollar amounts cover. Relatively small numerical shifts in these formulas can equal hundreds of millions of dollars over time. The state controller reported that by May 2015, receipts from all sources had outstripped projections in the previous year's budget by *$10.7 billion*, or 6.2 percent—a sign of a strengthening economy. Larger economic forces produce discrepancies like these that simply cannot be estimated precisely in advance. Nevertheless, sophisticated assumptions about how much will be coming into the state's coffers serve as a foundation for balancing the budget—or at least making it temporarily *appear* balanced.

Revenue is another word for income. The largest revenue streams are provided by **taxes** and **fees** for services, and in fiscal year 2015–16 these helped raise the state's general fund revenues to $117.5 billion (slightly less after $1.9 billion in emergency set-asides, or "rainy day funds" are taken out), or a total of $162.5 billion if special funds are taken into account.[1] Taxes are deposited into the state's general fund or redistributed to county and local governments; special taxes go into separate funds, such as gas taxes that are funneled into the transportation fund. It should be noted that property taxes are raised at the local level and mainly used to fund schools; they do not augment the general fund.

A separate stream of revenue, **federal grant money**, is funneled through the federal fund, representing billions of dollars from the U.S. government that go to state and local governments to subsidize specific programs, such as job retraining, or to local entities for a variety of items, such as low-income housing or school lunches. The Department of Finance estimated federal transfers to be $98 billion for FY 2015–16. When these federal dollars are included, the entire state budget in FY 2015–16 is actually close to *$266 billion*.

The state relies on several major categories of taxes, all of which are highly sensitive to larger economic trends. In other words, taxes rise and fall with the economy, creating unpredictable swings in tax collection. **Personal income taxes** represent the greatest portion of state revenues in California (as they do for virtually all states), totaling $77.7 billion in FY 2015–16, *two-thirds* of the state's general fund revenue. California's personal income taxes are *progressive*, meaning that tax rates increase along with income so that people at the higher end of the income scale are charged a greater percentage in taxes than those at the lower end. On top of base taxes, marginal tax rates (as of 2015) for single or married individuals range from 1 percent to 13.3 percent, reflecting a temporary increase of 1 to 3 percent for those making $250,000 or more, tax hikes approved by voters in 2012 (Proposition 30). Tax rates are also indexed to inflation (2.2 percent in 2014). To illustrate how this works, a single person making $15,000 would pay a base tax of $77.49, plus a 2 percent "marginal rate" on the amount over $7,749, for a tax bill totaling $222.51. A person in the next bracket would pay a 4 percent marginal rate. For someone making $300,000, the base tax is $21,674.39 plus 10.3 percent of the amount over $254,250, for a total of $25,810.46. Millionaires also pay 1 percent extra to help fund mental health services. This policy of "soaking the rich" means that California relies disproportionately on higher-income taxpayers to fill its coffers, although taxpayers can receive various exemptions and credits to offset the total they owe. In fact, in 2012, some 2,472 Californian taxpayers with incomes of over $200,000 paid no state income tax because of the deductions, credits, or tax breaks they were allowed to take.[2] Even so, in 2012 the top 1 percent of personal income tax filers paid more than half of all income taxes in California.

Retail sales and use taxes are the second-largest source of California's income, accounting for almost one-third of the state's general fund revenue (23.4 percent of total revenues). Sales are anticipated to bring in $38 billion in taxes in FY 2015–16, an amount based on the base state sales tax rate of 7.5 percent, a rate that voters temporarily raised 0.25 percent through Prop 30 to help fund education. Of the taxes on every dollar spent, 6.5 cents go to the state (some of which funds local activities), and 1 cent is reallocated to local governments (and extra sales taxes can be imposed in counties and cities). Consumer spending on everything from cars to clothing directly affects how much money is available to cover state expenses.

Corporate income tax revenues have declined over time and represent a much narrower piece of the budget pie (estimated to be $10.34 billion in FY 2015–16, or 6.4 percent of the total budget). A smattering of other sources include motor vehicle fees (4 percent), fuel taxes (3 percent), insurance taxes (1.6 percent), and taxes on tobacco and alcohol (less than 1 percent). The remainder of revenues comes from fees and fines imposed on a wide range of activities (parking at state parks, fines for crimes, professional licensing, and so forth), rental income on state property, and surcharges on energy and other commerce; these total approximately 12 percent.

Apart from taxation, **bond** funds are borrowed funds that supplement the budget and are designated for specific purposes. In 2015–16 bonds contributed $6.5 billion to the total state budget.

FIGURE 8.1 State Revenue, Fiscal Year 2015–16

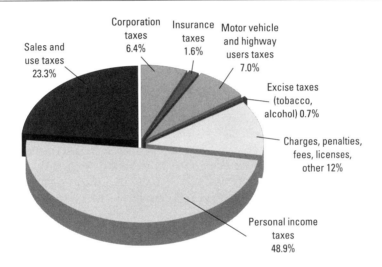

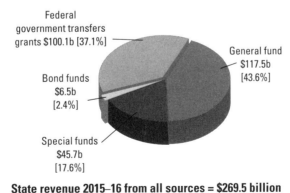

State revenue 2015–16 from all sources = $269.5 billion

Sources: California Department of Finance, "California Budget," http://www.ebudget.ca.gov.

Note: Percentages in top chart are based on general fund and special funds of $162.5 billion (bond funds excluded). Figures may not add to 100 percent due to rounding. General fund of $117.5b includes prior year surplus of $2.4 billion.

Borrowing to finance megaprojects has become so commonplace that the average bond measure is in the $5 billion range, and the state now carries more than $76 billion in bonded debt, excluding $30.5 billion more in bonds that have been authorized and will be issued in the coming years. Most of the debt comes from voter-approved general obligation bonds dedicated to school construction and remodeling, public transportation projects (including a record-setting $19.9 billion omnibus transportation bill approved in 2006), and environmental and natural resource projects such as beach restoration or above-ground water storage. These measures veer sharply from the "pay-as-you-go" schemes typically used to finance large infrastructure projects in the past. Unfortunately, bonds will cost about twice their "face value" in the long run because of compounded interest, though the total cost is lower if inflation is taken into account, and if lower interest rates can be obtained. The state's credit ratings (assigned by the nation's independent credit-rating agencies) dictate the interest rates: dismal credit ratings force the state to borrow at higher interest rates, adding billions more to the state's bond repayment obligations; higher credit ratings translate into lower interest rates. In the first half of 2015, the controller relied on improved credit ratings to renegotiate terms for six bonds, saving taxpayers $1.79 billion over the life of those bonds.[3]

Mechanics of Budgeting: Expenditures, Deficits, and Debt

The state commits to a spending plan before it knows how much will actually arrive in the state coffers. Legislative and Department of Finance analysts do their best to predict how much unemployment benefits, welfare, housing assistance, health coverage, and a host of other services will be needed, but the costs of these services depend on how the economic winds blow. A struggling economy typically means that more residents lose jobs and pay less income taxes; financially distressed consumers also spend less, so the state's sales tax collections falter. Meanwhile, the state has already committed to a spending plan, but government expenses in the form of unemployment checks, health coverage, and other social services spike during economic hard times, and these imbalances translate into billions of dollars that policymakers cannot quickly replace. In one year alone (FY 2008–09), the state's collections for three major taxes—personal income, retail sales, and corporate—declined $12.1 billion,[4] and as already mentioned, in FY 2014–15 the state underestimated revenues by $10.7 billion, ending the year with a surplus.

When expenses exceed revenues, **deficits** result. Legislators and the governor must return to the negotiating table to "close the budget gap," which they can accomplish through reducing benefit checks, cutting state workers' salaries and/or benefits, eliminating or reducing services, changing tax policies, borrowing, deferring payments to schools or other government agencies, or any combination of these. Elected officials have relied on all available options, including borrowing billions to cover portions of the deficit during the 2000s, deferrals, and "borrowing" from the state's other accounts, such as those dedicated to schools—about $35 billion, a large chunk of what Governor Brown has called the state's "wall of debt" (see Table 8.1). State officials also sliced state programs by billions of dollars (more than $14 billion in cuts negotiated in spring 2011 alone) and resorted to "gimmicks" such as unrealistically assuming a much higher employment rate. Governor Brown rejected some of these tactics in June 2011 by vetoing the budget for the first time in state history, calling it "unbalanced" and citing "legally questionable maneuvers, costly borrowing and unrealistic savings."[5] In 2013 the state hit a milestone when Brown erased a long-term structural deficit, which refers to a built-in imbalance between the amounts the state spends and collects.

TABLE 8.1 California in Debt (as of end of FY 2014–15)

California carries several types of debt. **General obligation bonds** or lease-revenue bonds generally cover investments in infrastructure that shape the quality of life and commerce, such as better roads and abundant water supplies. When times got tough in the late 2000s, to cover general fund expenses the state "raided" special accounts and also deferred payments that had been guaranteed to schools with promises to repay what it borrowed. That kind of **budgetary borrowing** amounted to a $35 billion "wall of debt" in 2011, which has been paid off. Then there are **unfunded liabilities**: promises made to future retirees in labor contracts, for example; they are the hardest to tame. The state's overall debt load looms large.

Category	Description	Main types	Amounts owed
Bond debt	Long-term loans to cover infrastructure that shapes quality of life and commerce, authorized by voters or the legislature. Must be repaid in time (often 5, 20, or 30 years) with interest.	• General obligation bonds (GO) • Lease-revenue bonds (LR)* • Other; self-liquidating special funds (SF)	GO: $76 billion LR: $11.4 billion SF: $.7 billion
	*Approximate total bonded debt: $88.1 billion*		
Budgetary borrowing	Long-term loans taken or payments deferred to cover shortfalls in the annual budget (most were incurred in late 2000s, forming what Governor Brown calls the "wall of debt")	• Bonds ("economic recovery") • Internal loans • Unpaid costs to local governments and schools • Underfunding of mandated programs • Deferred costs and payments • Borrowing from special funds • Unemployment Insurance Fund loans (to U.S. government)	~~$27.8 billion~~ (paid) $1.76 billion remaining $10.9 billion owed to U.S. government (unemployment trust fund account)
	Approximate amount owed from budgetary borrowing: $12.7 billion		
Unfunded liabilities**	Promised benefits for current and future state retirees, negotiated and set in labor contracts but underfunded based on obligations	• Underfunded (future) pension payouts for state employees (CalPERS, CalSTRS, UC, Judges) • Future health care liabilities	Pensions: $127.5 billion Health care: $86.3 billion
	Estimated total unfunded liabilities: $213.8 billion; TOTAL ALL CATEGORIES: $314.6 billion		

Sources: Bill Lockyer, "2014 Debt Affordability Report," California State Treasurer's Office, October 2014, http://www.treasurer.ca.gov/publications/2014dar.pdf; California Department of Finance, "California Budget 2014–15, Introduction," June 2014, and "California Budget 2015–16, Introduction," June 2015, http://www.ebudget.ca.gov; California State Treasurer's Office, "Authorized and Outstanding General Obligation Bonds, As of June 1, 2015," http://www.treasurer.ca.gov/graphs/authorized.pdf. See also, Ed Ring, "Calculating California's Total State and Local Government Debt," April 26, 2013, http://californiapolicycenter.org/calculating-californias-total-state-and-local-government-debt.

*"Lease-revenue" refers to debt incurred for facilities construction that will be paid through lease payments over time—hence "self-liquidating."

**Unfunded liabilities are generally difficult to estimate because fund levels depend on fluctuating rates of return over time, human longevity, and unknown future costs. CalPERS is the California Public Employees' Retirement System; CalSTRS is the California State Teachers' Retirement System. Health care costs will also be affected by the enactment of the Affordable Care Act.

What does the state pay for? **Education** dominates the budget, and funding levels for this area are typically locked in through initiatives and statutes. For example, except in times of fiscal emergency, Proposition 98 mandates a minimum spending threshold that usually results in 40 percent of the budget being dedicated to K–12 schools and community colleges, systems that include 6.2 million schoolchildren and 2.1 million full- and part-time community college students. Annual K–12 per-pupil spending dropped precipitously from 2000 to 2012, to about $7,600 per student, but Prop 30 funds have helped stopped the downward slide, and the governor boasts that spending is now $9,080 per pupil.[6] With increases through FY 2015–16, California should rise above its ranking of thirty-fourth in state spending on the U.S. Census Bureau's list, but spending would need to at least double to launch it into the top five.[7] Funding for the two major public university systems, California State University and the University of California, is not included in Prop 98. After billions were slashed from *each* university system and tuition hikes became regular for all 690,600 students, Governor Brown banked on Prop 30 and stabilized funding for higher education, initiating a freeze on resident tuition increases for 2013–17. All told, California spends about $65 billion on education annually.

Health and human services eat up the second largest slice of the budget pie, representing almost 28 percent of the general fund in 2015–16 and totaling $52.3 billion in expenditures. This category

---

FIGURE 8.2   State Expenses, Fiscal Year 2015–16

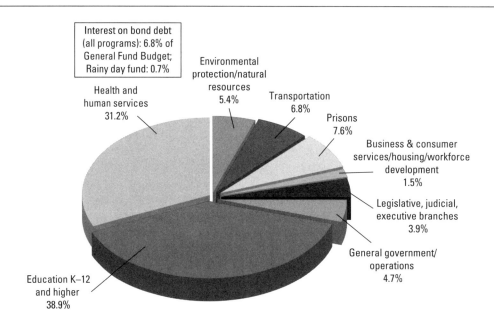

Source: California Department of Finance, "California Budget," http://www.ebudget.ca.gov.

Note: Percentages are based on combined general, special, and bond fund expenditures of $167.6 billion. Total state revenues were projected to be $267 billion, including $162.2 billion in general and special funds (an additional $1.9 billion was diverted to a "rainy day" fund), $6.5 billion in bond funds, and $100 billion in federal transfers and grants. Figures may not add to 100 percent due to rounding.

---

encompasses a range of essential services such as Medi-Cal, food stamps, residential care for the elderly, health care for children, and benefits for the disabled and unemployed. Health care spending dominates. To help meet the state's needs, the federal government transfers billions of dollars in welfare and other payments, which are both coordinated and redistributed through state agencies such as the Department of Health and Human Services. To implement the Affordable Care Act, total Medi-Cal coverage has been expanded to include 12.4 million people, such as adults near the federal poverty level and low-income children regardless of immigration status. The state has recently expanded coverage for dental and mental health services, including behavioral treatment for individuals with autism, up to age 21. In FY 2015–16, $27.7 billion from the general fund will cover Medi-Cal.

The newly reorganized Transportation Agency manages over $11 billion for the state's **transportation** infrastructure, which encompasses Caltrans, the California Highway Patrol, and the Department of Motor Vehicles. Much of the agency's budget is derived from bonds and special funds in the form of fuel taxes, which cover the construction of state highways, rail routes, mass transit projects, and maintenance of fifty thousand miles of road and highway lane miles, all overseen by Caltrans. The

FIGURE 8.3   Full-Time Undergraduate Tuition for California Residents Attending Public Universities and Colleges, 1994–2015

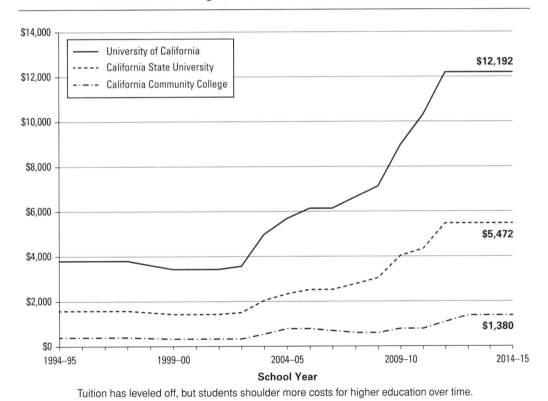

Tuition has leveled off, but students shoulder more costs for higher education over time.

Source: California Legislative Analyst's Office.

governor and legislature are seeking ways to supplement the shrinking pool of transportation funds, as gas tax receipts continue to sink as hybrid, electric, and alternative fuel vehicles swarm the roads.

State government also incurs **general operational** costs: about $6.5 billion is spent to run the state's judicial, legislative, and executive branches, including the state administration, which directs all government programs, from running elections to running state hospitals. This cateogry also includes the courts and lawmaking operations. Other government operations entail a category that includes running the state's employee retirement systems (CalPERS, and CalSTRS for teachers), supplying administrative support for independent agencies and commissions, and providing tax relief to local governments ($7.9 billion total).

At least another $13.5 billion goes to fund **prisons**, covering inmate medical care and rehabilitation programs as well as prison guard salaries and operating costs. About $10 billion of this comes from the general fund. As discussed in chapter 6, on average it costs California over $66,000 annually per adult inmate, a price tag that reflects the high costs of medical care and correctional officer compensation. Prison spending is at its highest in state history.

Finally, it should be noted that about 6.8 percent of the budget is dedicated to paying interest on general obligation or lease-revenue bonds, which represent the state's investments in infrastructure. This figure has risen as the state has assumed more debt over time, but it also varies with market conditions, such as the rates at which different bonds were (and are) sold.

Political Constraints on Budgeting

The budgeting process is far more than a series of steps. By nature it is political, involving many factors that condition and constrain policymakers' ability to make collective decisions. These factors help explain how budgets can be late and out of balance by billions of dollars within weeks of their passage, and why millions of Californians are skeptical of elected officials' ability to solve problems and remain dissatisfied with the budget in any form.

Above all, the budget reflects the **larger economic climate**. State governments suffer the same economic miseries when the U.S. economy falters, and rise with the tide when the economy recovers. As unemployment climbs, recessions decimate revenue sources such as personal income taxes ("the PIT") and sales taxes, which happen to be the state's top two largest sources of revenue—quite volatile, unpredictable sources on which California stakes its fortunes. Moreover, the state's tax policies have recently shifted some of the tax burden away from corporations onto high-income individuals who largely rely on earnings from capital gains and business activity. The top 20 percent of taxpayers (those making more than $237,000 per year) paid 89.4 percent of all personal income taxes in the 2013 tax year. *The top 1 percent of taxpayers paid 45.5 percent of the state's income taxes.* Thus, the entire state budget critically depends on the financial fortunes of this small group.[8]

The **political climate** also influences what kinds of programs receive funding and how much. Public opinion shifts, and public pressure causes some issues to gain political traction; sometimes this happens in response to sudden events or changes in environmental conditions. In the 1990s, crime dominated the political agenda; the drought now tops the public agenda. For instance, the 2015–16 budget contained $1.8 billion to address local water supplies, conservation efforts, and drought-related emergencies, on top of billions spent the prior year, and a $7.5 billion water bond measure passed in 2014. Furthermore, lawmakers know who the loyal supporters are, and they privilege some "special" issues and interests over others. Citizens who don't share the values of those in charge will view these choices as wasteful, offensive, or just plain ridiculous.

Anyone who has observed lawmaking will know that **special interests** and their **lobbyists** also unduly prevail throughout the process. Not only do they actively "educate" legislators about the effects of proposed budget changes, but they also threaten to use the initiative process to achieve what legislators may not deliver. Because they are usually "at the table" when the language of laws is being spelled out, their concerns are heard and can be accommodated. Business and union lobbyists vigorously promote their own companies, workers, industries, and causes, but among the most active advocates in California are those who work for local governments of the type described in chapter 7, "**stakeholders**" that include schools, counties, cities, and special districts. All send swarms of policy experts and lobbyists to press their cases to the state lawmakers, who help determine how much money they will receive and how it must be spent. Well-organized special interest groups are also behind some of the initiatives deliberately designed to limit legislators' budgeting flexibility. For example, a coalition of educators successfully endorsed Proposition 98, which guaranteed funding levels for public education.

Term limits have also contributed to the tangle by continually stocking and restocking the legislature with many novice lawmakers who lack big-picture understanding of how systems in the state interrelate and how cuts in one area will affect others. It takes more than one budget cycle for a legislator to gain a working understanding of how the process itself unfolds, and much longer to grasp how different constituencies are affected by changes. The ability to stay twelve years in one house may mitigate these dilemmas.

Use of the ballot box, or **ballot-box budgeting,** has fundamentally reshaped budgeting practices throughout the state as well. **Proposition 13** is a case in point. Prior to 1978, cities, counties, and schools relied on property taxes to finance their budgets. When Prop 13 capped property taxes at 1 percent of a home's or commercial building's purchase price and limited property assessment increases to no more than 2 percent per year, local governments were forced to look for other ways to pay for services (now mainly sales taxes and fees), and state government assumed responsibility for refilling local government accounts and funding schools. However, when times got tough, as they did in the early 1990s, the state substantially changed the way it allocated education funds, resulting in the redirection of yet more revenues away from local governments. Since then, state lawmakers have adopted the practice of occasionally "borrowing" property taxes from local jurisdictions to pay for schools or simply to plug large holes in the state budget. Thus, the burden of low property taxes has been shared by local governments, which have struggled to find alternative sources of revenue, and the state government, which must borrow to meet its obligations to fund local governments and schools when the general fund is empty. Governor Brown has accelerated his plan to erase indebtedness to local governments that accrued through unfunded mandates and deferrals, aiming to pay them off by 2019. Other ballot measures, such as mandatory minimum sentences for repeat or drug offenders, unintentionally impose costly obligations on the state that drive up prison budgets.

In all of this, **rules matter**. Today the **two-thirds supermajority vote requirement to raise any tax or fee** hamstrings the majority Democrats, which must secure a few votes from the minority Republicans, who consider raising taxes a nonstarter. Unless 54 Assembly members and 27 Senators are willing to hike sales taxes or vehicle license fees, or unless one party has supermajority status in both houses, the majority party needs several minority-party members' votes to implement such increases.[9] California is only one of seven states to impose this stringent threshold. Ironically, however, it takes only 50 percent plus one to *reduce* taxes and fees. Until 2010, one rule mattered most above all others: the two-thirds vote requirement for passing the budget. Because of their power to control the budget vote, minority-party members regarded the budget as their only opportunity to

FIGURE 8.4 The Annual Budget Process

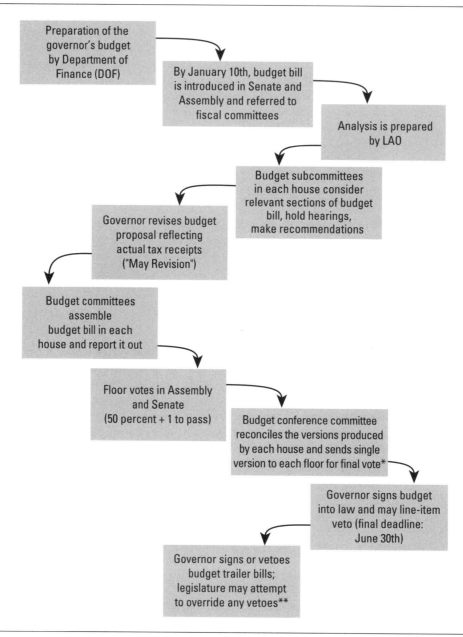

Preparation of the governor's budget by Department of Finance (DOF)

By January 10th, budget bill is introduced in Senate and Assembly and referred to fiscal committees

Analysis is prepared by LAO

Budget subcommittees in each house consider relevant sections of budget bill, hold hearings, make recommendations

Governor revises budget proposal reflecting actual tax receipts ("May Revision")

Budget committees assemble budget bill in each house and report it out

Floor votes in Assembly and Senate (50 percent + 1 to pass)

Budget conference committee reconciles the versions produced by each house and sends single version to each floor for final vote*

Governor signs budget into law and may line-item veto (final deadline: June 30th)

Governor signs or vetoes budget trailer bills; legislature may attempt to override any vetoes**

*More **typically, the Senate and Assembly leaders debate and negotiate with the governor** over final figures, with their staff members working overtime. If a conference committee meets, usually three people from each house participate. From this point, **permutations of the process occur with regularity.**

Leaders in each house help members construct many separate, omnibus **"budget trailer bills" that contain new policies or formalize legal changes reflected in the final budget figures. Trailer bills are processed through the houses, and the governor signs (or vetoes) each one. The legislature may attempt to override the governor's vetoes, but achieving the required two-thirds threshold is rare.

meaningfully influence public policy and force the majority to meet their demands. For years, long delays resulted from the parties' inability to reconcile fundamental political differences (in 2010 the budget was one hundred days overdue), compelled by the minority Republicans' stand-pat refusal to compromise on tax increases and the majority Democrats' opposition to cutting certain services. In 2010, Californians lowered the threshold for passing the budget to a simple majority, meaning 50 percent plus one (41 Assembly members and 21 Senators), thus shifting the burden of constructing a balanced budget entirely to the Democratic majority.

Generally speaking, representatives would rather give their constituents what they want than risk losing the next election because they "caused" their constituents to lose an important state service such as in-home elderly care for an aging mother, or receive a lower unemployment check, or lose health care coverage, or be unable to find day care for a child whose school year was cut short. Thus, **risk-averse politicians** who may want to promote the general welfare but shy away from making painful cuts help drive up deficits. This underlies the phenomenon of giant structural budget deficits. In other words, when times are good, lawmakers are happy to commit higher revenues to neglected or underfunded programs, but find it agonizingly hard to reduce spending levels when revenue sources dry up. Imbalances carry over to the following year, further deepening the hole and underscoring the fact that every budget builds on the prior one. A structural deficit that existed from 2000 was finally plugged with state program reductions, higher revenues from an improving economy, and a temporary sales tax hike (Prop 30), all of which has finally brought state spending in line with income.

Tax Burden: Highest in the Nation?

It is a common complaint among Californians that they pay more in taxes than the average person in other U.S. states. California's ranking in terms of overall state and local debt burden tends to justify that view: according to the state's nonpartisan Legislative Analyst's Office (LAO), the state placed tenth among the fifty states in 2010. However, if state and local revenues are considered as a share of economic wealth or income, the state's ranking is considerably lower.[10] The LAO calls the overall burden "somewhat above average" based on its calculation of state and local taxes: $11.30 per $100 of personal income, just above the national U.S. average of $10.59.[11] The bottom line is that whether one feels overburdened tends to be a function of one's place in the economy.

The statewide base sales and use tax rate of 7.5 percent places California among the highest in the nation (the national median is 6 percent), and because localities can charge extra sales taxes, California ranks ninth for combined state and local tax rates, which are 8.4 percent on average across the state.[12] New carbon taxes help boost California's gas taxes into the highest tier among the states (but Hawaiians, New Yorkers, and Pennsylvanians still pay more in state fuel taxes).[13] Corporate taxes are relatively high on paper, but because of tax credits and changes to corporate tax law in recent decades, corporate taxes as a percent of profits have sharply declined, so many firms pay a fraction of the 8.84 percent main rate. Personal income taxes are also deceiving: the top rate is among the highest in the nation, but as of January 2015, Californians who make less than $28,995 pay 4 percent, which is about average for all states. The rate jumps up for those making over $51,000 a year (9.3 percent, highest among all states), and voters imposed even higher rates on those earning $312,000 or more—but again, deductions and tax credits often reduce their tax burden significantly. On the other hand, thanks to Proposition 13,

Californians pay among the lowest property taxes in the nation, and comparatively low "sin" taxes on alcohol and tobacco.[14] For example, as of 2013, California ranked thirty-second in cigarette taxes and in beer taxes ($0.20 per gallon), and only Louisiana had lower taxes on table wine ($0.11 versus $0.20 per gallon in California; by comparison, both Florida and Alaska tax wine more than $2.00 per gallon). It should be noted that this category represents less than 1 percent of the state's revenues; sales, income, and corporate taxes make up the lion's share of the state's general fund revenues.

These figures show that the amount of taxes paid varies greatly from individual to individual and among socioeconomic classes. It is critical to note that on an individual basis, whether a Californian pays more or less than taxpayers in other states depends greatly on which tax is being considered, how much the person earns, home owner status, regional location, and what goods and services that person consumes. These factors also influence individuals' perceptions of being overtaxed at least as much as their attitudes about public spending and the proper role of government do.

Yet when it comes to budgeting, not enough revenue has been collected to cover all that Californians appear to collectively want. Solid majorities oppose spending cuts to education and health and human services, but less than half support higher sales taxes, and the only category most citizens

TABLE 8.2   State and Local Governments Rely on a Variety of Taxes

Type of tax	Current basic tax rate
Personal income	Marginal rates of 1 percent to 13.3 percent*; additional 1 percent surcharge for taxable income over $1 million
Sales and use	7.5 percent, but an average rate of 8.4 percent,* varies by locality
Property	1 percent of assessed value, plus rate needed to pay voter-approved debt (Assessed value typically grows by up to 2 percent per year.)
Corporation	8.84 percent of net income apportioned to California (10.84 percent for certain bank and financial companies)
Insurance	2.35 percent of insurers' gross premiums
Vehicle license	0.65 percent of depreciated vehicle value
Cigarettes	87¢ per pack
Alcoholic beverage	Varies by beverage, from 20¢ per gallon of wine or beer to $6.60 per gallon of spirits (over 100 proof)
Vehicle fuel	30¢ per gallon (plus 2.25% state sales tax, plus local sales tax, plus 2¢ per gallon UST fee)**
Diesel fuel	13¢ per gallon (plus 9.25% state sales tax, plus local sales tax, plus 2¢ per gallon UST fee)**

Sources: Mac Taylor, *Cal Facts* (Sacramento, CA: Legislative Analyst's Office, December 2014), 17, http://www.lao.ca.gov/reports/2014/calfacts/calfacts-2014.pdf. Board of Equalization, "Tax rates for motor vehicle and diesel fuels, in effect through June 30, 2016," http://boe.ca.gov/pdf/1413.pdf.

*Includes temporary tax increases imposed by Proposition 30 (2012).

**In September 2015, Governor Jerry Brown proposed raising fuel taxes by 6¢ per gallon, but the increase was still being debated as this book went to press. Also, federal taxes of 18.4¢ per gallon are added to vehicle fuel, and 24.4¢ per gallon are added to diesel fuel. "UST" refers to underground storage tank fees.

would slash is prisons and corrections—which federal courts have determined to be *under*funded in recent years.[15] Majorities of Californians say that spending more money on roads, bridges, and infrastructure is very important for California's vitality and future, but they balk at raising the gas tax or vehicle license fees (82 and 77 percent oppose those options).[16] However, it is worth noting that while Californians seem to have a penchant for keeping taxes low, time and again it has been shown that while they oppose general tax increases, they are much more willing to support specific taxes if they are assured the funds are designated for specific purposes—as they did in 2012 when they approved temporary tax hikes to pay for education.

Conclusion: Budgeting under Variable Conditions

As a U.S. state, California faces most of the same basic challenges as the other forty-nine, but as one of the world's largest "countries," its economy is intimately tied to global fortunes, and its fiscal dilemmas are comparable in scope and depth. The sheer volume of issues generated by its 39 million residents is staggering, and the majority of those issues are reflected, though not always resolved, in the state's annual budgets. Above all, annual budgets provide a blueprint for the state's priorities, and the governor's perspective in particular. When one party controls both the legislature and the governor's office, as has been the case since Democrat Jerry Brown retook office in 2010, the budget reflects that party's outlook, and it becomes easier for voters to hold that party to account for policy decisions and consequences.

Budgeting by nature is a rough-and-tumble business. Financial analysts in the executive (DOF) and legislative (committee consultants and LAO) branches must perform the wizardry of forecasting without a magic crystal ball, relying on feedback, data, experience, statistical indicators, history, and tested formulas to predict the economic conditions for the coming year. Political representatives must then square their ideals with economic realities and reevaluate their preferences in the context of what is politically possible. Choices must be made, bargains must be struck, and solutions must be fashioned through compromise. Legislators' behavior is incentivized by majority rules such as supermajority votes that encourage hard bargains at the expense of simple majority rule, or exclusionary tactics that marginalize a minority party if its votes aren't needed. Budget meltdowns, delays, and austere spending cuts during the late 2000s and early 2010s illustrated that effective governing requires rules to facilitate rather than obstruct compromise.

After negotiations have ended, the legislature has passed the budget bill, and the governor has signed it into law, the $100 billion (or so) annual budget is then assaulted by forces largely beyond the government's control. National and international crises may trigger severe and unanticipated drop-offs in tax revenues, leaving the state in the lurch. In times like those, representatives have almost no fiscally sensible ways to deal with such short-term crises because they cannot legally cut services immediately without undermining the state's contractual commitments to people and companies. On the other hand, unanticipated surpluses allow state officials opportunities to fulfill more promises. Although the budget is assembled for the coming year only, its very design conditions future choices by shrinking or expanding the state's commitments, paying down old debts or incurring new ones, spending cash or stashing away funds for emergencies, and/or making investments in infrastructure or ignoring other long-term projects. Whether or not California is livable is a reflection of the annual budgeting process and the set of compromises it ultimately yields, and the budget provides one yardstick for measuring the effectiveness of state government.

Notes

1. All taxes plus motor vehicle fees brought the total revenues to $116.887 billion, of which $1.854 billion was diverted to a "Rainy Day Fund." See the full budget summary for 2015–16, http://www.ebudget .ca.gov/2015-16/pdf/Enacted/BudgetSummary/FullBudgetSummary.pdf.

2. William Chen, "Who Pays Taxes in California?" California Budget and Policy Center, April 2015, http://calbudgetcenter.org/wp-content/uploads/Who-Pays-Taxes-in-CA_Issue-Brief_04.14.2015.pdf.

3. State Controller's Office, "News Release: Chiang Refinances $1 Billion in State Bonds," April 22, 2015, http://www.treasurer.ca.gov/news/releases/2015/20150422.asp.

4. California State Controller's Office, "Statement of General Fund Cash Receipts and Disbursements," press release, July 2009, http://www.sco.ca.gov/Press-Releases/2009/07-09summary.pdf.

5. Shane Goldmacher and Anthony York, "Governor Vetoes 'Unbalanced' State Budget," *Los Angeles Times,* June 17, 2011, http://articles.latimes.com/2011/jun/17/local/la-me-0617-state-budget-20110617.

6. Mac Taylor, *Cal Facts* (Sacramento, CA: Legislative Analyst's Office, December 2014), http://www.lao .ca.gov/reports/2014/calfacts/calfacts-2014.pdf.

7. Educational Finance Branch, "Public Education Finances: 2013," GS13-ASPEF, June 2015, http://www2 .census.gov/govs/school/13f33pub.pdf. Amounts quoted in text have been supplied by the Legislative Analyst's Office and are calculated differently from those listed in the U.S. Census Bureau's report.

8. Figures are from the California Franchise Tax Board for the most recent tax year available, 2013. See Franchise Tax Board, "Exhibit A-10: Personal Income Tax Changes in Income Distribution, 1994-2013, Resident Returns," https://www.ftb.ca.gov/aboutFTB/Tax_Statistics/Reports/Revenue_Estimating_Exhibits/05312015.pdf.

9. The only exception involves the risky move of including one or more fee hikes in the budget itself, which requires just a simple majority vote for approval, such as when the majority Democrats raised vehicle license fees an additional $12 through the 2011–12 budget without the approval of Republicans.

10. Tracy Gordon, "California Budget," Public Policy Institute of California, July 2009.

11. Based on the most recent figures available, 2009–10, in Taylor, *Cal Facts 2013,* 11.

12. Federation of Tax Administrators, "Table 15: Comparison of State/Local Retail Sales Tax Rates, 2014," updated January 1, 2015, http://dor.wa.gov/docs/reports/2014/Compare14/Table15.pdf.

13. As of October 1, 2015, the American Petroleum Institute pegged California's total state taxes on motor vehicle fuel at 40.92 cents per gallon, compared to 43.15 cents in Hawaii, 44.27 cents in New York, and 55.3 cents in Pennsylvania. California's excise tax per gallon decreased 6 cents in April 2015, but Governor Brown sought to raise it to compensate for falling fuel sales. Negotiations between legislators and the governor were ongoing at the time this book went to press. For a comparison of fuel tax rates across the U.S. states, see American Petroleum Institute, "State Motor Fuel Taxes, Rates Effective 10/01/2015," API, http://www.api.org/~/media/Files/Statistics/ State-Motor-Fuel-Excise-Tax-Update-October-2015.pdf.

14. Federation of Tax Administrators, "Tax Rates/Surveys," accessed June 20, 2015, http://www.taxadmin .org/Fta/rate/tax_stru.html#Excise.

15. According to a 2011 survey by the Public Policy Institute of California: "When asked about cutting spending to help reduce the state budget deficit, solid majorities of adults and likely voters oppose cuts in three of the four largest budget categories: K–12 public education (76% adults, 73% likely voters), higher education (68% adults, 64% likely voters) or health and human services (66% adults, 61% likely voters). But they support cuts in the fourth category: prisons and corrections (62% adults, 70% likely voters)." These statistics are roughly mirrored in past state surveys that asked similar or the same questions. See Mark Baldassare, Dean Bonner, Sonja Petek, and Jui Shrestha, "Californians and Their Government" (San Francisco: Public Policy Institute of California, May 2011), http://www.ppic.org/content/pubs/survey/S_511MBS.pdf.

16. Mark Baldassare, Dean Bonner, Renatta DeFever, Lunna Lopes, and Jui Shrestha, "Californians and Their Government", March 2015, http://www.ppic.org/content/pubs/survey/S_315MBS.pdf.

CHAPTER 9

Political Parties, Elections, and Campaigns

Political scientist E. E. Schattschneider wrote in 1942 that "modern democracies are unthinkable save in terms of political parties,"[1] and the same can be said of elections. Without parties, the scale and scope of conflict produced by countless unorganized groups would be unmanageable. Without elections, citizens would lack the means to hold their representatives accountable. Through both parties and elections, diverse interests are voiced, aggregated, and translated into policy.

Many Californians remain unconvinced. Almost three-quarters of voters believe that state government is run by a few big interests, and strong majorities across parties think they make better public policy decisions than elected officials do.[2] Most voters have faith in an initiative process that allows them to bypass a state government they generally despise—although less than half have confidence in their fellow voters when it comes to making public policy at the ballot box. The "no party preference" or independent voter category is the only one to have climbed upward since 1980, surpassing the 20 percent mark in 2009. Increasing percentages of college-educated and younger people (ages 18 to 34) refuse to affiliate with either of the two major parties. Voter turnout consistently remains low among Latinos, the state's largest ethnic group; although they are 34 percent of the state population, only 17 percent are eligible, likely voters.[3]

Political communities define themselves by how they use parties and elections, and in California, these institutions reflect an antigovernment political culture and a strong independent streak. Furthermore, an **east-west divide** has formed along liberal-conservative lines, whereby the more urbanized and suburbanized coastal regions are heavily liberal to moderate and trend Democratic, and rural, inland counties are much more

MAP 9.1 California's East-West Partisan Divide

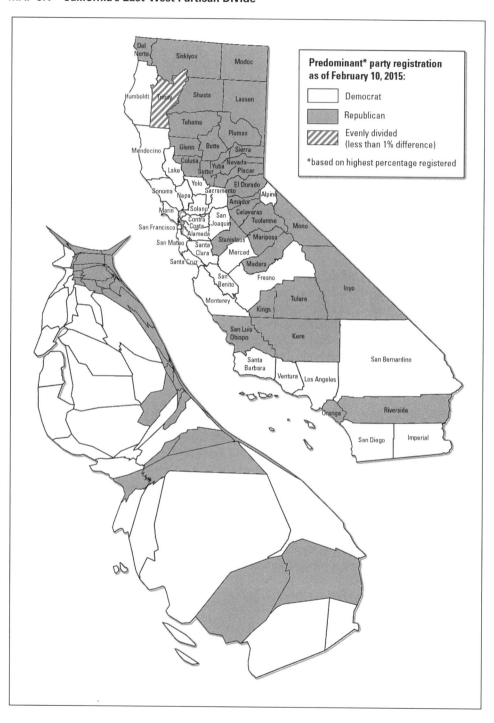

Predominant* party registration as of February 10, 2015:

- Democrat
- Republican
- Evenly divided (less than 1% difference)

*based on highest percentage registered

FIGURE 9.1 Party Registration in Presidential Election Years, 1924–2012

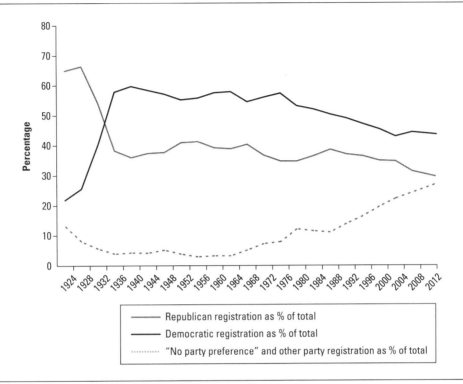

Source: California Secretary of State, "Report of Registration," November 2012.

Note: Percentages are based on numbers from the closing date for registration in the general election.

conservative and strongly Republican. This active fault has displaced the old north-south divide that is still visible in policy disputes over water distribution (and maybe sports rivalries) but little else. Urban Californians share more with other urbanites today, and rural residents have more in common with each other than urban dwellers; their politics are reinforced by their sociopolitical environments and the ground rules they have laid for political parties, candidates, incumbents, special interests, and each other.

Democratic Stronghold, but Weakly Partisan

Historically speaking, political parties in California have struggled for survival, not prospered. Much of their troubles date to Progressive reforms in the early twentieth century deliberately designed to strip them of their power. Idealizing politics without partisanship, Progressives overhauled election law by establishing new mechanisms for voters to sidestep parties altogether—the initiative, referendum, and recall being foremost among these. Other innovations included nonpartisan elections for local officials and judges and cross-filing at the state level for statewide elected officials (discussed in chapter 2). Through secret ballots, direct primaries, nonpartisan local elections, and a ban on parties' preprimary endorsement of candidates, party members were able to choose their nominees without the blessings of party bosses.

A good deal of the Progressives' antiparty program flourishes today. Cross-filing was eliminated long ago,[4] but the long-term consequences of the Progressives' attack on parties are still visible: there is no absolute majority political party in California, state party organizations remain relatively weak, special interests can affect some campaigns decisively through independent spending, and candidates tend to self-select and draw on their own resources rather than those of their parties. Almost one in four California voters (23.6 percent) lands in the "no party preference" category, having chosen to register with no political party at all.

Parties are far from ineffective in the state, however, and they thrive within government. The goals, values, and agendas of the two major parties remain far apart. Democrats dominate. Yet, on balance, the evidence supports the judgment that California is not a strong party state. This can also be seen through a more systematic examination of four interconnected parts of the party system: party *in the electorate* (PIE), party *in government* (PIG), party *as an organization* (PO), and party in *informal networks* (PIN).

Party in the California Electorate

In one respect, a political party is made up of members who share similar beliefs about the role that government should play in their lives, but "party in the electorate" also refers to the generalized sentiment a party's members share about what it means to be a Republican, Democrat, or member of any other party. It is this sentiment that leads them to vote for certain officials and reinforces their attachment to the party's "brand name."

Seventy percent of registered California voters belong to one of the two major parties, Republican and Democratic, but that number is somewhat deceiving. According to a 2012 statewide survey, a majority of Californians think the state needs a third political party.[5] Because neither party has absolute majority status, independent, "no party preference" voters provide the swing votes necessary to win in general elections, and generally speaking they side with Democratic candidates. While California is commonly labeled a "blue state" based on registration statistics and statewide elections that have overwhelmingly favored Democrats, the reluctance of more people to join a party and the defection of many from the major parties have turned the state's political complexion slightly purple.

In terms of party registration, California was an absolute majority-Democratic state between 1934 and 1989; since then Democrats have made up the state's plurality party, topping Republicans by more than 15 percent in February 2015. Democrats today are first in registration at 43.2 percent, Republicans take second at 28 percent, and other parties collectively hold third place with a combined membership of just over 5 percent. Individuals who affiliate with no party constitute 23.6 percent of the state's electorate.[6] A minority of "no party preference" voters actually consider themselves politically independent (31 percent), with the majority leaning toward the Democrats

(40 percent) rather than toward Republicans (21 percent), even as they profess to dislike the parties (59 percent of independents rate the Democratic Party unfavorably, but they rate Republican Party even more unfavorably at 73 percent). Historically they have cast more votes for Democrats than for Republicans in California elections. For example, exit polls showed that 57 percent of independents chose Democrat Jerry Brown over Republican Neel Kashkari in the November 2014 governor's race, evidence that corroborates political scientists' findings that self-identified independent "leaners" usually vote for the parties they prefer.[7] Slightly more men have registered independent; independents also tend to be young and college educated and are about as diverse as the Democratic Party. Half of them are college graduates, surpassing members of both major political parties in educational attainment (41 percent of Democrats and 37 percent of Republicans are college grads). San Francisco has the highest percentage of no party preference registrants in the state, nearing a third of all voters (31.5 percent in that city/county).

Current members of the Democratic Party in California tend to be ethnically diverse, in the low-to-middle income bracket, and younger than in the past. About one out of two Democrats is Latino, African American, or Asian, and 51 percent are White.[8] About a third of likely Democratic voters have household incomes of $40,000 or less per year, and a quarter of them are renters rather than home owners. Approximately 16 percent more women than men are registered as Democrats.

Republicans, meanwhile, tend to be White and middle- to upper-class, and they count more evangelical Christians among their ranks. In contrast to Democrats, 76 percent of likely Republican voters are White, and 50 percent are over the age of 55, compared to 45 percent of Democrats and 40 percent of independents. Majorities in both parties are college graduates, but almost half of Republican likely voters make $80,000 or more annually (47 percent), compared to 38 percent of Democrats and 42 percent of independents.[9] Overall, these trends mirror those across the states.

About three out of four California Republicans describe themselves as **conservative:** they generally want strictly limited government, oppose taxes, respond more favorably to business than to labor, favor strong laws restricting illegal immigration, and believe that "individual destiny should be in the individual's hands." Those who are strongly conservative defend gun rights and oppose homosexual marriage and legalizing marijuana. About 75 percent of Republicans want lower taxes and fewer government services.[10] California Democrats, on the other hand, tend to hold **liberal** views: 66 percent of them would pay higher taxes in exchange for more government services; they want the government to promote equal opportunity in education and the workplace, they want wider access to health care, they favor pro-choice laws, and they are more responsive to labor than to business. They feel government doesn't regulate or control guns enough (72 percent).[11] There is nearly universal belief among Democrats that immediate steps should be taken to curb the effects of global warming or climate change, compared to about half (54 percent) of Republicans who hold that view. Slightly over half of Democrats say they are liberal, and about a third consider themselves moderates. In contrast, independents are distributed widely across the ideological spectrum: about a third of likely independent voters describe themselves as moderate or **middle-of-the-road**, and equal proportions (one-thirds) consider themselves liberal or conservative. They are about evenly split on raising taxes for more services or lowering them for fewer services (48 percent would pay more).[12]

To qualify as a new political party in California, a group must first hold a caucus or convention at which officers are elected and a name is chosen. Qualification may then proceed either by petition or by registration. Petitioners need to gather 751,398 signatures, a number equal to 10 percent of the total number of people who cast votes in the most recent gubernatorial (governor's) election, and they must file those petitions in several counties at least 135 days before the next election. The more complicated registration option requires that 0.33 percent of registered voters complete an affidavit of registration at least 154 days prior to the next election (or 123 days prior to a presidential election) where they indicate their preference for the new party, affidavits that must be verified by county elections officials. The latter process is difficult to coordinate statewide, but a new party cleared those hurdles in 2012: Americans Elect, which qualified for the June 2012 primary election, was then disbanded in May 2012 because the party was unsuccessful in nominating a candidate through its online voting process.

Registered Parties in California as of June 2015

- American Independent: http://www.aipca.org
- Democratic: http://www.cadem.org
- Green: http://www.cagreens.org
- Libertarian: http://www.ca.lp.org
- Peace and Freedom: http://www.peaceandfreedom.org
- Republican: http://www.cagop.org

Parties That Have Failed to Qualify

- California Pirate Party
- California Moderate
- God, Truth, and Love
- No Corporate Money
- Pot
- The Good Party
- Reform Party
- Superhappy Party
- United Conscious Builders of the Dream

Source: California Secretary of State, "Qualified Political Parties," accessed June 25, 2015, http://www.sos.ca.gov/elections/political-parties/qualified-political-parties.

Party in Government

Those most responsible for advancing a party's brand name through policymaking are current elected officials: the party in government. Approximately twenty thousand officials in California hold elective office; of them, 132 hold statewide office and 55 represent Californians in the U.S. Congress. Governors, Assembly members, senators, federal representatives, and others pursue agenda items that become associated with a party's name through fulfilling their chief purpose: *to organize government in order to achieve their policy aims.* Through their decisions and also by what they choose not to do, those in positions of power communicate what it means to be a member of a particular party.

Democrats have held the title of majority party for more than forty years in both legislative houses. The Assembly and Senate have been majority Democratic almost continuously since 1971, interrupted only by Republican rule in the Assembly in 1995–96. A high degree of ideological polarization pervades the capitol, especially with regard to taxation and spending: Democrats are more willing to raise certain taxes (income taxes paid by millionaires, for example), and Republicans are unwilling to raise them, period, instead insisting on shrinking government through cutting services.

Although neither Democratic legislators nor Republican legislators are all exactly alike, they have expressed strong party solidarity and ideological rigidity over the years, which voters hoped to alleviate through redistricting and the Top Two Primary. In the past, district lines were engineered to guarantee the election of Democrats or Republicans, which led to the election of the most ideologically extreme candidates. The "real" competition took place during primary elections, as candidates of the same party vied for the votes of strong partisans in those low-turnout elections. Despite voters' intentions, however, the nonpartisan, citizen-led redistricting process created by Prop 11 did not eliminate the tendency for districts to favor one party or the other (more often the Democrats). Likewise, preliminary research shows that the Top Two Primary has fallen short of expectations that it would bring about the election of more moderates, but it has not been an utter failure. There is some evidence that in particular cases, the relative moderate has been chosen over the more ideologically extreme opponent, even if the legislature has not noticeably moderated overall. Also, more Democrats have supported business-friendly agenda items, but it is not clear whether that tendency can be attributed to the top-two system.[13] Underwhelming outcomes may be attributed to the difficulty average voters have in discerning candidates' positions, and voters usually resist crossing over to support opposing party candidates.

Democrats now dominate state government, having captured every executive office up for grabs in 2014 and a supermajority in the legislature for much of the 2012–13 term. What accounts for their domination? Historically, much success has come from Democrats' influence in the redistricting process. Competitive districts have not consistently materialized because of *natural sorting* and attempts at *gerrymandering*. **Gerrymandering** refers to the act of manipulating district boundaries to include or exclude certain groups in order to benefit a party or an incumbent. Until 2010 state lawmakers—in actuality, the majority Democrats, in concert with the governor, and ultimately the courts—were in charge of redistricting and tended to draw maps that guaranteed a Democratic majority and few competitive seats. "Bipartisan gerrymanders" were created when both sides agreed to maintain the status quo. In 2010, Californians joined a category of twelve states that entrust redistricting authority to citizen-controlled independent commissions. Under Prop 11, party leaders and legislators are barred from playing an active role in forming their own districts, although they are allowed to plead their cases to fourteen citizen mapmakers—along with every other Californian. So far the commission and its maps have survived state court challenges by Republicans who charged that the commission had gerrymandered districts to Democrats' advantage; a statewide referendum; and a U.S. Supreme Court case where citizens commissions' right to draw Congressional lines was challenged. Other factors help determine the level of competitiveness in districts: higher statewide Democratic registration, the Republican Party's relative unpopularity in the state, and natural **sorting**—that is, like-minded people with similar values tend to live near each other. These settlement patterns have produced a densely populated coastline that is more "blue" (Democratic) and an inland that is more "red" (Republican). Competitive districts are difficult to construct because the mapmakers must draw districts containing numerically equal populations that are as compact as possible, respect

FIGURE 9.2   Registration by Political Party in California, 2015

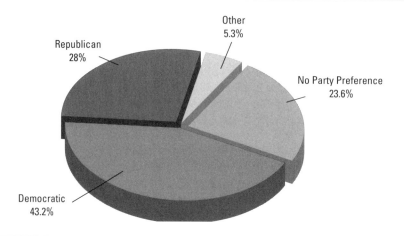

Other
5.3%

Republican
28%

No Party Preference
23.6%

Democratic
43.2%

Source: California Secretary of State, "Odd-Numbered Year Report of Registration, February 10, 2015," http://elections.cdn.sos.ca.gov/ror/ror-pages/ror-odd-year-2015/hist-reg-stats.pdf.

city and county lines, and cannot split communities of interest. These conditions pit practicality against ideals, and, in the end, electoral interparty competition suffers. Regardless, citizens have been swayed by the argument that lawmakers in principle should not be in charge of drawing their own districts, whether or not more competitive districts are created.

The governor's office remains one place where Democrats' hold has been historically weak. Republicans held the seat for almost fifty of seventy years after World War II. They have also managed to secure other statewide executive offices over the decades, preventing Democrats from monopolizing state administrative power. As of the 2014 elections, two constitutional officers of twelve were Republican (two of four elected Board of Equalization members).

Party Organizations

The concept of party also encompasses organizational bodies and their rules. It should be noted that when citizens register to vote they actually become members of their *state* parties, organized according to election codes in the fifty different states and the District of Columbia. This is why voter registration forms are addressed to a country registrar of voters rather than a national party association, and voters are given the option to register when they visit the Department of Motor Vehicles, a state agency. The national organizations known as the Democratic National Committee and Republican National Committee have little to no control over the state parties.

Party organizations are well suited to fulfill another key party role: that of *nominating candidates for election and getting them elected.* At the top is the party **state central committee**, responsible for coordinating the local bodies that exist below it, for strategizing to win seats, and for assisting candidates with funding and other resources. These committees run their respective state conventions every year.

A state party chair acts as "CEO" of the party, and members of the state central committees include current statewide elected officials, nominees for statewide office, county-level party officials, and appointed and elected members from across the state. Democratic members of their state central committee number about 3,000, evenly divided between men and women and roughly balanced among age groups and races/ethnicities. The Republican state central committee has approximately 1,650 members and there are no gender, age, or race/ethnicity quotas. Beneath the major state party organs are fifty-eight **county central committees** for each party, also organized by the state election codes. Further down are low-membership local and regional clubs, which are home to impassioned party volunteers.

Party in Informal Networks

In California as elsewhere, informal political party groups formed through alliances among local powerbrokers also hold important keys to elections, thereby shaping the nature of the parties and their parties' sphere of influence.[14] These informal groups include partisan business leaders, campaign donors and spenders, local officials, luminaries, and retired officeholders who may also participate in formal party committees. Located up and down the state, in and across cities and counties, they network in order to elect the candidates they prefer. Working "behind the scenes," often unofficially with the formal party apparatus but outside it, they seek and recruit candidates for all offices who embody their political values. They identify potentially viable candidates from their communities, invite them into their circles of influence, provide needed endorsements to cue voters, and work to get their picks elected. They might pressure competitors to drop out of a race to clear the field for a preferred front-runner. Increasingly, they are influencing elections by independently spending huge amounts of money for candidates they endorse and to defeat candidates they oppose. These well-networked, ideologically driven groups of elites and party activists have a high degree of success in influencing elections, although their members and power remain largely invisible.

Elections: Continuity and Change

Like political parties, elections are a keystone of democracy, and voters continue to find ways to improve them, usually in order to address what they perceive as unfair advantages held by groups or individuals. Elected officials also occasionally initiate electoral changes, which might take the form of readjusted rules targeting the conduct of parties or candidates. Sometimes those reforms perform as intended, but often there are unanticipated or unintended consequences.

Propositions 11 and 14, already discussed elsewhere in this text, illustrate such outcomes. For example, newly redistricted maps in 2012 forced many incumbents into the same districts, which caused an unprecedented number to decline to run for reelection (six Democrats, nine Republicans, one independent). New challengers entered the fray, and in the end thirty-nine first-time legislators were elected, two seats switched parties, and only two Assembly incumbents were defeated (compared to *zero* incumbent defeats in 2010).

Proposition 14, the "Top Two Primary," triggered a different set of outcomes. For years, reformers tried to unlock primary elections so that a larger electorate (independents) could participate. Through normal **primary elections** for various offices, party members nominate candidates who will later compete head to head with the other party's nominees in the general election. For instance, six Republicans may jump into an Assembly primary race, but only one will receive enough votes to become the Republican nominee for that seat (an incumbent invariably receives his or her party's renomination). That person will face the Democratic nominee in the **general election**.

Until 1996, the state had a **closed primary** system, meaning that only voters who declared their party affiliation prior to the election could participate in their own party's elections. At the voting station, a person would receive a Republican or a Democratic ballot listing party candidates for each office. Independent voters could not vote for partisan nominees, although they could vote on statewide initiatives, local measures, and nonpartisan offices. Proposition 198 (1996) changed the rules but only temporarily. Californians approved the **blanket primary**, a type of open primary, in which all registered voters could vote for any candidate. In 1998, primary election voters were given a single ballot listing each office and every possible candidate for it, just as in a general election. Two years later, the U.S. Supreme Court ruled the scheme an unconstitutional violation of political parties' First Amendment right to free association. A **modified closed primary** took its place, and independents' votes counted if a party allowed it.

In June 2010, California voters decided again to switch to a system that resembles an **open primary**. In exchange for his vote to pass the budget in 2009, Republican senator Abel Maldonado demanded the legislature place a constitutional amendment on the ballot creating a nonpartisan **"top-two candidate"** voter preference election, in which any registered voter may select a top choice from among all candidates for office. The system is not a traditional political party primary, because even if one candidate receives a majority of all votes cast for that office, the top two winners advance to the general election for a runoff, be they two Republicans, two Democrats, one from each party, or otherwise. Reformers hoped to shake up the status quo by encouraging the election of moderate candidates who would need to appeal to a wider electorate and discouraging the election of ideologically polarizing lawmakers; they also sought to allow greater ballot access. One consequence has been longer ballots, because all candidates for an office are listed, and "wilder" outcomes that have earned it the name "jungle primary." As noted above, preliminary analyses of the first two elections have obtained mixed results about its moderating influences.

Ironically, legislative parties in Sacramento work hard to keep their members in line, discouraging all forms of moderation that undermine party unity.[15] Another extremely significant reform has been **term limits** for elected state officials, which have generated a slew of electoral consequences since their adoption in 1990. For one, the game of political office "musical chairs" now extends to all levels of government: competition for "down-ticket" elections such as seats on county boards of supervisors and big-city mayoralties has increased, and pitched contests over congressional seats have also multiplied as the pool of experienced candidates looking for jobs continues to swell. About two-thirds of all statewide officials attempt to run for another office within two years of being termed out. In the crusade to stay in office, it is also fairly common now for incumbents to be challenged by members of their own party—rivalries that used to be adroitly managed by party leaders or preempted by the advantages of incumbency that scared off good challengers (those with experience and money). Ironically, term limits have not affected incumbents' chances for reelection, however; officeholders continue to be reelected at near-perfect rates. Modifications to term limits affecting officeholders elected after 2010 will likely suppress the rate of turnover (they can now stay up to twelve years total in one or either house), although the goal of staying in public office will continue to motivate individuals to run when new opportunities arise.

Special elections to fill vacant seats are commonplace due to term limits, as politicians leave one office for another that opens up. The "domino effect" occurs when a state senator runs for an open U.S. Congress seat and a member of the Assembly then runs for the subsequently vacated state Senate seat; this then creates a third election needed to fill the empty Assembly position, and so on down the line. Between January 2011 and June 2015, twenty-six stand-alone special primary and runoff elections were held to fill congressional or state legislative seats, most of which were vacated by ambitious elected officials. Candidates who win a special election with over 50 percent of the vote are considered elected and no runoff election will be held. Unfortunately for cash-strapped counties, the average price tag for special elections can approach $1 million, and voter turnout for these elections is usually dismally low, averaging *below 15 percent* turnout from 2013 to 2015. Turnout rates for special statewide elections called by the governor are usually only a little higher and cost upward of $100 million.

A few other noteworthy reforms continue to reshape California elections. First, the failings of punch-card systems laid bare by the 2000 presidential election between U.S. vice president Al Gore and Texas governor George W. Bush prompted the U.S. Congress to pass the Help America Vote Act of 2002. Every state received millions of dollars to replace older voting equipment with more accurate touch-screen and optical-scan machines. California's secretary of state monitors the new equipment for software glitches and intentional mischief. All counties are now outfitted with advanced voting technology—the need for which is increasingly offset by the numbers of registered California voters who "**vote by mail**" or are "permanent absentee" voters, meaning they receive and submit their ballots only through the mail. Voters are briskly opting for "permanent absentee voter" status; more than 47 percent were permanent absentee voters in the general election of 2014, compared to 16 percent a decade earlier. About two-thirds of the 2014 primary and general election ballots were cast by mail.

One of the biggest technological developments affecting elections is **online voter registration**. As of 2012, Californians can register to vote via the Internet, a service offered in twenty-four other states and D.C. (including Arizona since 2002), plus three more states that will implement their systems soon. To register, applicants can go to *http://registertovote.ca.gov*. If an individual does not have a signature that can be accessed from his or her California driver's license record, then a hard copy of the form that the applicant fills out online will be mailed for a signature. It is too early to discern whether voter registration rates have increased because registration can be done online, but it appears that young voters prefer this method of registering over mail-in forms, so this change has the potential to improve this voting group's historically dismal registration rates. Another change that could affect turnout is **same-day registration**, a process that already has been approved but delayed. If the system becomes operable sometime after 2016, voters will be able to show up at the polls on election day and effectively register to vote and cast a ballot all at once.

Eliminating barriers to vote is a priority in California, and voters are NOT required to show a form of identification at the polls. A new "**motor voter**" law reduces barriers to vote even further: effective January 1, 2016, Californians will be **automatically registered to vote** when they renew their driver licenses or register their cars with the Department of Motor Vehicles (DMV) unless they opt out. **Automatic vote-by-mail** (absentee) ballots could also effectively bump up turnout

FIGURE 9.3 Vote-by-Mail Statistics, 1976–2014

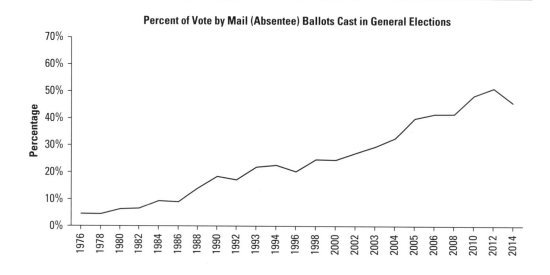

Percent of Vote by Mail (Absentee) Ballots Cast in General Elections

Source: California Secretary of State, "Historical Vote-By-Mail (Absentee) Ballot Use in California," http://www.sos.ca.gov/elections/historical-absentee/. Data for 1993, 2003, and 2005 are for statewide special elections.

at least marginally, and cut election costs by automatically sending every registered voter a ballot in the mail, a proposal the legislature is now developing with the secretary of state. One other important change could take effect for the 2016 or 2020 presidential elections: how California allocates its Electoral College votes for U.S. president. Under the U.S. Constitution, each state determines how it will cast its electoral votes. In order to avoid the dilemma that arises when a candidate receives the U.S. popular vote but loses the election, as was the case with Al Gore in 2000, California will direct its electors to cast their votes for the presidential candidate who wins the most popular votes in the United States. This proposed change will take effect only when enough states enact this **"national popular vote" law** (collectively they must possess 270 Electoral College votes, a simple majority). California was the ninth state to commit to implementing this plan.

California Campaigns

Given parties' relatively weak hold over Californians, the frequency of elections, a mobile population, and the immense size and density of districts, campaigns serve the important role of connecting citizens with candidates and incumbents. Across the state, virtually all campaigners face the same basic challenges: raising huge sums of cash to buy access to potential voters and convincing enough of those voters to reject their opponents.

Former Assembly speaker Jesse Unruh once proclaimed, "Money is the mother's milk of politics."[16] Indeed, incumbents cannot afford to stop raising money, waging what is known as the nonstop "permanent campaign." On average, a successful Assembly campaign costs about $750,000, and a Senate campaign can easily run more than $1 million.[17] But those costs depend critically on how strong the competition is: incumbents running in a general election usually face "sacrificial lambs" who spend almost nothing in their own defense, and some incumbents without serious challengers still spend in excess of $2.5 million "defending" their seats (leaders can't afford to lose, so they might spend *thirty-five times* as much as their competitors, as Senate Pro Tem Kevin DeLeon and Speaker Toni Atkins did in 2014). These sums do not include multi-millions more that outside groups expend independently to influence electoral races.

Open-seat elections, created regularly now by term limits, require far higher sums. Candidates for open Assembly seats spend upward of $1 million on average; the most exorbitant races can cost each candidate more than $3 million. Costs are also higher when there is a good possibility that the other party could win the seat: in the most expensive race in 2014, recently elected Republican Senator Andy Vidak and his opponent spent $6 million, following up the most expensive electoral contest in Fresno history, which had taken place the previous year;

Steve Glazer for California State Senate Campaign

Campaigning for the state legislature involves "retail politicking," or interacting face-to-face with potential or existing constituents. Here, soon-to-be-State Senator Steve Glazer talks with Bay Area students while on the campaign trail.

Vidak's victory denied Senate Democrats supermajority status. Candidates must raise these funds from individuals who are limited to donating up to $4,200 per candidate, small contributor committees that can donate up to $8,500 per candidate, and political parties, which may give unlimited amounts.[18]

Among the most generous contributors to campaigns (by industry) are trade and public employee unions, banking and securities/investment, energy or oil and gas companies, general business (manufacturing, chemicals, food and beverage, tobacco), law, the two major state political parties, agriculture, real estate, health, and ideological or single-issue groups. Tribal governments also continue to donate and spend; the top ten tribes spent over $20 million on state contests in 2014, down from $163 million in 2008 when a tribes-related initiative was on the ballot. There are no limits on how much can be donated to ballot campaigns. In addition, candidates enjoy the constitutional right to spend as much as they want of their own money in pursuit of a political office, but all other donors are subject to strict limits on how much money they may give directly to candidates. Out-of-state contributors are allowed to participate in campaign financing, and they, along with everyone else, must report to the secretary of state how much they spend independently plus the source of their contributions, a point the Fair Political Practices Commission (FPPC) drove home in 2013 when they fined two out-of-state nonprofits $1 million for improperly disclosing their contributors' names.

To clarify these rules further, all campaign contributions and expenditures must be reported to the California secretary of state's office, which makes fund-raising activity publicly available pursuant to Proposition 9 (see http://cal-access.ss.ca.gov). The state's disclosure rules (dictating that information about donors must be made available to the public) survived a legal challenge after the U.S. Supreme Court ruling in *Citizens United v. Federal Election Commission* (2010) lifted a seventy-year-old ban on independent federal campaign expenditures by corporations and unions in the name of free speech. Large sums are now being spent in independently run *federal* (Congressional and presidential) campaigns without strict reporting and disclosure requirements, principally in the form of

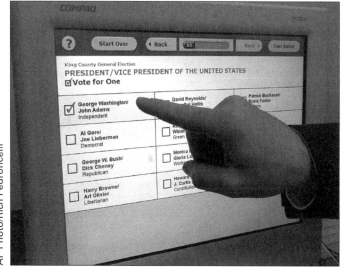

AP Photo/Rich Pedroncelli

The secretary of state has certified a variety of touch-screen and optical scan voting machines for use in California elections. In case of failure or if votes need to be recounted, by law all direct recording electronic (DRE) voting machines in California must produce a voter-verified paper audit trail.

TABLE 9.1 Top Independent Spenders in the 2014 Race for Superintendent of Public Instruction

	Marshall Tuck/Parents and Teachers for Tuck for State Superintendent, 2014			Tom Torlakson/Torlakson for Superintendent of Public Instruction, 2014 (Winner)		
Rank	Contributor	State	Total Contributions	Contributor	State	Total Contributions
1	William E. Bloomfield Jr.	CA	$2,550,000	California Teachers Association Expenditure Committee	CA	$5,520,000
2	Eli Broad	CA	$1,000,000	California State Council of Service Employees Political Committee	CA	$950,000
3	Julian H. Robertson Jr.	NY	$999,000	American Federation of Teachers, AFL-CIO Committee on Political Education	DC	$250,000
4	Doris Fisher	CA	$950,000	PACE of California School Employees Association Local, State, Federal Candidates	CA	$225,000
5	Michael R. Bloomberg	NY	$500,000	California Federation of Teachers COPE	CA	$190,000
6	Powell Jobs, Laurene; including Emerson Collective LLC	CA	$500,000	Faculty for our University's Future, a committee sponsored by the California Faculty Association	CA	$115,000
7	Carrie Penner	CA	$500,000	Service Employees International Union local 1000	CA	$100,000
8	Alice L. Walton	AR	$450,000	SEIU Local 99 Los Angeles City and County School Employees Union	CA	$50,000
9	Cyrus Hadidi	CA	$300,000	American Federation of State, County and Municipal Employees, AFL-CIO	CA	$50,000
10	John and Laura Arnold	NJ	$300,000	Standing Committee on Political Education of the California Labor Federation AFL-CIO	CA	$50,000
11	–			American Federation of State, County & Municipal Employees—CA People	CA	$50,000
12	–			Committee for Working Families, sponsored by the California Labor Federation, AFL-CIO	CA	$50,000
TOTAL			**$8,049,000**			**$7,600,000**

Source: FPPC, "Top Contributors to Committees Formed to Support or Oppose State Candidates (Independent Expenditure Committees), November 2014 Election." http://fppc.ca.gov/TopContributors/past_elections/nov2014/candidatenov.html.

mass mailings and television and radio ads designed to defeat or endorse candidates. However, in California, large sums could already be spent independently on state elections, so these were minimally affected by *Citizens United*.

Why do candidates require colossal amounts of campaign cash? In California's populous districts, paid media are the only realistic way to reach large numbers of potential voters. Advertising is especially pricey in urban media markets already crowded with commercial ads. Most candidates in the state invest heavily in this type of **wholesale campaigning**, or indirectly contacting voters through the airwaves and direct mail.

This is not to say that knocking on doors, attending community events, and "pressing the flesh"—types of **retail campaigning** that require a comfortable pair of shoes rather than large amounts of campaign cash—are unimportant in modern campaigns. Personal contact is particularly beneficial in local contests in which friends and neighbors help turn out the vote.

Professional campaign managers and consultants help candidates build efficient money-raising machines by coordinating other critical aspects of successful campaigns: access to donors, polling data, media buys, social media, targeted messages, and volunteers. Still, money isn't everything, even in statewide elections: in her losing gubernatorial contest with Jerry Brown, Republican candidate Meg Whitman spent a total of $178.5 million, or $43.25 per vote, compared to Brown's $36.7 million, or $6.75 per vote. Whitman, former president and CEO of eBay, spent $144 million of her own fortune on the race.

Conclusion: A Complex Electorate

Parties, elections, and campaigns have been the instruments of change and the targets of reform. Historical disdain for parties lingers in California's state election codes and permeates the conduct of elections, surfacing in initiatives that seek to empower individuals over organizations, such as Proposition 14, the "Top Two Primary," which reformed primary elections by opening them to all voters, regardless of political party affiliation. It is also manifested in relatively weak formal party organizations, active informal party organizations, and ever-increasing numbers of independents.

Political parties are far from dormant, however, and the strident partisanship that is displayed at times by legislators accentuates their viability. They are relevant at every level of government, from running elections to organizing government, and they still provide the most important voting cues for the average citizen. The ideological divisions they represent are real, and the fact that Democrats hold a distinct party registration advantage and swept statewide elections in 2010, 2012, and 2014 signals their advantage over Republicans in the state, as well as Republicans' need to regroup in order to regain lost ground. Democratic consolidation of power in both legislative chambers and executive offices enables greater accountability, in that the voters can blame or reward one entity, one party, for the governance provided. However, many voters aren't paying close attention to politics (the topic of the next chapter), and Democrats' consistent electoral successes tend to mask citizens' growing detachment from parties. Voter-related reforms now in the pipeline are unlikely to strengthen partisan connections, but they intend to increase political participation, however incrementally. It remains to be seen whether same-day voter registration, expanded motor voter registration, or switching to permanent absentee voter elections results in campaigns, candidates,

Mailers like these are designed to persuade voters and often are produced independently by outside spenders. This mailer, produced by Andy Vidak's 2013 state Senate campaign, was distributed in a special election race in which more than $5 million was spent overall. Vidak's victory cost the Democrats their supermajority status in the Senate.

and winners that embody the spirit of moderation and citizenship that Californians yearn for, or whether these will bring about the effective governance that citizens so strongly desire, but the abiding hope is that they will.

Notes

1. E. E. Schattschneider, *Party Government: American Government in Action* (New York: Holt, Rinehart & Winston, 1942), 1.

2. The Public Policy Institute of California (PPIC) reports that 72 percent of Californians feel this way. See Public Policy Institute of California, "California Statewide Survey," May 2015, http://www.ppic.org/content/pubs/survey/S_515MBS.pdf. A 2010 PPIC survey found that 44 percent have little trust in their fellow initiative voters. See Mark Baldassare, Dean Bonner, Sonja Petek, and Nicole Willcoxon, "Californians and Their Government" (San Francisco: Public Policy Institute of California, December 2010), http://www.ppic.org/content/pubs/survey/S_1210MBS.pdf.

3. One reason for the discrepancy is that many of these Latino adults are noncitizens. Mark Baldassare, Dean Bonner, Sonja Petek, and Jui Shrestha, "Just the Facts: Latino Likely Voters in California," PPIC, August 2014, http://www.ppic.org/main/publication_show.asp?i=264.

4. Cross-filing—the practice of allowing candidates to file nomination papers with any party, appear on multiple ballots, and gain the nomination of more than one party—was finally eliminated through legislative action in 1959, and a ban on preprimary endorsements was found to be unconstitutional in 1989.

5. Mark Baldassare, Dean Bonner, Sonja Petek, and Jui Shrestha, "California's Independent Voters," Public Policy Institute of California, August 2014, http://www.ppic.org/main/publication_show.asp?i=784.

6. Data from California Secretary of State, "Odd-Numbered Year Report of Registration, February 10, 2015," http://www.sos.ca.gov/elections/voter-registration/voter-registration-statistics/ror-odd-year-2015.

7. Baldassare et al., "California's Independent Voters"; national election data compiled from CBS News National Election Pool poll results reported on CBS Campaign 2014, "Exit Poll for Governor Race," http://www.cbsnews.com/elections/2014/governor/california/exit.

8. Baldassare et al., "California's Independent Voters."

9. Public Policy Institute of California, "California's Likely Voters," August 2015, http://www.ppic.org/main/publication_show.asp?i=255.

10. Mark Baldassare, Dean Bonner, Renatta DeFever, Lunna Lopes, and Jui Shrestha, "Californians and Their Future," PPIC, December 2014, http://www.ppic.org/content/pubs/survey/S_1214MBS.pdf; Public Policy Institute of California, "Statewide Survey Interactive Tools," accessed June 26, 2015.

11. Public Policy Institute of California, "Statewide Survey Interactive Tools," accessed June 26, 2015.

12. Baldassare et al., "California's Independent Voters." See also PPIC, "Statewide Survey Interactive Tools."

13. See the special journal devoted to research on the topic, beginning with Betsy Sinclair, "The California Top Two Primary," *California Journal of Politics and Policy* 7, no. 1 (2015), http://escholarship.org/uc/item/4qk24589.

14. See Seth E. Masket, *No Middle Ground: How Informal Party Organizations Control Nominations and Polarize Legislatures* (Ann Arbor: University of Michigan Press, 2009). See also Seth Masket, "Polarization Interrupted? California's Experiment with the Top-Two Primary," in *Governing California: Politics, Government, and Public Policy in the Golden State,* 3rd ed., ed. Ethan Rarick (Berkeley, CA: Berkeley Public Policy Press, 2013).

15. See Masket, *No Middle Ground.*

16. Quoted in Lou Cannon, *Ronnie and Jesse: A Political Odyssey* (New York: Doubleday, 1969), 99.

17. Based on 2008 and 2010 data; see Follow the Money, "California 2008," accessed September 3, 2013, http://www.followthemoney.org/database/state_overview.phtml?s=CA&y=2008, and "California 2014, Candidates," accessed June 28, 2015, http://www.followthemoney.org/election-overview?s=CA&y=2014. Averages reflect sums spent by winners. For the midterm 2010 election, the average was slightly lower for winning Senate candidates, at approximately $885,000.

18. Figures obtained from Fair Political Practices Commission, California State Contribution Limits, Effective January 1, 2015 through December 31, 2016, http://www.fppc.ca.gov/bulletin/007-Dec-2014State ContributionLimitsChart.pdf.

CHAPTER **10**

Political Engagement

Citizens and Politics

The Greek words *demos* and *kratos,* or *democracy*, translate literally as "the people rule." Democracy is therefore rightly associated with voting, but self-governance requires more than filling in bubbles on a ballot. Being informed, discussing public affairs, and contacting elected officials are essential elements of self-governance that allow a citizenry's will, demands, and needs to be expressed, and are a mere sample of the ways a person might engage politically. Subgroups of citizens with similar interests try to influence the political system through political parties (the subject of chapter 9) or organized interest groups, of which there are thousands in the state of California alone. In addition, the mass media play a critical role in linking residents, interest groups, and government by distributing, analyzing, and framing information that influences how Californians behave politically.

News Sources and Media Habits

Californians know extremely little about state politics unless a scandal breaks, a crisis develops, or an election occurs, and their attitudes, opinions, and beliefs about government are molded by the way public affairs are reported or "framed" in the press. For instance, a protest group might be portrayed as a motley collection of out-of-work complainers, or contrastingly, as honest patriots who are overcoming adversity. Different frames of reference can strongly affect how fellow citizens, groups, and government are perceived.

Television news broadcasts remain the most popular sources of political news overall, but barely. Just 38 percent of Californians get their news from television, a number that shrinks each year as the Internet becomes the "go-to" source for more and more people; already the Internet is the main news source for 32 percent of Californians.[1] Half of all young people (age 18–34) primarily rely on the Internet for political news.[2] Televised political coverage tends to be scant, sporadic, celebrity-centered, scandal-oriented, and big-event-driven, and it appeals to viewers who are voters over age 49.[3] Several large **newspaper** operations provide investigative journalism and in-depth treatment of political issues (*Los Angeles Times, Sacramento Bee, San Francisco Chronicle,* and several other major city papers), but independent sources continue to wither away. In 2015, for example, the parent company of the *Los Angeles Times* bought the *San Diego Union Tribune* for $85 million. Information seekers can look to **minority newspapers** and publications such as the Spanish-language *La Opinión* for alternative coverage of politics, yet even as newspapers continue to struggle for readership, almost 40 percent of all voters still read their local newspaper daily (reported in 2012).[4] Among all Californians aged 18–34, almost none of them—*just 3 percent*—reported reading a printed newspaper.[5] Only 9 percent of Californians get their news from the **radio**.[6] Other sources such as Cal-SPAN, the state's version of C-SPAN, which provides cable feeds of government agency meetings and the state legislature's committee hearings and floor debates, attract tiny audiences. Today more than half of young voters turn to **Facebook** for daily news and information.[7]

National trends affect state and local news coverage and consumption, with **media consolidation** topping the list. "One-newspaper cities" abound following the disappearance of local papers during the past few decades, and most of the state's major newspapers are owned by out-of-state corporations. This translates into far less original local and state-level investigative reporting of the kind that has been pivotal in uncovering wrongdoing or political corruption in the past. Reporting news in entertaining ways, or "**infotainment**," has also entered the mix. At least 8 percent of registered California voters admit to getting their information about California politics regularly from *The Daily Show* on Comedy Central (12 percent nationwide).[8] The trend of getting **news through mobile devices** also bodes ill for investigative journalism but well for headline writers who can condense news into "byte-sized" pieces. **Tweeted** or **texted** information tends to be shallow and lacking context, misinformation can spread like wildfire without the ability to retract it fully, and public authorities tend to "script" their appearances because they know their gaffes could be broadcast on YouTube. More research is needed to determine whether news and information derived from social media lead to a more informed public or whether they affect a person's level of political interest, two phenomena that are associated with political participation.

Despite the proliferation of social networking and expanded forms of instant communication, like other Americans, most Californians do not follow state politics closely. Fewer than half of registered voters (41 percent) say they follow what's going on in government and politics most of the time, and about a quarter do not follow politics at all.[9] Certain groups in California, however, are more closely attuned to politics than others, and their news consumption patterns reflect behavior that has been well documented: younger people of all ethnicities, education levels, and income levels are far less attentive to government affairs than are older, White, more educated, and wealthier citizens. *Almost two-thirds* (63 percent) of Hispanics/Latinos have "only a little" interest in politics or "none" at all, compared to 28 percent of non-Hispanic Whites. Interest in politics is generally higher among likely voters across all racial/ethnic groups.[10] These trends demonstrate that **political interest** makes a huge difference in helping people connect to politics, and those who feel the impact of policies, recognize the immediate relevance of state government, and feel as if they can make a difference tend to seek more information that can lead to becoming involved politically.

Political Engagement and Disengagement

Feeling informed contributes to the sense that one can personally make a difference by participating in public affairs, and this sense of "efficacy" provides a stepping stone to active participation in civic or political settings. In addition to voting, which will be discussed below, Californians partake in a wide range of civic and political activities, though they rank lower than most U.S. citizens on most measures of civic engagement.[11] Studies consistently find that people are not more likely to engage in political activities online than offline.

At the lowest level of political involvement, individuals might indicate their political **likes and dislikes** on their Facebook pages, **follow** a political candidate or figure on Twitter, or join a **social networking group** dedicated to politics or a social issue (12 percent of adult Californians have joined online political groups).[12] They might also **discuss politics** with their friends and family, and just over a third of Californians report doing so weekly, while 25 percent of Californians report that they never discuss politics.[13] Like most Americans, more Californians of all ages still discuss politics *offline* rather than online, preferring to do so in person, on the phone, or through letters.[14] With some effort they might post a campaign **yard sign**, sport a campaign **sticker or T-shirt**, **encourage others to vote**, or try to **influence how others vote.** Higher up the scale, Californians **sign petitions** and may do so easily when electronic versions show up in their e-mail in-boxes; still, easy access has not translated into higher rates of petition signing (nationwide, 22 percent of adults signed paper petitions within the period of a year, whereas 20 percent signed Internet petitions).[15] It takes progressively larger investments to **call** or write **e-mails** or letters to elected officials in response to their solicitations for feedback or voluntarily to complain about a problem or ask for help with an issue or to **boycott** a product for a political or social reason. About 14 percent of Californians have done at least one of these during the past year.[16] They also **attend local meetings** (9 percent), **attend rallies** or demonstrations, **work with informal groups** to address local problems, **work for campaigns**, or even **donate** to campaigns or incumbents. A tiny fraction become **active party members or officers**.

The same kinds of class biases and socioeconomic factors associated with use of news media are found in general patterns of political participation that political scientists have long observed at the national level. In addition to the variables already mentioned (age, ethnicity, income, nativity, and education), home ownership and length of residence are positively associated with civic behavior and activism; retirees and older residents who have lived in their own homes for more than two decades are among the most reliable political participants. On the other hand, while disengaging from politics can certainly be a conscious choice, *not participating* is associated with these same factors, which are often beyond an individual's control. Poverty and lack of education limit an individual's skill set, leading to language deficits, a smaller knowledge base, a lower sense of efficacy, fewer chances to be contacted or mobilized, and/or less disposable time to participate in activities. Those who feel as if they will never be taken seriously will hardly waste their time trying to voice their opinions, and continuing disengagement leads to even greater disparities in skills and high levels of frustration and political apathy.

MAP 10.1   Eligible Youth Voter Turnout, 2014

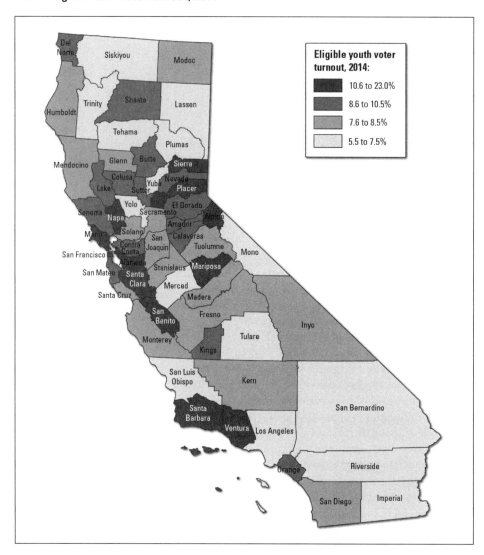

Source: California Civic Engagement Project, UC Davis Center for Regional Change, Table G14-1: California Eligible Voter Turnout by Age: 2014 General Election.

Of all these variables, **race/ethnicity** and **nativity** (whether one was born in the United States) are the strongest predictors of political nonparticipation and help explain why participation rates in California generally lag behind the rest of the nation. California contains disproportionately large Latino and Asian populations with high percentages born elsewhere, and they are less inclined to discuss politics and to participate politically than are others. They are also less likely to register to vote, the topic of the next section.[17]

FIGURE 10.1 Party Registration by Race and Ethnicity, 2015

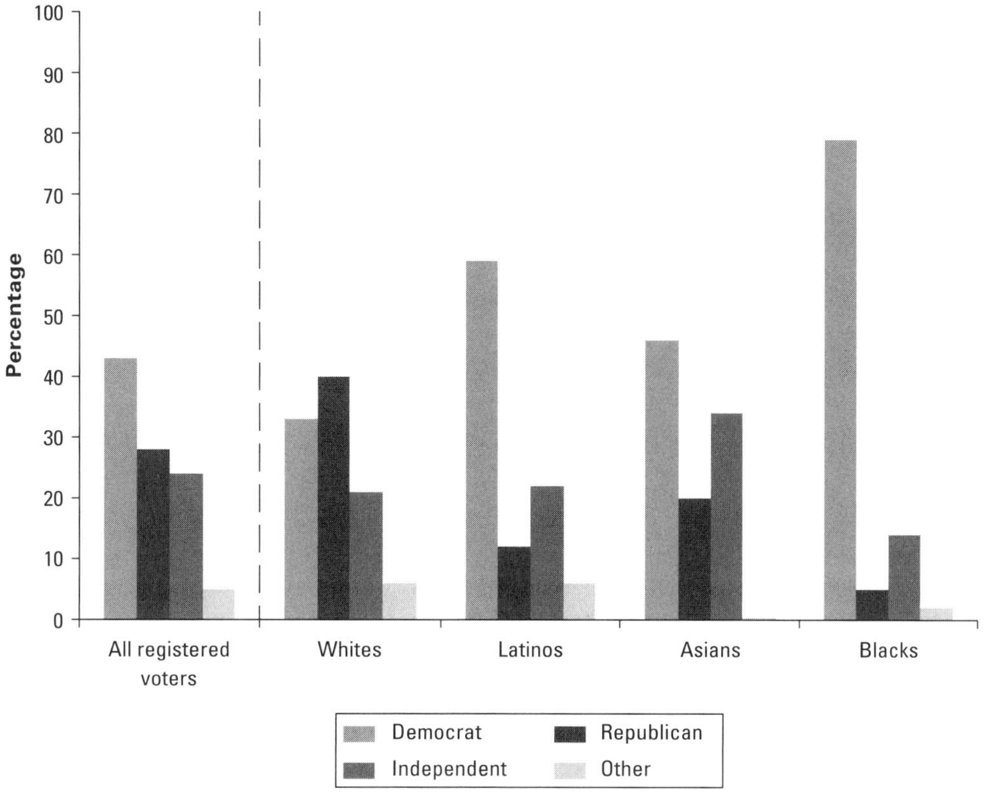

Bar chart showing percentage of party registration (Democrat, Republican, Independent, Other) across All registered voters, Whites, Latinos, Asians, and Blacks.

Sources: Combined data from Public Policy Institute of California Statewide Surveys: January 2015 (1,377 registered voters), March 2015 (1,427 registered voters), April 2015 (1,405 registered voters), and May 2015 (1,374 registered voters).

Major Voting Trends

"California's turnout was even worse than you thought," taunted one headline following the November 2014 general election, in which only *8.2 percent* of eighteen- to twenty-four-year-olds voted.[18] Widespread apathy and abstention contributed to record low voter participation in a regular election: the worst in California history. Only 42.2 percent of registered voters took part, or by a different measure, less than a third—just 30.9 percent—of eligible voters bothered to cast a vote. Of those who did, grandparents crushed the other age groups: nearly 60 percent of voters in the sixty-five to seventy-four-year-old category carried the election.

In a representative democracy, the act of voting provides a critical check on officeholders, as it not only offers a means to reject undesirable representatives but also supplies cues about what

@ Ariel Skelley/Blend Images/Corbis

A disproportionate number of potential voters between the ages of eighteen and thirty-four are not registered to vote, despite their ability to do so online (http://registertovote.ca.gov). An enhanced "Motor Voter" law proposed by secretary of state Alex Padilla would enable automatic voter registration through the Department of Motor Vehicles. In-person voter registration drives add names to the rolls, but getting those new voters to cast ballots often requires additional mobilization efforts.

policies a constituency prefers. In a direct democracy, the voters represent themselves and "check" each other by casting votes, but *the majority of whoever turns out to vote wins.* For these reasons, "who votes" in a hybrid democracy such as California's has profound implications for electoral outcomes, policymaking in the public interest, and, ultimately, the quality of representation and governance.

California's electorate is an exclusive, self-selected group. Voters neither represent all Californians nor reflect the size, growth, or diversity of the state's population, and there are several reasons for this. First, among those who cannot vote are approximately 3.3 million legal permanent residents, another estimated 2.67 million undocumented immigrants who reside and work in the state, and approximately 182,500 in prison or on parole.[19] Second, about one of four adults who are eligible to vote don't register; this equates to more than 6 million people who are not among what the Public Policy Institute of California calls the state's "exclusive electorate." Those who are not registered to vote differ from the pool of registered voters in several significant ways: more are renters (63 percent of all unregistered potential voters), have only a high school diploma or less (68 percent), and are racial or ethnic minorities (77 percent).[20] They make

less money overall than those who vote: 70 percent of unregistered, voting-eligible adults make under $40,000 a year.[21] Not registering to vote largely accounts for the low Latino vote share in comparison to that of Whites. A U.S. Supreme Court case slated for 2016 could scramble the political landscape as they consider whether to count non-citizens for the purposes of drawing district boundaries, or in essence, determine which people "matter" in elections that determine political representation.

Third, not all eligible voters vote in every election. Presidential elections combined with supercharged ballot issues such as the legalization of marijuana lure many more voters than off-year midterm elections, special elections, or primaries, which draw far fewer voters but more loyal partisans. Turnout over the past four presidential elections averaged 75 percent of all registered voters, and a much lower percentage—56 percent—of all *eligible* voters (2000–2012). Turnout sinks in the off-year elections, averaging 52 percent of all registered voters (for the past four midterm elections, 2002 to 2014), or just *37.5 percent* of all those eligible to vote. Stand-alone municipal elections obtain gravely low turnout rates, usually ranging between 15 percent and 35 percent of registered voters. On the other hand, the revved-up presidential election of 2008 that resulted in the election of Barack Obama and the passage of Prop 8, the constitutional amendment defining marriage as between a man and a woman (invalidated in 2013), drew out 79.4 percent of registered voters (or 59.2 percent of those eligible to vote), one of the highest turnouts since the mid-1970s.

Fourth, among those who actually vote, different combinations of voters produce different electoral outcomes. For instance, voters "grouped" into Assembly districts choose candidates who tend to reflect their characteristics and preferences, and, as a result, elected legislators resemble those localized voters. Initiative voters, on the other hand, hail from the entire state, and they reflect a different set of characteristics and preferences. The same is true for governors and statewide executives, whose constituency is the entire state. Fifth, the phenomenon of "roll-off" means that many voters cast their ballots only for the "big-ticket" offices such as president, the races that appear first, skipping lower offices and ballot measures located further down the ballot, often because they do not feel informed enough to vote on them or because they view "down-ticket" items or offices as unimportant. Fewer

FIGURE 10.2 Racial/Ethnic Makeup of California's Likely Voters

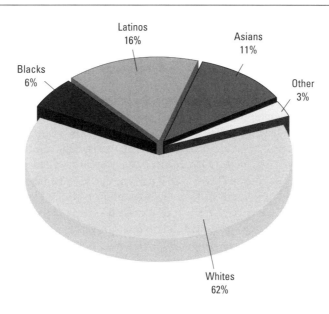

Source: Mark Baldassare, Dean Bonner, and Jui Shrestha, "California Voter and Party Profiles," Public Policy Institute of California, August 2014, http://www.ppic.org/content/pubs/jtf/JTF_VoterProfilesJTF.pdf.

people actually choose the officials who are geographically closest to them, either because they don't reach the end of their ballots or because the many candidates for local offices remain unrecognizable.

Who are California's likely voters? Non-Hispanic Whites total just under 40 percent of California's resident population, but they constitute close to *two-thirds* of all voters, who also tend to be slightly older, U.S.-born, and more conservative than nonvoters. Other important vote predictors are **age** (younger residents are more likely to be Latino, and both of these groups vote at the lowest rates), **nativity** (native-born residents are more likely to vote than foreign-born citizens), **education** (more highly educated individuals vote more), **home ownership** (renters are far less likely to vote), and **income** (the higher the income, the more likely one is to vote). Clearly, the "haves" outshout the "have-nots" in elections.

As with other forms of political participation, differences in turnout are also related to variables such as **time pressures** (nearly 20 percent of Californians as well as all Americans report being "too busy" or having conflicting work or school schedules, which may be related to the 6 percent of Californians who simply forgot to return their absentee ballots on time[22]) and **disposable time** (most nonvoters work more than forty hours per week, and it takes time to become educated about the issues and candidates and to vote). Structural factors also matter greatly, including **registration requirements** (see chapter 9 for pending changes to the state's election and voter registration systems), **timing of elections**, and the **perceived importance** of a given election. **Political interest** and **beliefs about government** are significant predictors of voting: two out of three nonvoters and infrequent voters believe that politics is controlled by special interests, and many of them find no candidates to believe in.[23] Having friends and family who value voting, or **living in a "pro-voting" culture**, also matters: two-thirds of those who speak Spanish and rarely vote also say that their friends hardly ever talk about politics.

Almost all of these characteristics are at least indirectly related to race/ethnicity and go a long way in explaining the large voting-related disparities that exist among groups. Nearly 40 percent of Californians are Latino, but they represent less than 20 percent of voters—the lowest turnout among all major racial and ethnic groups.[24] Stated differently, more than 70 percent of eligible Latinos didn't participate in the 2014 midterm election, compared to 51 percent of non-Hispanic Whites who failed to cast ballots.[25] In the presidential election two years earlier, the gap was almost identical, although more people showed up to vote overall.[26] Latinos participate at lower rates than their population numbers would predict, and the same is true for Asian Americans, a trend that was less pronounced in the 2012 presidential election than it was in the midterm elections two years later. For instance, Latinos' votes were 19.7 percent of all those cast in California in 2012, but based on eligible voters it should have been closer to 26.3 percent that year, still far below their 34 percent of the adult population and 39 percent share of the population overall.[27] Eligible African American voters tend to cast a high percentage of votes in relationship to their share of the population.

Finally, different groups of voters represent different sets of values and priorities, determine who gets elected and who loses, and control which initiatives pass or not. Those who cast ballots generally hold distinctly different views about the proper role of government than those who don't vote. For instance, income bias and economic inequality affect voters' policy and candidate choices; for example, more California voters would prefer to pay lower taxes and have a state government that provides fewer services, while those who are not registered to vote would prefer more services and higher taxes.[28] Similar patterns have been identified at the national level.[29] Likewise, among the youngest group of voting-aged Californians (aged 18 to 34), 44 percent believe state government wastes "a lot" of money, compared to 60 percent of older Californians who share that belief (those over age 55 and who are far more likely to vote). The results of low-turnout elections magnify the biases of narrow electorates.[30]

Special Interest Groups: Indirectly Connecting Citizens to Government

Interest groups representing practically every aspect of the human experience advocate for government policies that will advance or protect their causes, and the benefits or changes they seek often extend to anyone who shares a key characteristic—which could be a medical condition, a position on offshore oil drilling, or a business or professional affiliation. An organized group that makes its case to the government about its goal, or "special interest," is known as a **special interest group**. Such a group might therefore be an entity such as the Catholic Church or a pro–gun rights organization, or a set of interrelated businesses such as the film industry. The term *special interest* can also be a vague reference to any group whose members share the same concerns and are willing to fight for them, such as beachfront property owners who want to protect their homes against erosion or nosy tourists trying to access the beach. In all cases, special interest groups are directly affected by public policy, and often they want something from government.

Though special interest groups are often regarded as self-interested, greedy political creatures, most citizens are unaware that they are indirectly linked to government through the interests and goals they share with many of them. A typical California college student is "represented" in the public sphere by a multitude of interest groups, among them the university or college itself; the city, county, and region in which the student resides; hobby-, sports-, or activity-related groups such as the National Collegiate Athletic Association (NCAA); groups based on demographic characteristics such as economic status, ethnicity, religion, and more; health-related groups focused on chronic conditions such as diabetes; values-based associations concerned with rights, the environment, moral issues; and too many more to name. That student might also be linked to politics through employment or a parent's affiliation with a trade association for professionals such as the 170,000-member California Association of Realtors, which facilitates state licensing requirements and advocates for laws and tax policies that will affect real estate agents or their clients, or a labor union, such as the mighty California Correctional Peace Officers Association (CCPOA), which represents more than thirty thousand prison guards and parole officers. If that student comes from a family that owns a business, then the California Chamber of Commerce, which represents almost thirteen thousand California businesses both large and small (see Box 10.1), offers a symbiotic connection to politics.

TABLE 10.1   Top Fifteen Spenders on Lobbying in California, 2013–2014

Name	Industry	Total amount spent
Western States Petroleum Association	Oil and gas	$13,553,943
California State Council of Service Employees	Labor unions	$9,993,316
Chevron Corporation	Oil and gas	$8,257,361
California Chamber of Commerce	Business	$7,639,130
City of Los Angeles + County of Los Angeles	Government	$5,252,458
Kaiser Foundation Health Plans	Health services	$5,237,233
California Medical Association	Health services	$4,125,207
AT&T	Telecommunications	$3,929,936
PG&E	Electric Utilities	$3,701,041
California Teachers Association	Public-sector unions	$3,605,398
Southern California Edison	Electric Utilities	$3,506,398
California School Employees Association	Labor unions	$3,486,958
California Manufacturers and Technology Association	Manufacturing	$3,451,786
Howard Jarvis Taxpayers Association	Taxpayer advocacy	$3,199,131
Consumer Attorneys of California	Legal	$3,146,909

Source: California Secretary of State, http://cal-access.sos.ca.gov.

BOX 10.1 **The Power of Organized Interests**

The California Teachers Association: Major Player in Education

If education was in the news this morning, chances are the powerful California Teachers Association (CTA) had something to do with publicizing it. As the state's largest professional employee organization representing more than 325,000 teachers, school counselors, and librarians, the CTA is a union that helps bargain for higher salaries and benefits in local districts and provides assistance in contract disputes. As an advocacy group, the CTA is committed to "enhance the quality of education for students" and "advance the cause of free, universal, and quality public education" through influencing state education policy.

Closely aligned with Democratic interests, the CTA participates at all stages of the bill-passage process by writing bills, testifying before committees, shaping legislation through suggesting amendments, donating to initiative campaigns, mobilizing citizens to support measures, and encouraging legislators either to support or to oppose bills. Most of this work is done through lobbyists, but members also are highly active, holding public demonstrations in local districts and loud rallies at the state capitol, organizing massive postcard campaigns, calling legislators to voice their views, and contributing to both candidates' and initiative campaigns. When Governor Schwarzenegger proposed altering Proposition 98 to balance the budget in 2009, the CTA roared to life with a statewide ad campaign attacking his plan to "rob millions of dollars from public schools." In 2012, the CTA donated to and ran independent expenditure campaigns in support of local school bonds and candidates, organized volunteers, and contributed large sums to pass Prop 30 and defeat Prop 32—a whopping $43 million in all. They spent over $20 million in the 2014 elections. The CTA also retained seven lobbyists and spent $3.6 million on lobbying activities in 2013–14.

Sources: California Teachers Association, http://www.cta.org; California Secretary of State, http://cal-access.sos.ca.gov.

Kevork Djansezian/Getty Images

When teachers speak, Democratic legislators—and sometimes powerful people—listen. The group spent was instrumental in mobilizing support for Prop 30 in 2012, helping to reelect the superintendent of public instruction in 2014, and generally influencing education policy.

California Chamber of Commerce: Major Player in Business

Ever heard of a "job killer" bill? The California Chamber of Commerce (or CalChamber) has, and it aims to identify and destroy such bills before they impose new "expensive and unnecessary" regulations on California businesses. What is CalChamber, and why is it so powerful?

Unlike professional associations that represent individuals (such as the CTA), the Chamber's members are 13,000 California-based companies, from local shops to Microsoft, enterprises that employ a quarter of the state's private-sector workforce. The motto of the state's largest and arguably most important business organization is "Helping California business do business." Aided by seven in-house lobbyists, the Chamber tries to help shape laws or administrative rules by educating policymakers about how proposed laws will critically affect California companies. It also donates to sympathetic candidates and officeholders through its political action committees, supports and opposes ballot campaigns through independent expenditures and direct donations, and files friend-of-the-court briefs in court cases, among other activities. The member companies often team up to advocate for or against important bills. The Chamber reported lobbying expenditures during 2013–14 totaling $7.639 million and campaign donations of about $1 million. These figures represent a fraction of what businesses spend to protect their interests in California. For example, the Walt Disney Company pays hundreds of thousands of dollars a year for ongoing lobbying activities, as do other California businesses.

Sources: California Chamber of Commerce, http://www.calchamber.com; California Secretary of State, http://cal-access.sos.ca.gov.

Dennis McCoy/Sacramento Business Journal

Calling attention to business-related issues is part of CalChamber's strategy to influence lawmaking and the regulatory environment. Chamber president and CEO Allan Zaremberg's days are filled with media appearances and interviews, meetings with policymakers, and more.

Special interests are not all equal, however, and some in California carry disproportionate political weight because of advantages stemming from their resources, size, and/or perceived importance. In other words, legislators pay more attention to some interests than others. Among the most prolific, active, and influential special interests in Sacramento are actually **local governments** and **public entities** that carry out state programs for thousands or millions of Californians: public officials and experts working for cities, counties, and special districts often are in the best positions to judge the impacts of programs or predict how proposals will affect the public. Other groups are valued for their important roles in communities, such as **large employers** that provide jobs and subsidize local economies through the taxes they collect and pay, and **labor groups** that defend workers' rights. Representatives have incentives to please politically active constituencies, so any group or business that has the **ability to mobilize voters** and **influence public opinion** possesses significant advantages over those that cannot do so. Lawmakers also pay attention to organizations that share their issue positions or values, and they respond to individuals and groups that provide **support for their campaigns** through financial or in-kind donations.

The political power of special interests, therefore, is largely derived from what they can provide to decision makers, principally in the form of **information, voters,** or **money**. In lawmaking environments, good information is always in demand, and legislators and their staff members crave answers to questions about the potential impacts of their bills. To provide persuasive information, groups hire **professional lobbyists** who can be "educators" about the negative or positive effects pending legislation may have—framing a case that is sympathetic to their own interests, of course. So powerful are special interest lobbyists in Sacramento that they are collectively known as the "**third house**," a reference to the fact that they are crucial players in the lawmaking process. Lobbyists can make their clients' cases in face-to-face meetings with legislators or staff, but more often they do so by testifying in committee hearings where bills are vetted. They also perform research for bills and draft client-friendly legislation for lawmakers to sponsor.

Lobbyists also gain access to legislators by buying tickets to expensive fund-raising events (happening daily around Sacramento and elsewhere) and funneling **campaign donations** to state representatives, making sure that the interest groups they represent donate the maximum allowed. Although state law caps the amounts of direct donations that individuals, unions, and corporations can give to candidates, special interest groups may spend as much as they want independently to influence elections, and lobbyists help them decide how best to spend that money. A record $564 million was collectively spent on lobbying activities during the 2011–12 term, and even higher records were set in 2013–14 by organizations that spent $579 million on lobbying.[31] In state politics, organization, information, money, and status amplify voices and provide critical linkages to decision makers. The well-heeled few tip the playing field in their favor with the access their resources can buy. By extension, the unorganized and the poor are the biggest losers in politics.

Conclusion: An Evolving Political Community

Social media, traditional mass media, and interest groups provide the means for citizens to connect to government affairs, officials, and each other. Californians used to rely most heavily on traditional media such as television, newspapers, and radio for news, but the Internet is fast becoming the favored hub for political news. Regardless, most people scarcely pay any attention to state or local politics, even though their livelihoods are tied more closely to decisions at those levels than at the national level. Being informed helps empower citizens to be politically active, and there is plenty of room for more citizen participation in all types of governments and in politics generally, because even though political scientists disagree about the minimum levels of knowledge, trust, and engagement needed to sustain a governing system for the long term, they generally recognize that "inputs" taking the form of civic involvement generally lead to more positive government "outputs." As it stands, rich corporations, well-heeled unions, and well-organized, resource-rich groups are perpetual, outsized contributors to California's political system and, consequently, benefit from their investments in politics. As the saying goes, the squeaky wheel gets the grease.

The most recognizable form of political participation—voting—carries intrinsic value as a democratic exercise and plays a vital role in linking citizens to their representatives. Uneven levels of participation, however, and higher rates of nonvoting among Latinos contribute to the governing dilemmas of policymakers as they weigh their responsibilities to serve the greater public interest but also respond to those who actually cast their ballots and are politically active. Those who are White, established, educated, and affluent tend to speak louder than the rest. Until the electorate more accurately reflects the entirety of the state's population, elected officials' decisions will continue to reflect the political, cultural, geographic, and demographic biases of those who vote, a dynamic that ultimately constrains how effective government can be. Government will also continue to be viewed as particularly ineffective by those who feel unable to influence it, regardless of its performance. In the search for greater governability, expanding the electorate and raising levels of political participation would be surefire ways to make California's government more accountable and representative.

Notes

1. Mark Baldassare, Dean Bonner, Lunna Lopes, and Jui Shrestha, "Californians' News and Information Sources," PPIC, October 2014, http://www.ppic.org/main/publication_show.asp?i=770. Respondents were 2,003 registered voters statewide, surveyed October 2014; margin of error ±3.5 percentage points.

2. The exact figure reported was 51 percent. "Californians' News and Information Sources," October 2014.

3. Seventy percent of all viewers who watch televised news broadcasts are over age 49, according to the USC Annenberg–Los Angeles Times Poll on Politics and the Press, August 2012. Respondents were 1,009 registered voters nationwide, surveyed August 13–19; margin of error ±3.1 percentage points.

4. USC Annenberg–Los Angeles Times Poll on Politics and the Press, August 2012.

5. "Californians' News and Information Sources," October 2014.

6. Ibid.

7. USC Annenberg–Los Angeles Times Poll on Politics and the Press, August 2012.

8. Mark DiCamillo and Mervin Field, "Release #2382," The Field Poll, June 27, 2011. Survey was conducted on 950 registered voters in California by telephone in English and Spanish, June 3–13, 2011, sampling error ±3.3 percent. The figure of 12 percent nationwide was reported by the Pew Research Center, "Where News Audiences Fit on the Political Spectrum," October 21, 2014, http://www.journalism.org/interactives/media-polarization/table/consume.

9. Ibid.

10. Public Policy Institute of California, California Statewide Surveys, 2015 aggregate file.

11. This deficit was recently verified by James Prieger and Kelly Faltis, who analyzed data from the Civic Engagement Supplement to the Current Population Survey, U.S. Census Bureau, collected November 2009. See James E. Prieger and Kelly M. Faltis, "Non-electoral Civic Engagement in California: Why Does the State Lag the Nation?," Social Science Research Network, Working Paper Series, January 2, 2013, http://papers.ssrn.com/sol3/papers.cfm?abstract_id=2195770. See also National Conference on Citizenship, California Forward, Center for Civic Education, and Davenport Institute for Public Engagement and Civic Leadership, *California Civic Health Index 2010: Financial Crisis, Civic Engagement and the "New Normal"* (Washington, DC: National Conference on Citizenship, November 10, 2010), http://www.ncoc.net/Political_Civic_Engagement.

12. Aaron Smith, *Civic Engagement in the Digital Age: Main Report, Part 1* (Washington, DC: Pew Internet & American Life Project, April 25, 2013), http://pewinternet.org/Reports/2013/Civic-Engagement/Main-Report/Part-1.aspx.

13. See National Conference on Citizenship et al., *California Civic Health Index 2010,* 5; Prieger and Faltis, "Non-electoral Civic Engagement," 8, 18.

14. Smith, *Civic Engagement in the Digital Age.*

15. Ibid.; and Aaron Smith, Kay Lehman Schlozman, Sidney Verba, and Henry Brady, *The Internet and Civic Engagement* (Washington, DC: Pew Internet & American Life Project, September 2009), http://www.pewinternet.org/Reports/2009/15--The-Internet-and-Civic-Engagement.aspx.

16. Prieger and Faltis, "Non-electoral Civic Engagement." (Note that the data were collected in 2009.)

17. Ibid., 27.

18. John Myers, "California's 2014 Voter Turnout Was Even Worse Than You Thought," *KQED News*, February 11, 2015, http://ww2.kqed.org/news/2015/02/11/california-2014-voter-turnout-was-even-worse-than-you-thought. Note that the figure is 8.2 percent of all Californians, regardless of eligibility.

19. Bryan Baker and Nancy Rytina, "Estimates of the Lawful Permanent Resident Population of the United States: 2013," U.S. Department of Homeland Security, last updated March 4, 2015, http://www.dhs.gov/sites/default/files/publications/ois_lpr_pe_2012.pdf; and Laura E. Hill and Joseph Hayes, "Undocumented Immigrants" (San Francisco: Public Policy Institute of California, July 2015), http://www.ppic.org/main/publication_show.asp?i=818; California Department of Corrections, Office of Research, "Weekly Report of Population as of July 1, 2015," http://www.cdcr.ca.gov/Reports_Research/Offender_Information_Services_Branch/WeeklyWed/TPOP1A/TPOP1Ad150701.pdf.

20. Mark Baldassare, "Improving California's Democracy" (San Francisco: Public Policy Institute of California, October 2012), http://www.ppic.org/content/pubs/atissue/AI_1012MBAI.pdf.

21. Mark Baldassare, Dean Bonner, Sonja Petek, and Jui Shrestha, "California's Likely Voters," PPIC August 2014, http://www.ppic.org/main/publication_show.asp?i=255.

22. Pete Peterson, "The Real Reason Why Californians Don't Vote," June 23, 2014, *Zocalo*, http://www.zocalopublicsquare.org/2014/06/23/the-real-reason-why-californians-dont-vote/ideas/nexus; see original table for all U.S. households, based on Current Population Survey, generated by the U.S. Census Bureau, "Voting and Registration in the Election of November 2012," http://www.census.gov/hhes/www/socdemo/voting/publications/p20/2012/tables.html.

23. U.S. Census Bureau, "Voting and Registration in the Election of November 2012," and California Voter Foundation, "California Voter Participation Survey," 2005, http://www.calvoter.org/issues/votereng/votpart/index.html.

24. See Mark Baldassare, Dean Bonner, Sonja Petek, and Jui Shrestha, "Latino Likely Voters in California," Public Policy Institute of California, August 2012, http://www.ppic.org/main/publication_show.asp?i=264.

25. Myers, "California's 2014 Voter Turnout Was Even Lower Than You Thought." Statistics supplied by Paul Mitchell, Political Data, Inc.

26. Mindy Romero, "Changing Political Tides: Demographics and the Impact of the Rising California Latino Vote," U.C. Davis Center for Regional Change, California Civic Engagement Project, Policy Brief Issue 6, May 2013, http://regionalchange.ucdavis.edu/ourwork/publications/ccep/ucdavis-ccep-brief-6-impact-of-ca-latino-vote.

27. Ibid.

28. Time-series data supplied by the Public Policy Institute of California, California Statewide Surveys, May 2004 through December 2014. The average difference ranged from one to four points (in the expected direction; however, no difference of means tests were performed on these data).

29. See Jan E. Leighley and Jonathan Nagler, *Who Votes Now? Demographics, Issues, Inequality, and Turnout in the United States* (Princeton and Oxford: Princeton University Press, 2014).

30. See Public Policy Institute of California, California Statewide Survey (Interactive Tools), May 2015.

31. Follow the Money, "California 2012, Overview," accessed September 4, 2013, http://www.followthe-money.org/database/state_overview.phtml?y=2012&s=CA; Sharon Havranek, "Behind the list: California's top lobbying firms … and their top clients."; *Sacramento Business Journal,* March 27, 2015, http://www.bizjournals.com/sacramento/news/2015/03/27/behind-the-list-californias-top-lobbying-firms-and.html.

CHAPTER 11

Concluding Thoughts: Political Paradoxes and Effective Government

"**E**ffective governance" suggests a good fit between the demands of the people and what their institutions deliver, that representatives understand their constituents' needs, and that decision makers grasp the dimensions of pressing problems and devise fair, responsible, timely solutions that make economic sense. Rules that encourage participation, deliberation, and compromise form the core of an effective political system, and some combination of strong leadership and cooperation among representatives can enable a government to be effective. How does California measure up?

In thinking about state government, how any individual answers that question largely depends on how much that person depends on the state for certain services and the size of those benefits, his or her socioeconomic status, and whether he or she is sympathetic to the party in power and the values it enshrines in public policy. If a Cal Grant isn't available when needed, or in-home services payments for a disabled parent are cut, or one's income taxes appear wildly higher than those of friends living in other states, government may seem downright ineffective. In 2015, a contingent of parents passionately opposing mandatory vaccinations for schoolchildren failed to stop that bill from passing both chambers of the legislature and becoming law; to them, government probably seems like an abject failure. Whether government is responsive to him or her profoundly affects how one appraises government's effectiveness.

From a wider, macro perspective, government can rate high or low on some "big" measures: does it balance the books, and does it use taxpayer dollars wisely? Do representatives cooperate and respond to pressing problems such as drought or a crashing housing market, and do they also plan for the future by taking into account changing demographics and reasonable estimations of an expanding population's needs—as well as their demands?

A few short years ago, predictions of the state's demise rose to a fever pitch as multibillion-dollar structural budget deficits reigned, the amounts of the deficits dwarfed the economies of small countries, and finally mushroomed to a stunning $27 billion in one year. Democrats and Republicans in the legislature boxed each other into stalemates that delayed budgets and policy decisions for months. Observers shared the general perception that California was on the verge of economic and political ruin. Perceptions have shifted. Today some conspicuous improvements must be weighed against problems that simmer on the backburner. Budget surpluses have materialized with a better economy, and budget cuts made previously to social programs that Democratic legislators had wanted to protect are being restored. A gross backlog of infrastructure projects remains virtually untouched. The stubborn problems of unemployment and long-term debt in the form of unfunded liabilities loom large; pension plans remain a hot topic for the cities, counties, and state governments. Yet Brown's 2015 budget pays down other types of debt substantially, and he has a payment plan. Political reforms have also eased some tensions and altered the balance of power, paving the way for one party, the Democrats, to consolidate their hold on state offices—reforms such as citizen-driven redistricting processes that created new districts for the next decade, the Top Two Primary, and Prop 25, which allows the political majority to enact budgets without the encumbrance of supermajority rules. Under the revised term limits law, incoming legislators will accumulate more policy expertise as the game of musical chairs slows from a frenzied scramble to a more measured pace.

These reforms scratch the surface of California's deeply rooted problems, some of which stem from the very design of its government. California's self-styled hybrid democracy splices the power of direct democracy with political representation, and the two coexist in a state of uneasy tension. This can be seen most clearly in voter-imposed laws intended to restrict political choices, such as in annual funding guarantees for big-ticket items like schools and practically unattainable two-thirds thresholds for raising tax revenues. Ballot-box reforms also obstruct comprehensive approaches to problem solving, complicating the job of governing. Ironically, Californians demand strong and efficient leadership from all elected officeholders, yet ballot initiatives often limit authorities' power and therefore the ability of these officials to perform efficiently and effectively.

Furthermore, what was supposed to be a stopgap for keeping legislators in check—the ballot initiative process—is now an overloaded policymaking machine, the gears of which are oiled by oversimplified messages and shifted into overdrive by massive amounts of campaign cash. Lower signature requirements for ballot measures have invited yet more activity. Special interests parade as public interests, trying to drown out other voices in the political marketplace. The initiative process is ripe for reform.

California politics is riddled with other ironies and paradoxes that go a long way toward explaining the current state of affairs. For example, even when things are going well, Californians generally distrust politicians and disdain political conflict, so they continue to reach for ways to take politicians—and politics, for that matter—out of politics; they resort to initiatives like term limits and open primaries that will automatically toss people from office at prescribed intervals and lessen political party control. Disappointment with politics continues, however, because political systems are by nature designed to expose conflicting interests in the struggle to reach consensus, and the people not only need politicians to govern what is effectively one of the largest countries in the world, but also need to organize in order to win, and political parties provide that reliable structure. Nevertheless, many Californians are unconvinced that parties matter, and increasingly they are registering as "no party preference" voters.

Paradoxically, Californians also expect that the public good will automatically be served when their personal needs are met. This may be possible with a government service like public education, a "good" that yields private gains with long-term public benefits, but this approach does not necessarily produce sustainable economic policies for large and diverse communities. To wit, Californians generally choose to pay lower sales, income, and property taxes if it helps their own bottom line and if they believe government is incompetent. Generally speaking, this attitude has led to chronic underfunding of infrastructure and services such as education, health, and transportation that local and state governments must provide for all. The irony is that when infrastructure fails because governments have stretched scarce dollars too thinly, citizens are quick to blame politicians for wasting or misspending funds, and therefore are even less willing to help government do its work. However, voters do tend to make exceptions for new taxes that have concrete, dedicated purposes and when they believe that their money will be well spent, allowing most local governments to meet residents' most immediate demands but often to the detriment of long-term critical needs.[1] These tendencies have resulted in a heavy reliance on upper-income taxpayers to foot the state's bills, as well as a shift away from paying up-front costs and a pivot to long-term bond debt that costs about twice as much in the long run, generating interest payments that place stress on the state's general fund and local treasuries by siphoning off money that could be used for other necessary budget items.

Quite apart from the institutional aspects of governing are socioeconomic issues that determine the political state of affairs—issues that involve 39 million people who place myriad conflicting and ever-changing demands on the state. Growth rates have actually slowed and now hover near 1 percent, yet 300,000 new people add the equivalent of a Riverside or Anaheim to the state year after year. The multiethnic mix of children signals momentous change: 53 percent of all schoolchildren in 2013–14 were Latino/Hispanic; non-Hispanic Whites just 25 percent.

Cartoon by Tom Meyer

Latinos constitute the largest ethnic group in the state, and California is projected to be an absolute majority-Latino state around 2050, just as the population reaches 50 million.[2] How will decision makers nurture the educated workforce that will be needed to drive the state's service-based economy? Will voters be willing to extend helping hands to those on the bottom end of the socioeconomic scale? Nearly a quarter (22.5 percent) of all Californians will be sixty-five years of age or older by that time: how will the state provide for a humongous elderly population that places immense demands on health and residential care systems?[3] To accommodate such growth, the state will need to invest more than $500 billion to upgrade, add, and expand crumbling transportation, school, water, and other systems in the next twenty years.[4] How will Californians be able to raise that kind of cash?

In many ways, political reforms brought California to this point, and political reforms will help transform its future. Yet institutional reforms can go only so far. Rules set boundaries for decision making but do not determine the choices people make, and choices must be based on realistic understanding about government's capabilities if the state's policies and laws are to work. For instance, many Californians presume that rooting out existing government waste would uncover enough revenues to pay for large government programs, as if saving millions of dollars could compensate for not raising billions through higher taxes. Voters' expectations and attitudes about government underscore its perceived effectiveness, but competent leaders who can convince citizens to reshape their expectations can counteract this drift.

California's government faces the same challenges as the governments of other states. What makes it distinct are the scope and scale of the state's issues, a hybrid governing structure in which voters can change the rules of the game for representatives, and constrain authorities' power through reforms such as term limits or supermajority rules that sacrifice majority will to the rival demands of a minority (political party, usually). The issues are mostly the same across the nation, however, and they pose enormous challenges for state government now and for the foreseeable future. The extent to which elected officials can offer comprehensive solutions that stretch across a range of policy areas is another measure of effective governance:

- *Education:* Only an educated workforce can sustain a sophisticated, diverse, service-oriented modern economy. California spends the most of all states on its K–12 students but ranked thirty-fourth in 2013 for per-pupil spending, equaling inadequate instructional materials, lower pay for teachers, fewer days of instruction, and shortages of reliable after-school care and programs.[5] How will California schools bridge the gap to prepare future citizens to meet state, national, and global communities' changing needs? The fastest-growing segment of the population is Latino, but as a group, these students trail behind in graduation rates and test scores. How will achievement gaps be closed and graduation rates be improved? State colleges and universities are still a bargain, but California's master plan for providing tuition-free higher education has been abandoned, forcing students to bear the escalating costs of tuition and fees. How will the state's education funding habits affect students' future job prospects and the higher education system's competitiveness nationally and globally?
- *Immigration:* California's immigrant population is the largest in the nation at about 10.6 million, equating to 27 percent of residents who were born outside the United States. Will voters be willing to extend to immigrants the same rights and public benefits that they have

enjoyed? If not, how might a service economy accommodate massive numbers of low-skilled, unemployed, low-educated residents who require state services to fulfill basic needs, from food to housing to employment? Should representatives push policies that advance assimilation or accommodation?

- *Environment:* Climate change threatens California's basic lifelines. Erratic weather patterns are difficult to plan for. Rising temperatures bring less rain and lighter snowpack, translating into limited water supplies for thirsty farms, manufacturing plants, and homes. Alternatively, unpredictable weather events such as El Niño can produce severe and costly flooding. Volatile weather patterns place stress on traditional recreation and tourism-related industries. Lower rainfall increases the risk of wildfires in bone-dry areas and increases airborne fine-particle pollution; wildlife unaccustomed to higher-than-average temperatures cannot quickly adjust, so biodiversity suffers. Rising sea levels threaten a densely populated coastline and imperil the Delta agricultural region (the source of drinking water for two-thirds of Californians and irrigation for 750,000 acres of croplands) with rising levels of salinity. California's AB 32, the nation's first greenhouse gas emissions law, remains under siege by those who object to the high costs of implementing its requirements. Can California continue to make the investments necessary to bring about a "green" economy without creating a more hostile business environment? Emergencies take huge tolls; the state Geological Survey estimates that a 7.8 earthquake on the San Andreas Fault would cause over $210 *billion* in damages in Los Angeles, and a 7.0 quake in San Francisco would cause even more losses.[6] Could local and state governments adequately respond if environmental crises like earthquakes, heat waves, extensive wildfires, extended droughts, and torrential rains and resulting mudslides hit in quick succession?
- *Poverty and Income Inequality:* The gap between rich and poor continues to widen in the United States, and about 17 percent of Californians live below the poverty line, pegged at $24,000 a year for a family of four. When costs of living are taken into account, it's closer to 8 million Californians in poverty.[7] Without CalWorks (temporary assistance for needy families); refundable tax credits; or CalFresh, a "food stamps" type program, a much larger number would slip below the threshold. Still, many taxpayers believe the state pays too much for safety net programs. What can and should the state do to address poverty rates?
- *Business and labor:* A large majority of California's 875,000 small and large business employers complain about the regulatory difficulties they face, and *Forbes* ranks California near the bottom of U.S. states (thirty-seventh in 2014) in business climate. Unemployment persists. Meanwhile, multibillion-dollar unfunded liabilities, existing mostly as health care insurance and pension obligations for teachers and other public employees, menace the state's long-term financial outlook. How will the state balance its books, protect 13.4 million private-industry workers with legal safeguards while enticing businesses to stay and also make public service attractive to "the best and brightest" who can make government run effectively?
- *Drought and Water:* Extended, severe drought has parched all parts of the state. (See Map 11.1.) For the first time, groundwater usage will be managed under state law and local governing regimes, but it takes time to develop plans. As of June 2015, over nine thousand junior and senior water rights holders had been directly affected by state-imposed water restrictions, and urban Californians were told to cut back usage by 25 percent. Population collapses of freshwater-dependent animals are predicted. Water-dependent hydroelectric facilities that provide 10 to

MAP 11.1   U.S. Drought, 2015

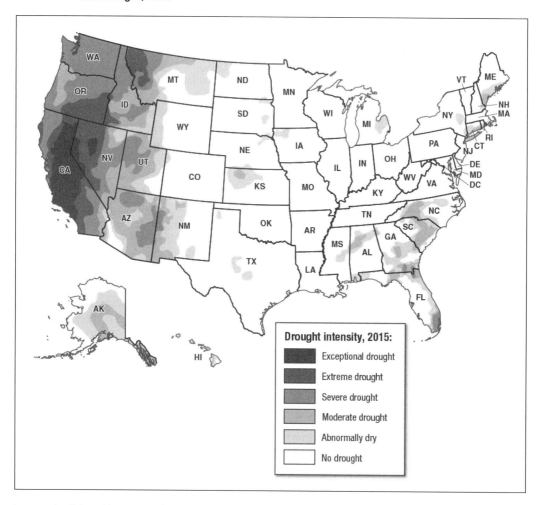

Long-term drought has stricken western U.S. states and California most brutally. As of July 2015, the entire state was experiencing severe, extreme, or exceptional drought. Even heavy winter rains, such as those an El Niño weather event could bring, will not erase the ecological or hydrological drought that has been building for four years. Lack of precipitation in the western region has strained relations among states interconnected by complex hydrologic systems, as well as by compacts detailing historical rights to water from the Colorado River (especially neighboring Nevada and Arizona). Considered the nation's breadbasket, the drought will reduce California's crop, dairy, and livestock revenues by an estimated $1.84 billion in 2015, and multiplier effects bring total losses closer to $2.74 billion plus twenty-one thousand jobs—a measurable hit to California's $45 billion agricultural industry.[8]

Source: David Simeral, Western Regional Climate Center, California, July 14, 2015, United States Drought Monitor, http://drought-monitor.unl.edu/Home.aspx. The U.S. Drought Monitor is jointly produced by the National Drought Mitigation Center at the University of Nebraska-Lincoln, the United States Department of Agriculture, and the National Oceanic and Atmospheric Administration. Map courtesy of NDMC-UNL.

15 percent of the state's power are drying out, and northern California utility customers are paying more for electricity. The northern part of the state receives about 75 percent of rainfall, but about 75 percent of residents live in Southern California. Water scarcity is pitting urban against agricultural users and farmers against fish as the state struggles to balance the rights of people, the environment, and businesses. Between droughts and floods, policymakers have a hard time organizing storage and distribution systems that move water where it's needed, when it's needed, and ensuring quality when water is fouled by agricultural activity, reduced water flows, and urban runoff. A voter-approved $7.5 billion bond barely begins to address water management needs, and emergency funds provide only limited relief to those whose wells are dry. Neighboring states and Mexico have prolonged disputes with California over equitable distribution of water from the Colorado River. Degraded and vanishing wetlands are the norm, as are declining native tree and fish populations and inexplicable bird die-offs. In many parts of the Delta region, where millions of people and animals reside and fertile lands are farmed, catastrophic levee failure due to earthquakes or flooding is a palpable risk. Are extremely costly solutions—such as Brown's proposal to construct giant tunnels—feasible? Will California's leaders be able to craft strategic plans that comprehensively address the entire state's long-term water needs or come up with the money to fix the damages from drought?

- *Transportation:* The nation's highest number of cars on roads and freeways travel California's roadways, which are the most congested in the United States, and they cross more than 13,100 bridges that are maintained by CalTrans. About 40 percent of California's 50,000 miles of highway lanes require fixing, and while Caltrans estimates needed repairs should cost $2.8 billion annually, typically only $685 million is available for repairs each year.[9] On top of a multi-billion dollar backlog of deferred state highway and road repairs, local government officials estimate a price tag of $82 billion to mend the local streets that form more than 80 percent of the state's roadway mileage. Ironically, alternative fuel vehicles benefit air quality but have caused a shortfall in gas tax revenues to pay for roads. New systems are needed to move people more quickly around the state, and Governor Brown endorses high-speed rail that will connect San Francisco to Los Angeles by 2029, but the price tag is nearly $100 billion even as work gets underway in Fresno, and all funds are not in the bank. Motorized vehicles, especially farm and construction equipment, also create dirty air that contributes to serious respiratory illnesses. California's airports, seaports, and railway systems pollute the air as well, an inevitable consequence of being a gateway to Asia and South America. Can lawmakers improve California's air and travel systems by making them cleaner, safer, more navigable, and more efficient, and can they do so in cost-effective ways? Can they ensure the safety of residents as those systems expand; can they get more than 5 percent of the population to use public transit? Is high-speed rail worth it? What will it take to reduce the state's extreme backlog of repair projects?

With an improving economy, small changes to budgeting rules, and Jerry Brown's leadership, conversations in and about California have shifted from doomsday scenarios to what might be improved. The debate is no longer about whether the state is governable, but rather, what can and should be done to make it work better, more effectively, and more efficiently. The list of suggestions remains long, and Californians will continue to chase better government through direct democracy and their elected representatives. The state of California politics is a testament to the power of rapidly changing social, economic, and political circumstances; the cumulative force of historical decisions; the power of culture; the consequences of rules; and the importance of collective choices. These conditions will continue to be at the heart of the policymaking that will define California's future and how well it will be governed.

Notes

1. For a study of these tendencies among Californians, see Kevin Wallsten and Gene Park, "Confidence, Perception, and Politics in California: The Determinants of Attitudes toward Taxes by Level of Government," *California Journal of Politics and Policy* 7, no. 2 (2015).

2. California Department of Finance, Demographic Research Unit, "Report P-1: State and County Population Projections by Race/Ethnicity, July 1, 2010–60 (by Decade)," December 15, 2014, http://www.dof.ca.gov/research/demographic/reports/projections.

3. Ibid.

4. Ellen Hanak, "Paying for Infrastructure: California's Choices" (San Francisco: Public Policy Institute of California, January 2009), 1, http://www.ppic.org/content/pubs/atissue/AI_109EHAI.pdf.

5. This ranking can be calculated using a variety of costs. California ranks 42nd as a ratio of public money spent to personal income. This ranking reflects the U.S. Census Bureau's formula; state rankings found in Table 11 of Educational Finance Branch, "Public Education Finances: 2013," GS13-ASPEF, June 2015, http://www2.census.gov/govs/school/13f33pub.pdf.

6. "The ShakeOut Scenario," California Geological Survey (CGS) Preliminary Report 25; U.S. Geological Survey Open File Report 2008-1150 Version 1, 2008, page 11, http://pubs.usgs.gov/of/2008/1150; "HAZUS Scenario and Annualized Earthquake Loss Estimation for California," CGS Special Report 222, 2011, page 36, ftp://ftp.consrv.ca.gov/pub/dmg/rgmp/2011%20Annualized%20Losses/CGS_SR222_%20Losses_Final.pdf.

7. Christopher Wimer, Marybeth Mattingly, Sara Kimberlin, Caroline Danielson, and Sara Bohn, "Poverty and Deep Poverty in California," The Stanford Center on Poverty and Inequality, October 1, 2013, http://web.stanford.edu/group/scspi/poverty/cpm/CPM_Brief_Poverty-Deep-Poverty.pdf; Sarah Bohn, Caroline Danielson, and Monica Bandy, "Just the Facts: Poverty in California," PPIC, June 2015, http://www.ppic.org/main/publication_show.asp?i=261.

8. Richard Howitt, Duncan MacEwan, Josué Medellin-Azuara, Jay Lund, and Daniel A. Sumner, "Harsher Drought Impacts Forecast for California Agriculture," California Water Blog, UC Davis Center for Watershed Sciences, June 2, 2015.

9. California Department of Transportation, Caltrans, "2013 State of the Pavement Report," December 2013, http://www.dot.ca.gov/hq/maint/Pavement/Pavement_Program/PDF/2013_SOP_FINAL-Dec_2013-1-24-13.pdf.

Index

About the Author

Renée B. Van Vechten is associate professor of political science at the University of Redlands, where she teaches courses primarily in American government and California politics. She received her PhD in political science from the University of California, Irvine. In 2002–03, she was a Kevin Starr Fellow in California Studies, and in 2008, was honored with the Rowman and Littlefield Award for Innovative Teaching in Political Science, the American Political Science Association's national teaching award at that time. She is also engaged in the scholarship of teaching and learning. A lifelong resident of Southern California, she has spent the better part of her professional life studying, writing, and lecturing about California institutions.